Now Playing

THE SUNY SERIES

HORIZONS OF CINEMA

MURRAY POMERANCE | EDITOR

Also in the series

William Rothman, editor, *Cavell on Film*

J. David Slocum, editor, *Rebel Without a Cause*

Joe McElhaney, *The Death of Classical Cinema*

Kirsten Thompson, *Apocalyptic Dread*

Francis Gateward, editor, *Seoul Searching*

Michael Atkinson, editor, *Exile Cinema*

Bert Cardullo, *Soundings on Cinema*

Now Playing

Early Moviegoing and the Regulation of Fun

Paul S. Moore

STATE UNIVERSITY OF NEW YORK PRESS

Cover photograph: Cosmopolitan Theatre, Yonge Street, Toronto. Photograph by Ernest Hoch, *ca.* 1914. Provincial Archives of Ontario, William H. Hammond Fonds, Image 21957.

Published by
State University of New York Press, Albany

© 2008 State University of New York

For information, contact State University of New York Press, Albany, NY
www.sunypress.edu

Production by Marilyn P. Semerad
Marketing by Anne M. Valentine

Library of Congress Cataloging-in-Publication Data

Moore, Paul S., 1970–
   Now playing : early moviegoing and the regulation of fun / Paul S. Moore.
      p. cm. — (Suny series, horizons of cinema)
   Includes bibliographical references and index.
   ISBN 978-0-7914-7417-4 (hardcover : alk. paper)
   ISBN 978-0-7914-7418-1 (pbk. : alk. paper)
   1. Motion picture audiences—Canada. 2. Motion picture audiences—United States. 3. Motion pictures—Social aspects—Canada. 4. Motion pictures—Social aspects—United States. 5. Motion picture theaters—Canada. 6. Motion picture theaters—United States. I. Title.

PN1995.9.A8M66 2008
302.23'430971354109041—dc22   2007032230

10 9 8 7 6 5 4 3 2 1

Contents

Illustrations

Figures

Tables

Acknowledgments

I must first acknowledge my doctoral supervisor, Alan Blum. His inspiring mentorship within the Culture of Cities Project at York University was invaluable and will always remain a model for my own career. Many others played a part: also at York, Fuyuki Kurasawa, Engin Isin, and the Citizenship Studies Lab; at the University of Chicago, my postdoctoral supervisor Tom Gunning, the Committee on Cinema and Media Studies, and colleagues at the Mass Culture Workshop; Richard Abel and colleagues at Domitor; Richard Sklenar and the late Joseph R. Ducibella of the Theatre Historical Society of America; at the State University of New York Press, Interim Director James Peltz, Horizons of Cinema Series Editor Murray Pomerance, Director of Production Marilyn Semerad, as well as manuscript reviewers and editors. P. Paul Hadian, Sheila Lewis, and Anne Beresford helped immensely in preparation of the final manuscript, financially supported by the Dean of Arts at Ryerson University, Carla Cassidy. Thanks also to my chair, Terry Gillin, whose support included funds for the superb indexing help of Camille Hale. The strength of the book comes largely from the collections of public archives and libraries across North America. The City of Toronto Archives and Archives of Ontario must be singled out, not least for photographs reproduced herein. Travel to libraries and archives was funded by doctoral and postdoctoral grants from the Social Sciences and Humanities Research Council (SSHRC) of Canada. My parents, Joseph and Margaret, have offered constant support in every possible way. Above all else, the daily presence of Andrew Paravantes underpins all my work.

Parts of chapter 5 were previously published as "Everybody's Going: City Newspapers and the Early Mass Market for Movies," in *City and Community* 4, no. 4 (2005). Parts of chapter 2 are forthcoming as "Socially Combustible," in *Cinema and Technology*, edited by Bennett, Furstenau, and MacKenzie. Parts of the conclusion have been submitted to the proceedings of the 2006 Domitor meetings on *The Nation and Nationalism in Early Cinema*, edited by Richard Abel.

The cover photograph shows the Cosmopolitan Theatre downtown in Toronto, near my present-day office at Ryerson University. The picture was taken around 1914 by Ernest Hoch, and is Item 21957 from the William H. Hammond Fonds of the Archives of Ontario.

Introduction

Early Moviegoing and the Regulation of Fun

In May 1909, a local newspaper surveyed the "fad" of moving pictures in Toronto. Considering whether the picture show was becoming part of everyday urban life, the writer surveyed the opinions of politicians and film business people, detailed the bureaucratic efforts that had to be made to open a show, considered issues of fire safety and profitability, compared the scene to Montreal, and finally listed which city streets already had picture shows and how many on each. A city official was quoted, "Let them multiply like rabbits and they'll soon sign their own death-warrant. They are almost overdoing it already, and if we get a few more of them the moving picture fad will soon fall flat" (*Toronto Star* [henceforth *Star*] May 22, 1909). With the twenty picture shows that had opened since the first in 1906, that the number of movie theaters in the city would multiply fivefold again to nearly 100 by 1914 was still unimaginable to some. Rather than being a fad, moviegoing would become fully integrated into the rhythms of city life. With pessimism and prescience, the journalist himself interjected, "How can they be stopped? . . . They can't." The article describes the emergence of a mass market for moviegoing as it was happening before the idea of a mass audience was well-defined. At this point, the future of moviegoing was conceived strictly in local, municipal terms: whether to regulate the market for this fad or take a laissez-faire approach. None of the official voices imagined a future when movies would become a form of mass communications pervasive enough to anchor a modern, mass culture. The journalist himself happened to be the only one who guessed correctly that the movies could not be stopped.

1

Picture shows turned experience and perception into a mass marketed commodity, within the budgets of almost anybody, and soon promoted as open to "everybody." However, that power of movies as a force for integration, a mass practice, was not inherent in its technology, nor simply a result of more people gathering to watch shows. It was carefully constituted by local showmen, by municipal and state legislators, influenced by reformers, by journalists, and by audiences themselves. For the movies to become a mass practice, they first had to be integrated into existing cultures of cities. They first had to fit into everyday life as a legitimate, collective pursuit. The fun they provided had to be regulated. Once moviegoing became routine and the movies a mass practice, however, the fun they provided helped to regulate society in turn, not least the nationalist homefront of World War I.

Movies were not simply imported to cities and towns, although the content of a picture show program was strikingly similar from place to place. Before the U.S. film industry became a big business eventually known as "Hollywood," competing showmen began to organize regionally as a new profession, presenting what they each did as a common industry. They did this partly in response to local authorities and institutions as everyone from parents to ministers to policemen had their say in stipulating local conditions for moviegoing. Perhaps most important, the movies were not really promoted as a form of mass communications until newspaper journalists began addressing readers as the subject of moviegoing and until local showmen began using newspaper advertising to signal how the entire city was invited. This civic aspect of showmanship and the regulation of amusement is the subject of *Now Playing*.

This book does not focus on how individuals experienced filmgoing nor how film functioned structurally in modern society. Although it does offer a generalized theory of spectatorship, the book considers early filmgoing through its urban social history with a midlevel focus on situated institutions. The result is a method that mirrors the substance of the main argument that film had first to be integrated into the culture of particular cities to become a national or global mass practice. Chapters on showmanship, regulation, and promotion trace how the novelty of moviegoing became a collective mass practice rather than a merely prevalent or routine pastime. Film history typically begins with the invention of the technology and focuses on filmmakers and studio production, as if the mass character of the movies follows automatically from its mass production and distribution. *Now Playing* deals with a neglected piece of the puzzle: mass reception, built on a situated social history of the movies becoming a mainstream pastime. Although the book compares cities throughout, the main focus is a single metropolis: Toronto, Canada—an ideal bridge between the United States and its global markets. The case is occasionally comparative, but only insofar as comparisons with other cities were made in Toronto at the time. A continental overview of the nickelodeon boom, gathering facts and figures applicable to any city, would have erased the importance of local civic cultures in anchoring the spread of mass culture. The point of focusing on a particular city is not just that regionalism was empirically important, but that integrating movies into urban cultures through municipal governance actually helped lay a foundation for the subsequent global culture of moviegoing.

Early moving picture shows had many names in their day, varying among places over time: Edison or electric theaters, five-cent shows, and especially nickelodeons. Harry Davis's Nickelodeon in Pittsburgh opened in June 1905 and quickly staked claim as the first storefront picture show (*Moving Picture World* [henceforth *MPW*] November 30, 1907, 629; McNulty 2005). Despite earlier "electric" theaters in 1902, for example in Los Angeles and Vancouver, there is some truth behind grounding the moving picture craze in the industrial heartland around the Great Lakes. Those earlier experiments on the Pacific Coast did not spark a new and enduring craze, while nickelodeons took root in 1905 and 1906 in cities and towns in Pennsylvania, Ohio, and the Midwestern states, and the craze largely spread across the continent from there.

The term "nickelodeon" was never used in Toronto, where a nickel show was called a "theatorium" instead. That was the name of the first to open in March 1906, but it quickly became the local generic term, appearing on about 100 building permits from 1909 to 1914. Journalists and bureaucrats perhaps signified the crass cheapness of these places by consistently writing the plural as "theatoriums" rather than the Latinate *theatoria*. An auditorium for visual attractions, the slightly pretentious word "theatorium" was used as early as October 22, 1882, for the opening of Kohl & Middleton's first dime museum in Chicago. The word "nickelodeon," too, carried over from earlier dime museums (precursors of vaudeville that combined variety burlesques with sideshow freaks and displays of technological marvels). However, cheap museums opened only in big cities in the 1880s and 1890s, unlike the ubiquity of picture shows in the early twentieth century. While early picture shows almost always included some live performance, moving pictures were most often interspersed with a program of popular music of "illustrated songs" whose slideshow images were as standardized as films themselves, mass produced and distributed in much the same way (Altman 2005). The moving pictures and illustrated songs of nickelodeons and theatoriums turned mass production and distribution into mass gathering, and made the mass market for entertainment an ordinary thing—no longer found only downtown in the biggest cities or at carnival occasions such as fairgrounds, rallies, and parades.

Picture shows also made crowded urban space more sensible by organizing bustling masses of city people into a more orderly audience—no longer the chaotic throng of sidewalks, streetcar transfers, or factory gates. Teeming at cross purposes in public spaces, city people then had an ordinary, everyday place to act together with a common focus—toward the screen, as an audience. Historians of U.S. urban culture point to concurrent forms of mass gathering at amusement parks, vaudeville theaters, industrial expositions, ballparks, and department stores (Barth 1980; Nasaw 1993). However, trips to ballgames, theaters, and even department stores were arguably still more of a special occasion than the ordinary, everyday routine of picturegoing. At the movies, the mass market of consumers became material in the mass audience, and the mass provision of commodities became the pretext for a common experience (Chandler 1977; Hobsbawm 1987; Strasser 1989). The mass interdependence and division of labor in modern society was thought to produce atomization and alienation (Haskell 2000). It could also magically materialize as the movies' mass audience. A collective pastime, a mass practice, was ironically built on the radical and unprecedented heterogeneity of urban populations in North America, the result of mass immigration and rural migration (Grossman 1989; Ward 1989). The movies are key to understanding the mass market, for better or for worse, as the culmination of modernization and urbanization, in the exemplary way they made a sensible, legible practice out of the cacophony of polyglot North American cities (Buck-Morss 1989; Frisby 2001).

Not far from Niagara Falls and its endless supply of electricity, Toronto was the metropolis and capital of the Canadian province of Ontario, which spanned the northern shores of four of the five Great Lakes. In the early twentieth century, Toronto was a rapidly growing city of several hundred thousand citizens. By 1920, when the movie industry was fully instituted, Toronto was the national center for film distribution and exhibition in theater chains. Although competition among picture shows never rose to the heights of the early years of the largest U.S. metropolises, Toronto's more gradual growth to a peak of about 100 picture theaters in 1914 was not unlike cities of similar size, such as Buffalo, Cleveland, or Detroit. In retrospect, Toronto's theatoriums eventually followed the same pattern of business conglomeration, centralized regulation, and architectural development as any other large city on the continent. Unlike the earliest nickelodeon years, by 1920 the quantity and concentration of movie theaters in all cities (even Chicago and New York) had become more predictably a matter of population density, competition, and neighborhood wealth (Gomery 1992, 34–82; Nasaw 1993, 221–240). In part this happened because it was typical by 1920 for companies affiliated with movie studios to build or buy the biggest and best-located movie theaters in almost every city. Social histories of early amusements easily claim a regional, distinct character in rural and small city entertainment (Fuller 1996; Goodson 2002; Waller 1995). But they draw the line with the emergence of a vertically integrated film industry and the loss of local ownership of theaters. On the other hand, the gradual convergence to homogeneity among regions and cities allows local histories, like this study of Toronto, to maintain the goal of saying something about filmgoing in general. The lessons learned from this regional case study will raise questions and provide some answers that are applicable to anywhere in North America, especially because many steps were taken to act or react explicitly to what was happening in Chicago or New York. The relation between Toronto and New York, or alternatively between Canada and the United States, is beyond the scope of this project. Even limited to the film industry, the border relation has been the subject of volumes on cultural policy and film financing (Dorland 1998; Magder 1993; Pendakur 1990). This story of early moviegoing begins before that border was important. Indeed, the federal government is curiously absent, not yet taking notice or exerting any jurisdiction over the urban novelty of picture shows.

In the U.S. film trade press, and beforehand in the amusement and theater trade press, Canada is the only foreign country treated as part of the U.S. domestic circuit, just another region on the continent. Of course, this region had its quirks; but canisters of film, song illustrations, and vaudeville acts, even theater managers and capital investments, crossed the border easily, paying duty or inspecting papers with little more than a rubber stamp. To this day, Canadian box office remains calculated as part of the U.S. domestic figures with films released within the same run-zone-clearance network of the United States. Charles Acland (2003) notes how this ambiguous relationship is well-entrenched for the U.S. film industry overall because Canada has historically been both inside and outside of the U.S. industry, part of the domestic network of film distribution, yet a foreign territory with its own cultural policies and protections. This book looks at a time before that distinct national policy was in place, when regions, states, and cities within the United States were often trying to assert their own distinct policies and protections. The economic, social, and cultural proliferation of picture shows was effectively the same in Ontario as in Ohio or Oregon, and central Canada is just another region like the Midwest or the Pacific Coast (although New York and Chicago perhaps remain exceptional altogether.) Thus, the bulk of *Now Playing* applies to the United States, in substance and methodology, given the caveat of regional variation.

The conclusion of the book ends up showing a distinctly nationalist practice of moviegoing emerged in Toronto, catalyzed by World War I. As a result of the regional aspects of movie showmanship, regulation, and

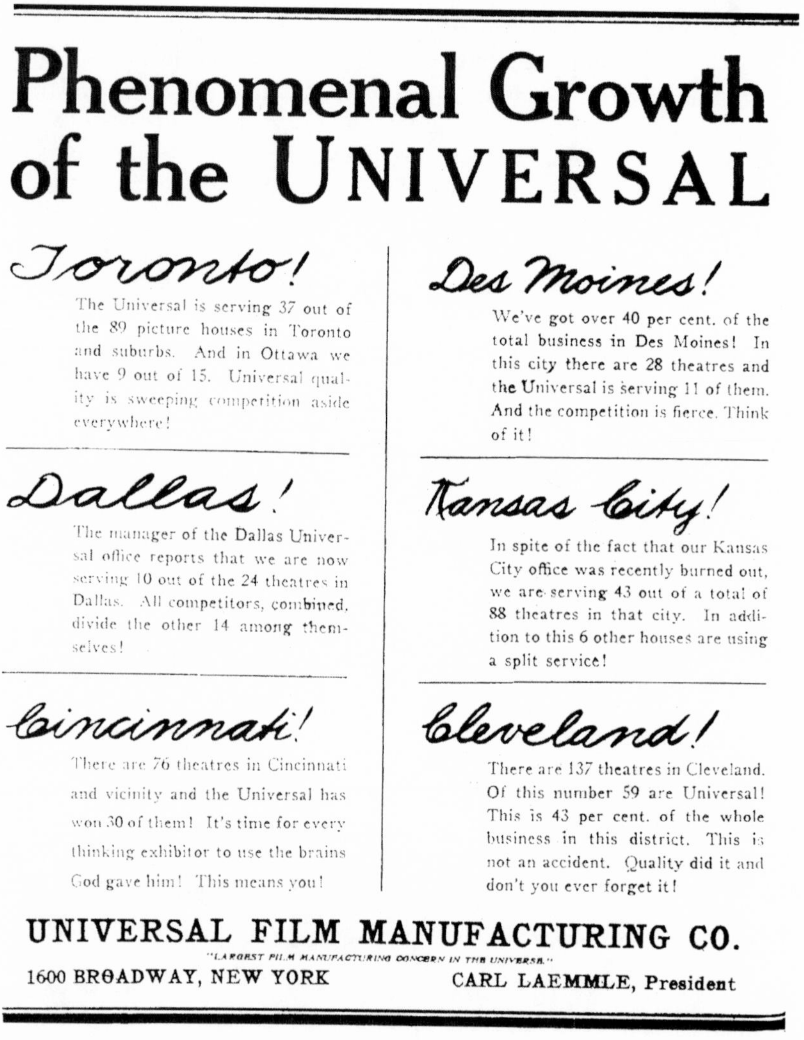

Figure I.1. Toronto was just one regional metropolis among many in North America, for example in this Universal Pictures trade ad, where the city had equal place with Des Moines, Dallas, Cincinnati, and Kansas City. (*Moving Picture World* November 7, 1914.)

promotion, Toronto ultimately positioned itself as a national prototype for a somewhat distinct Canadian mass practice, despite remaining thoroughly integrated into the U.S. domestic market for movies. The concurrent decline of regional variations within the United States was partly due to the Supreme Court denying First Amendment freedom of speech to moving pictures and partly to the federal jurisdiction over interstate commerce (Grieveson 2004). Neither of those factors applied to Toronto. Differences between Toronto and its sister cities in the United States emerged only gradually, although rather starkly by the end of World War I. Accordingly, *Now Playing* begins as a case study within the U.S. film industry and ends as a case also relevant to other countries that were similarly colonized by the U.S. studio system, but nonetheless constructed relatively distinct national practices of moviegoing. The stories of policing, showmanship, and early advertising are directly relevant to U.S. film history because the standardization of moviegoing happened first at the municipal level. But then, once regional conventions and routines were set, distinctions at the national level emerged. Indeed, the evidence of *Now Playing* supports the claim that modernity itself, at least as a global trend of rationalized governance, rests on the smooth ordering of everyday life in municipal spaces, increasingly equivalent across all North American cities (Novak 1996; Wiebe 1967). Within this emergent rationalization of everyday life, especially its commercialization through the mass market, regional differences emerged as a symbolic realm, at the level of the nation rather than the metropolis. Certainly for film in Toronto, the idea of a distinct national or nationalist culture of moviegoing and moviemaking did not come into view until the debates over ordinary showmanship and municipal regulation were more or less settled, until after a mass audience and a nascent mass communications network were understood.

Early filmgoing in Toronto provides the context to understand how and why Toronto continues to be a city whose population goes to the movies with expertise, supporting rather than opposing film production nearby in the United States. Nearly a century ago, the city adapted to the transnational context of the film industry, neither adopting nor rejecting it wholesale; instead, it set local conditions for how film was to be handled, sold, and seen. This book recovers the origins of the way Torontonians go to the movies but makes no effort to recount what the movies meant to historic audiences. More literally, it accounts for the circumstances that allowed audiences to gather and the way those in charge of stipulating the local conditions of viewing were acting on what they thought best for the particular people of Toronto.

Moviegoing developed very quickly into an exemplary civic practice, able to accommodate divergent claims about its ideal social role. Local showmen, city officials, journalists, and implicitly audiences as well, helped integrate the mass gathering of filmgoing into the established civic culture of Toronto years before the city's movie theaters became formally incorporated into an "institutional" or "Hollywood" cinema. The task of standardizing filmgoing was treated in Toronto as a local achievement despite how the issues were, in fact, debated continentwide. Even with a lack of Canadian filmmaking, during World War I moviegoing became overtly nationalistic, not primarily through propaganda but through ordinary movie exhibition. The local process of integrating filmgoing into the everyday life of Toronto was largely independent of, although concurrent with, conglomerating networks of film production and distribution in the United States. Toronto became a film metropolis for Canada not through producing films but by producing an exemplary form of moviegoing.

Now Playing traces the emergence of a mass practice, changing from a "Rendezvous for Particular People" to a place where "Everybody's Going," titles of the first and last chapters. Another important relation of the particular to the general in any sociological study of early cinema is in the sense that moviegoing is an opportunity to experience how ordinary life is embedded in a global modernity. The here and now in the moment of viewing was always the context for seeing a world beyond, captured on film. Although that could be true for theater or the circus, a movie was instead mass produced, available simultaneously elsewhere, in principle everywhere. While the imaginary world of art or literature, of newspapers or magazines, could be mass produced, part of the experience of joining a movie audience for a specific theater at a particular time was joining a mass audience for all movies everywhere. That relation of particularity to generality is crucial in studying the social context of moviegoing. The mass practice must be understood through a regional case of its emergence as well as its industrial and commercial networks of production, making the local an essential partner with the globally distributed reproduction of the world on film.

Now Playing has much in common with recent studies of early U.S. cinema and its reception. The broader context of film regulation and the influence of Progressive-era reformers on the shape of cinema draws on Tom Gunning's book on *D. W. Griffith* (1991), Uricchio and Pearson's *Reframing Culture* (1993), and Lee Grieveson's *Policing Cinema* (2004). One blind spot for these authors, which comes from focusing on changes in film production, is their emphasis on the local regulations of only New York or Chicago. Without disputing how those cities are key because their film regulations shaped production decisions, these world metropolises are unique rather than prototypical, exactly because they were centers of filmmaking. By removing production from the equation (by necessity, because Toronto had almost none), a more widely applicable story emerges of the role of local film regulations, that of creating a mass audience, at first on a regional scale. The emergence of the mass audience has been studied in relation to advertising and movie promotion, but usually through studio-run national campaigns, not local showmanship (Staiger 1990; Luckett 1999). In contrast to those studies of studio promotions, essays on exhibition and advertising by Gregory Waller (2005), Richard Abel (2006), and Michael Aronson (2002) have been invaluable for demonstrating how the situated presentation of movies owed as much to local innovations as studio promotional campaigns. And yet, they seem interested in early regional autonomy to show it slipping away with Hollywood's subsequent emergence as a big business. However, the initial care and attention to regional autonomy was precisely necessary for an interregional and transnational mass market in movies.

An earlier generation of film historians took up the challenging task of relating the historically and culturally particular to the general development of the mass practice. Miriam Hansen (1993) and Judith Mayne (1993), for example, have moved to historicize spectatorship by emphasizing the social context of viewing. But even these studies that counter an overly standardized "classical" spectatorship can unwittingly continue to assume what they criticize. Without being anchored in regions or locations, audiences and spectators remain somewhat interchangeable. An exception is Richard Maltby's (1983; 1996) articulation of the purposeful ambiguity and incoherence of classical Hollywood cinema under the Production Code. Against replicating models of decontextualized spectatorship, Acland (2003) notes how "our world is one in which time and space are expected to be made and remade on an ongoing basis, and film figures as symptomatic and emblematic of that expectation" (p. 50). Yet, the making and remaking of time and space is also what the city does, or rather what people do with the city. Well before film, the making and remaking of city spaces and routines was well established, managed through the bylaws and offices of municipal governance. Municipalities already had a process of making and remaking in the earliest articulations of film practices because film was being integrated into existing civic cultures of cities. In his work on movies, multiplexes, and global culture, Acland demonstrates how the standards of moviegoing are always changeable especially today. Instead of fluidity over time, this book finds a regional fluidity in the civic origins of those standards. The emphasis here is historical, looking in depth at a particular urban case in the moment before the U.S. film industry was known simply as Hollywood. Although the book agrees with film scholars who situate spectatorship historically, it only implicitly critiques theories of classical spectatorship. The aim here is to understand the generality of filmgoing as, perhaps paradoxically, something that was in part achieved locally and integrated into the particularity of various cities. This is especially important for Toronto as a foreign metropolis that was nonetheless effectively part of the American domestic mass market.

Now Playing: On the Basis of Standardized Showmanship, Regulation, and Promotion

Approaching early moviegoing through a wide range of acts that shaped its situation, the book addresses how conditions for watching film organized its social occasion within a logic of urban modernity. The study is thus also about the organization of city spaces and its relation to regions, nations, and modern society generally, and in particular the mediation of technologies through social relations. An audience was a social body, an instance of modernity, of *Gesellschaft*, rather than a traditional communal ritual, a matter of *Gemeinschaft* (Tönnies 2001). A significant part of what makes a film audience modern and urban is its temporary, optional, and public character as a gathering of strangers, oriented to a commercial, secular amusement. This aspect of filmgoing was more or less the same as any other theatrical entertainment or carnival site. What uniquely made a film exhibition modern was how this particular form of showmanship openly flaunted the electric technology and transnational distribution of its mass-produced industrial product. Although similar to the centrally administered routes of late-nineteenth-century theatrical shows and circuses, film based its appeal on the explicitly modern exhibition of mechanically reproduced scenes, not on the embodied talent of performance. Cinema produced experience, reproduced it, within a technological and industrial system that allowed perception and experience itself to become consumable and available among the goods for sale on city and neighborhood shopping streets.

The local efforts to make filmgoing a normative practice shaped filmgoing into a recognizable and meaningful part of everyday life in Toronto. Government representatives, parents, religious leaders, educators, journalists, and showmen themselves were all active in making moviegoing socially meaningful, giving it a standardized form. But social constraints on moviegoing rarely changed the apparatus of filmmaking or the commercial distribution of films. Sometimes the secular trend of commercialized leisure was at issue, especially how it was directed at children; but profit-seeking showmanship almost always remained intact. The industrial status of film as a modern product was ultimately distinguished from the cultural and social conditions of its exhibition. Cinema thus became regulated, that is, regularized and legitimated, in ways best suited to capitalist and urban forms of showmanship. *Now Playing* thus provides an exemplary case of an innovative place in modern society taking on cultural and economic form, becoming institutionalized after first being experienced as novelty.

Film drew the attention of a wide range of people and officials whose reactions covered an equally wide range from concern to curiosity. The multiple ways film appealed to people was at least implicitly considered when debates and standards were set, making the process a matter of pragmatic accommodation rather than strident or idealistic positioning. What all shared was a sense that the experience of viewing a film was fundamentally social, not an entirely psychological or personal pleasure. In a sense, each struggled to have his or her own understanding recognized. However, the plurality of uses for film was so evident that each seems also to have recognized the importance of alternative pleasures of moviegoing. Perhaps this occurred because the technology of cinema emphasized that it could be manipulated by editing and distributed widely after those changes were made.

As film became a mass medium, which is to say a *collectivizing* mass practice, it had to be integrated into local routines, despite its content being self-evidently transnational. Chapter 1 explores how this premise differs from social histories that treat film primarily as a technology that simply arrives in communities, and also distinct from sociologies of film that strive to capture the cultural or individuated effects of watching films. Instead, a social history of film documents how it gradually became part of the civic culture of the city. Toronto's difference from U.S. cities was that it was an overseas British colonial city in a newly independent country, positioning itself as a metropolis for that country and conducting its affairs accordingly, leading by example. Yet, initially Toronto encountered film much like any other industrial city of its size in North America, especially other cities in the Great Lakes basin such as Buffalo, Cleveland, Detroit, or Milwaukee. In the early 1900s Toronto was a rapidly expanding new home to hundreds of thousands of immigrants and rural migrants, dealing with women's suffrage, labor reform, and a creeping commercialization of family life and childhood. It was thus similar to U.S. cities, yet consistently and deliberately had its civic affairs molded to avoid corruption, vice, and graft, seen as problems endemic to U.S. municipal politics. In Toronto, such civic reforms dated to the mid-nineteenth century, so that the famous (or infamous) moral conservatism of the Queen City in the twentieth century, "Toronto, the Good," might even have been a result, not a cause, of how its early public culture was crafted. Despite this particularity of Toronto, moviegoing soon anchored its mass culture just as it did in every other place on the continent.

Early moviegoing was regulated in Toronto with urgency: at first as an imminent threat to the built form of the city because of celluloid's chemical combustibility, and subsequently in a variety of other ways, as a creeping threat to the pedagogical, moral, nationalist, and economic well-being of the city and its public. But why focus on the origins of its norms in a historical method, given that moviegoing exists in more or less similar form in the century since? Because people continue to leave their home and arrive at a box office to buy a ticket (albeit now sometimes vice versa) before sitting in an auditorium to watch a film, perhaps with family or friends, but always with strangers alongside. Films are still advertised and promoted with advance publicity in a style developed around 1914. In Ontario, children continue to be banned even today from attending certain films as first happened in 1911, and all films are still reviewed by the government's successor to the Board of Censors, also established in 1911. Many movie theaters continue to be owned and operated today by companies formed in 1920 and earlier. Theaters, equipment, and employees continue to be licensed by government agencies, and fire safety codes continue to be stipulated, all first articulated between 1908 and 1914. Ontario still has an amusement tax distinct from general sales tax, first implemented during World War I. This continuity of the standardized conditions of the business and regulations of filmgoing alone merits a sociological consideration of the terms in which cinema was first defined as a unique and special amusement. When, where, by whom, and how did that configuration of filmgoing become recognizable in those categories that endure today?

The story begins in 1906, the year the first theatoriums opened in Toronto, the first businesses managed and subsequently licensed, inspected, censored, written about, and promoted as a site for the everyday mass gathering of filmgoing. With emphasis on the local bureaucratic definition of moving pictures, chapter 2 provides an analysis of the broad social context of the first law specifically addressing film in Toronto. Subsequent chapters deal with the emergence of standardized showmanship, regulation, and promotion.

In 1908 a fire safety law mandated municipal police forces to inspect, with the option of licensing, all sites in Ontario handling or storing film. Before this moment of concern about the material combustibility of celluloid film, the occasional debates over film in Toronto each quickly subsided when the city's police force and its morality squad asserted they could handle the problem within the status quo. The chemical combustibility of films and the concurrent social combustibility of audiences, seen as prone to panic, required a novel articulation of procedures overseeing film in the city, indeed all of Ontario. In the case of film, this law provided a foundation for continuing to extend the jurisdiction of film regulation, ultimately in centralized bureaucracies. The invention of new bureaucracies for film is entirely different from the way other novelty amusements were handled. Chapter 2 thus contrasts the initial film regulations with concurrent debates in Toronto over billiards and bowling, ice cream and peanut vendors, and fortune tellers. These were also seen at the time as socially problematic, but unlike film, they quickly became socially innocuous.

Three relatively independent processes needed to occur at the urban and regional scale for the movies to become a mass practice. In more or less chronological but overlapping action, chapter 3 reviews how film *showmanship* offered filmgoing as a novel type of consumption and soon positioned it as a viable, everyday pastime, at times almost an essential service to the public. Then, chapter 4 explains how film *regulations* articulated and instituted limitations and directions for showmanship's provision of commercial amusement, necessary for film to be understood as a collective practice. Finally, chapter 5 explains how film *journalism* and *promotion* made sense of the novelty consumption and framed it as a common practice despite the diversity of audiences that coexisted. These three processes are explained as they occurred in Toronto with concern for how they contributed to the standardization of filmgoing in the decade following 1906. All of these processes articulated social standards and iteratively coordinated in response to conflicting concerns to reshape the conditions in which audiences gathered to watch films. However, the last process of promotion is crucial. Indeed, the crux of the book and perhaps its most original point is that newspaper advertising was key to making the movies into a mass medium by articulating and explaining them as such. Chapter 5 proposes that cinema became a mass practice only when it was promoted as something "everybody" could do. Not until 1914 did the film industry explain to the public that despite differences in location, cost, and filigree of theater, all classes of audiences were part of the same experience—a move that came with a film genre until recently dismissed as unimportant to film history: the serial film (Wilinsky 2000).

For chapter 3 on the standardization of film showmanship, classical sociological conceptualizations of urban commerce are foundational. Early theatorium managers had to balance an ambiguous status, both traders and artisans, both local representatives of the transnational film industry and situated merchants of a novel form of retail consumption. Competition among entrepreneurs was tempered by the need to respond to the continual reorganization of film production and distribution in the United States, and on the other hand, the constant reorganization of local regulation in Toronto. Collective representation occurred through formal economic conglomeration but more important, at first, through voluntary "protective associations" that opened a forum among competitors for social gathering, voluntary standardized practices, and political representation.

Chapter 4, tracing the emergence of centralized bureaucracies of film regulation, begins by gathering the various concerns and alternatives proposed to counteract the supposedly harmful social effects of entrepreneurial showmanship. The popular, cheap pastime of filmgoing was consistently noted as particularly welcoming of children, young women, and foreign-born families. As a commercial amusement inviting anyone with a nickel to enter, not corralled downtown but throughout the city on neighborhood avenues, the movies were infringing on the conduct of families, churches, and schools. Although film regulation began entirely as part of urban policing "on the beat," more efficient mechanisms were instituted, usually in agencies usurping what had been police patrol duties, through licensing, censorship, and inspection. Early suggested alternative forms of nonprofit filmgoing were thoroughly marginalized through the development of regulations. Police and government relied on standardized conditions of filmgoing for efficient surveillance as much as the film industry relied on routine practices for its profits.

Chapter 5 is crucial. It takes up the vital role of newspapers, translating and circulating knowledge about film to the public. Again, it starts with a sociological theory, in this case of newspapers and the early urban studies of Robert E. Park and the Chicago School. There was a general shift from investigative journalism about audiences to puff promotion of specific but constantly changing films. Reporting and promotion followed, but just by a half-step, the provision of filmgoing through showmanship and its regulation by civic officials. Newspapers organized the scattered options of urban consumption and experience into an idealized version of metropolitan living, demonstrating a possible urban world in relation to the domestic individual. Thus, journalism and promotion did not merely reflect and comment on the place of film in society. Newspapers fundamentally were agents themselves in reshaping the meaning and practice of going to the movies. Locally distributed forms of mass promotion communicated how individual people and audiences were actually engaging collectively in a *common* practice. Regular entertainment reporting, collective advertising umbrellas for showmen, and especially fiction tie-ins to serial films, each demonstrated not just how filmgoing was becoming respectable and mainstream, but also how "everyone" was doing the same activity when they went to the movies, despite the wide diversity of times, places, prices, and films.

A conclusion gathers developments during World War I, 1914 to 1918, and asks how an apparently national practice of filmgoing could emerge with almost no Canadian film production. Details of a short-lived exception, the Conness-Till studio in 1915, combined with the use of films in the war effort, allow for a speculative reflection on how moviegoing could be nationalist while relying on imported films. The inclusive space of mass gathering that had more or less settled into normative forms just before World War I was an ideal place to incorporate the disenfranchised masses into the homefront war effort. In Toronto, this was largely done without propaganda. Instead, patriotic intentions were simply attached to ordinary movie shows. Showmen collectively offered moviegoing as an ordinary way for the public to take part in the homefront war effort. The Ontario government introduced an amusement tax to make every act of filmgoing also an act of citizenship with a contribution to the war coffers. The war effort allowed the fun of moviegoing to be a form of citizenship, despite the near-total absence of Canadian-made films.

Rendezvous for Particular People

The Local Roots of Mass Culture

There was no age, I venture to say since the world began, in which the people would not have flocked to the moving picture shows. It remained for this age to produce this marvel, . . . If we continue along the lines followed in the present times we shall yet see in Toronto and other Canadian cities moving pictures as real as life.

—Editorial, *Star Weekly* June 3, 1911

O NE OF THE FIRST THEATORIUMS in Toronto to advertise regularly was the Garden on College Street. Opening July 30, 1910, it ran a small ad in just one of the city's six daily newspapers, the *Star*, initially for the theater's roof garden where a "good musical program" could be enjoyed nightly, admission ten cents. Throughout September and October 1910, ads for the Garden's moving pictures and vaudeville appeared in the same paper, each naming a live performer but describing the films only through various brand names of the technical apparatus, the kinetograph, the cymograph, and the cinematograph. Alfred and William Hawes constructed the theatorium for $8,000, replacing a storefront picture show they had opened only months before (*Building Permits* April 3, 1909, and November 25, 1909). The Garden was located neither downtown nor uptown, but on a neighborhood shopping street, bridging working-class and immigrant-associated areas to the south and middle-class suburban districts to the north. The University of Toronto nearby provided a consistent clientele for many decades (in its last years in the 1970s, it was an important art house called the Cinema Lumière). In 1911 the Garden was leased by a growing U.S. chain of picture shows, "which cater to the best class of citizens rather than the transient or tourist traffic, . . . situated in the best residential localities" (*Toronto World* [hence-forth *World*] June 11, 1911, 9). Still, the Garden, even with its rooftop garden, was only a modestly sized picture theater, neither the largest in the city nor the one with the most elaborate façade.

The theater's new manager was showman Leon Brick from Buffalo, and he was anything but modest when it came to promoting the neigh-borhood picture show. "Superior presentation, . . . first-class music, . . . just the place to spend an hour"; *World* October 30, 1911). It was rumored that Brick kept track of the number of automobiles lined up outside the theater to drop off patrons from uptown and the suburbs (*MPW* Novem-ber 28, 1914, 1257). With automobiles still a rare luxury, a traffic jam outside the Garden would indeed have been a measure of his boastful claims. In 1912, Brick's ad began to use the phrase, "A Rendezvous for Particular People," explaining in detail what to expect:

Figure 1.1. Leon Brick's ad in an American film trade paper prominently called the Garden Theatre, "A Rendezvous for Particular People." Photos of the façade and roof garden later appeared in a Canadian architecture journal. (Top: *Moving Picture World*, June 28, 1913. Bottom: *Construction*, April 1915.)

Devoted Exclusively to a High-class Exhibition of Motion Pictures which Include Travel Scenes, Interesting Dramatic Creations, Humorous Comedies and Novelties as Issued. Music of a High Order by the Garden Theatre Orchestra, which Is Composed of Versatile Performers. A Miniature Symphony Orchestra. (*Toronto Star Weekly* [henceforth *Star Weekly*] October 12, 1912, 32)

Gradually the description of the film and music program was shortened to "Motion Pictures—Music," but the slogan, "A Rendezvous for Particular People" stuck, appearing in ads for the Garden until 1914. A newspaper article introducing plans for the new season at the Garden in 1913 noted the audience was three-quarters "ladies," described the policy as "a clean show in a clean house," and reported that Brick would personally select films to ensure "thrillers and sensational, blood-curdling dramas are eliminated" (ad in *Star Weekly* August 2, 1913, 21). Brick even took the exceptional step of buying a large, half-page ad in the New York film trade paper *Moving Picture World* inviting other showmen to visit when vacationing in Canada (*MPW* June 28, 1913, 1395). The particular people of Toronto could accommodate American visitors easily.

The Garden's slogan is a crystallization of the question at the core of this study: Is a local case study of filmgoing particular to that place? On its surface, however, it is a deceptively simple marker of the upwardly mobile character of movie audiences at the time, described by Brick in the *Moving Picture World* ad as "representing the most respectable and influential element of Toronto." The act of moviegoing, too, was upwardly mobile, signaled not only by Brick's rhetoric, but also by the simple existence of ads in daily papers where there were almost none before. The Garden's slogan is one example of many, from almost any locale, of how moviegoing at small picture shows transformed from a cheap novelty to a mass practice with a specifically middle-class appeal. In every big city and many smaller towns and suburbs, authorities and moral reformers began censoring films and limiting children's attendance. Filmmakers, and in turn regional film exchanges and local showmen, carefully refined the moving picture program to appeal to the middle-class, especially women, the very same "particular" people who had been most active in agitating for regulation of the early nickel shows. On the surface, then, there is nothing particular to the Garden Theatre about its claim to be a rendezvous for particular people. The emergence of "refined" moviegoing was as much a transnational, standardized process as the parallel transition to a formally conglomerated Hollywood.

Although some Canadian theater chains had formal and arm's length ties to U.S. film interests, particular people in Toronto almost always managed, legislated, and advertised moviegoing with genuine concern for what was best for their own city. The general similarity between this process and what happened elsewhere, if not everywhere, cannot be explained by the "branch plant" links to the transnational companies that distributed and produced films. Especially during this transitional decade when regulations and routines specific to film were first articulated, there was an active process of deciding how to *import* this still-novel global export commodity. The form and forum of gathering for filmgoing, regardless of the film, allowed audiences, authorities, and showmen to treat the social context of viewing as equal in importance to the specific story or scenes viewed. Leon Brick himself explained this was exactly the premise of his management of the Garden Theatre and proposed that the role he played in exhibiting films to the particular people of Toronto was on par with the earlier production of the images. "The artistic presentation of a moving picture is now conceded to be in importance equal to its original reflection on the sensitive film" (*MPW* June 28, 1913, 1395).

The central premise of *Now Playing* is that the standardization of filmgoing in Toronto was articulated in forms of showmanship, regulation, and promotion that were indeed particular to Toronto. But then how did a global, mass culture take root in spite of such attention to local particularity? One commonsense explanation might be that the mass character of cinema was determined by its technology and production: because projection apparatuses and film prints, sheet music and song slides, were manufactured industrially and mass distributed, moviegoing of course had the same basic form everywhere. One might suppose in turn that mass communication would follow: because people saw similar films in similar ways, a type of universal spectatorship resulted. Neither of these approaches allows for a sense of the ways local and regional efforts to shape cinema seem instead to have contributed to its mass appeal, helping along the understanding that what we do here is the same as what they do there.

Of course, the apparatus and images were widely distributed and generally came from far away; but that aspect was not seen as problematic in local debates. Concerned about possibly immoral stories, people called for censorship to aid good parenting and civic education without assuming indecent images similarly affected everyone. Sometimes aspersions of profiteering were directed at showmanship, calls to discriminate against frivolous entertainment in favor of a more educational cinema, and concerns about flag-waving films from other countries. Even these local debates rarely questioned the technological apparatus, viewing format, or commercial and capitalist basis of moviegoing. Regional and municipal decisions about the movies dwelt almost entirely with regional and municipal concerns: the built spaces of theaters, the policing of indecent public conduct or its depictions, fair business practices, and moviegoing's intrusion onto the spaces and times of churchgoing, schooling, or family life. These local matters—the conditions of moviegoing, its places, rhythms, and manners—were not mere tangents and obstacles in the way of mass culture but were its building blocks. The process of setting local conditions *sanctioned* the practice in the dual sense of stipulating limitations but thus adding a stamp of legitimacy.

The Matter on Its Merits: Preempting the Problem of Moving Pictures

The first histories of film appeared almost immediately after the introduction of the apparatus to the public. As early as 1897, histories of film such as Cecil Hepworth's *The ABC of the Cinématographe* reviewed the technology as a scientific invention, framed by the biographies of its innovators (Chanan 1996; Popple & Kember 2004). In 1895 several machines debuted with varying degrees of success in an attempt to take Thomas Edison's Kinetoscope peepshow films and project them to an audience. Auguste and Louis Lumière perhaps most famously patented their Cinématographe and had a first public performance in Paris in December. In London in January 1896, Robert Paul and Brit Acres provided a demonstration of moving pictures to the Royal Photographic Society. In the United States, Edison purchased the rights to a similar adaptation of the existing technology Thomas Armat devised, renamed it the Vitascope, and gave it a commercial premiere in New York in April 1896. Most local histories of filmgoing, too, begin with the first projected film shows, making the technology the foundation for the subsequent social practice. Canadian film histories usually begin by citing the introduction of these technical apparatuses within the nation's borders. The first film show was long taken to be a demonstration of Edison's Vitascope in Ottawa on July 21, 1896. In fact, Lumière's Cinématographe had surfaced even earlier in Montreal on June 28, 1896, a day before its first showing in New York (Gaudreault and Lacasse 1996; Lacasse 1984; Morris 1992, 1–13). Histories of film in Toronto begin in this way, too, citing the appearance of the Vitascope at the Musée Theatre on August 31, 1896, just a day before Lumière's apparatus debuted at the Toronto Industrial Exhibition (Gutteridge 2000, 7–32; Morris 1992, 7–11).

From this origin, a conventional history of film proceeds to recount the patterns of progress of an industrial technique of storytelling toward the mature "institutional" cinema with the classical Hollywood style and studio system. On the one hand are the accounts of the history of filmmaking technique and narrative style (Bordwell 1985; Gunning 1991; Keil 2001). On the other hand are the business histories of the transnational industry, which ended up in the 1930s and 1940s fully vertically integrated, a global oligopoly with direct chains of management from film production through distribution and local exhibition (Balio 1976; Gomery 1992). Perhaps most numerous are local histories of theater building. The prototype remains Ben M. Hall's *Best Remaining Seats* (1966) and the Theatre Historical Society of America's magazine *Marquee*, which Hall helped create. Although the degree of nostalgia can vary greatly, these all recognize that movie theaters are important sites of local heritage. In this vein, I have examined the emergence of the movie palace in Canada and have read it as a signifier for downtown and urban history itself (Moore 2004). These variants of film history treat film as a technology that arrives in communities fully formed. The focus on the invention of the apparatus thus ignores how the arrival of the technology might have prompted a social process particular to the site, let alone how the apparatus helped institute a practice that was adjusted over time as part of the local situation.

Yet, many studies demonstrate that the technology of projected film from 1895 was just part of a long-standing technological, commercial, and social fascination with visual representation and illusion (Boyer 1994; Crary 1992; Friedberg 1993). In a less abstract way, this translated into film at first being attached to existing forms of exhibition and amusement. The first film shows in Canada demonstrate how the new technology was carefully inscribed within existing places of modern entertainment and spectacle: a variety show at an established theater in Montreal and later Toronto, a suburban amusement park in Ottawa, and the industrial exhibition in Toronto. A familiar air was felt when the Lumière Cinématographe was briefly set up after the Exhibition in a space of its own on the city's main shopping avenue, Yonge Street, in October and again in December 1896. Empty storefronts such as this were often used for temporary, special exhibits of artistic or novelty attractions. For example, a temporary art gallery was put in the same Yonge Street storefront as the Cinématographe, and promoted in the same tone: "The Rage of the Day—Historical Paintings, No Canadian Should Miss Them" (ad in *Star* November 6, 1896). The novelty of the attraction was initially carefully mediated through existing local practices. Film did not at first prompt local efforts to regulate and normalize its relation to society.

One succinct measure of how the 1896 introduction of film technology to Toronto was a moment of social continuity, rather than rupture, is the license fee schedule municipal authorities set to manage and monitor business operations in Toronto. The general category for entertainments charging admission had been set a yearly license fee of $50 before 1890 (Toronto Bylaw 2453). This license category, which would later apply to moving picture shows, was thus introduced more than a full decade before the first nickel show and years before the first projection using film technology. Commercial amusements were a regular and regulated part of the modern city before film technology came along. The novelty of cinema was not in itself socially problematic. Before the theatoriums opened in 1906, there was perhaps just one incident prompting a debate to regulate film in Toronto.

In August 1897, tickets for "Veriscope" pictures of the Corbett–Fitzsimmons fight were widely advertised as a forthcoming sensational extra attraction at the Toronto Opera House. The prizefight had taken place in March in Nevada where it was legal. But prizefights were illegal in Canada. In Toronto at the time, even amateur fights needed special permission from the chief constable. The week before the filmed attraction was set to open, Mayor Fleming became determined to stop the "disgraceful and demoralizing thing." The issue was addressed at a meeting of the Board of Control where the mayor was relieved to discover that Alderman Sheppard, manager of the Princess Theatre, had refused to book the films. The City Solicitor was instructed to draft a bylaw prohibiting the attraction, although not everyone agreed (*Toronto News* [henceforth *News*] August 6, 1897). The bylaw drafted was a $500 penalty per day for any exhibition or representation of any fight between individuals or of any prizefight "by means of a kinetoscope, cinematograph, veriscope, or any other instrument or otherwise," including pictures, drawings, photographs, models, wax works, or other devices.

Described in one report as a prohibitive license, all acknowledged that the city could not prohibit the film from being shown and could only impose penalties afterward. The managers of the Toronto Opera House arranged a special Saturday screening for councilors to view the moving pictures in preparation for an impromptu city council meeting Monday morning. If the bylaw failed, shows would begin just hours later. Because of the rushed timing, the bylaw required two-thirds consent of council to come into effect the same day as it was introduced (*News* August 7, 1897). The debate was lively, with the *Star* putting a small note within its synopsis to make the issue explicit, "The City Getting too Good." Alderman Sheppard, the theater manager, interrupted debate over proper jurisdiction, wanting first simply to know how many thought the picture actually should be banned. Alderman Hallam called out, "Never mind what I think. What do you think, yourself?" To which Sheppard parlayed, "Well, you have been to Paris, and seen everything which the human eye could see. Therefore I take [you] as a high authority" (*Star* August 7, 1897, 1).

The bylaw failed to get two-thirds support of council and the fight pictures played for two weeks to a packed house. The *Star* summarized the episode with the headline, "Fad Legislation Beaten by a Technicality," adding that the councilors were thankful that the two-thirds rule let them "escape the necessity of dealing with the matter on its merits and adjourn in good humor" (*Star* August 9, 1897, 1). Decades later columnist W. A. Craik (*Toronto Telegram* [henceforth *Telegram*] June 2, 1961) recalled this civic debate over the regulation of film in Toronto, noting that the Canadian federal parliament earlier in 1897 had considered a revision to the criminal code specifically to bar films of prizefights nationwide. No such federal provision was ever introduced and any federal concern over film had an impasse similar to what happened in Toronto. The failure to reckon with moving pictures "on its merits" is a sign that the place of film in society was still undefined. Because prizefights were prohibited, should films of them be banned, too? The answer was not obvious. Less obvious was the question of jurisdiction—federal, provincial, or municipal. Whereas prizefights were a special loophole, police had long been able to seize any representation of indecent or immoral conduct as a criminal matter just as they could arrest any person for indecent or immoral acts.

Even with theatoriums open in 1906, a full year elapsed before controversy erupted. By 1907 police were already inspecting and censoring films "on the beat" as they patrolled the city more generally for indecent acts. This time film censorship was considered in general for the city, not just for prizefight pictures but for everyday shows at the cheap theatoriums, a novel space of consumption that had existed in Toronto for only a year. In April 1907, a moving picture called *The Unwritten Law* was censored after playing a few days at the Star burlesque theater (*Toronto Mail & Empire* [henceforth *Mail & Empire*] April 13, 1907; *News* April 12, 1907). It depicted the notorious murder of Evelyn Nesbitt Thaw's lover Stanford White at the hands of her husband. Harry Thaw's defense was a supposedly unwritten law that a husband had a right to slay his wife's seducer. The film included a fictionalized not-guilty verdict, although the trial was still underway and making front page news (more recently popping up in the plot of the novel and musical *Ragtime*). Lee Grieveson (2004, 37–77) proposes the emergence of movie censorship in Chicago and throughout the United States can be traced directly to the controversy surrounding this film. As controversial as the trial itself, the film nonetheless played without getting censored in places such as Montreal and even in smaller cities in Ontario.

Soon after police banned the Thaw–White film in Toronto, a city councilor on the legislative committee proposed a city bylaw to specify police censorship of amusements and allow for an official play censor

(*Star* April 17, 1907). Just a week later, an amusement license application for a proposed theatorium was referred by the Board of Police Commissioners to the Board of Control. The *Star* (April 25, 1907) reported that Mayor Coatsworth and other controllers, with one exception, had no knowledge whatsoever of what went on in the moving picture shows. Although told they had nothing to worry about, they decided to temporarily require the property commissioner to inspect all proposed theatoriums. The legislative committee of the city council discussed the morality of plays as well as moving picture shows, considering inflammatory anecdotes about corrupted children who thieved and lied to get nickels to go to the picture shows (*Star* April 27, 1907; *World* April 27, 1907). Although picture shows were thoroughly mixed with stage theater in the discussion, Toronto clearly had potential to seize on moving pictures as an urgent problem in the city. This did not happen. Because it was embedded in the prospect of theater censorship, a forceful editorial in the *Star* compared the proposal to despotism and fought the idea as part of a "dangerous and growing tendency to meddlesome legislation, interfering with individual liberty, and substituting legal restraint for self-control and judgment" (*Star* April 25, 1907, 8). Another paper reported that the city's four or five picture shows were already well supervised by the police, who assured city officials no problem was beyond their capable grasp. The police made clear they already had been censoring and destroying scenes from films even before the recent Thaw–White picture (*News* April 27, 1907). The *Mail & Empire* (May 4, 1907) sent a reporter to spend time in the city's handful of five-cent theaters. The report provided a detailed survey of the inside and outside decorations, style of show available, some habits of the audience, and description of the film stories. Nothing objectionable was found, however. The headline read, "Five Cent Theatre Harmless Here, Merely Creates Taste for an Entertainment." Toying with stage censorship in tandem with film review, the newspapers refused to back the measures or enflame any sense of moral panic. The proposed regulations were abandoned.

These two incidents show how, after their bow in 1896, films continued for more than a decade without becoming problematic. Even when cinema became the focus of debate, the problem was not serious enough to meet the required consensus to take action. An impasse occurred with regard to articulating a solution to the problems raised, even in 1907 when a more generalized sense of some need for oversight was apparent. In 1897 technicalities preempted the disagreement about the harmful effects of represented images of fighting. In 1907 the public was relieved to have the assurance that police officers were already handling the problems raised. But in both cases, everyone was relieved that regulation addressing the particularity of film in society was not yet required. Avoiding novel regulation became the order of the day unless the need could be solidly verified. For film this verification came in 1908 with a law mandating the fire safety measures discussed in the next chapter. By then, two years had passed since the first five-cent picture shows opened in the city, and more than a decade had passed since Torontonians first had a chance to view films.

When local authorities were first prompted to regulate the fun and amusement of film, the concern was not with the commercial or technological form of cinema or its showmanship. The moral effects of viewing possibly indecent moving pictures were the first concerns. This puts the urban and regional process of regulating cinema in line with later academic studies of its media effects. Emilie Altenloh (2001) conducted an exceptionally early sociology of cinema through survey methods in Germany. Originally published in 1914, *Zur Soziologie des Kino* has only recently been recovered and translated into English; it is presented as an early model for the ethnographic study of the cinema audience. Much more widely known is Hugo Münsterburg's (2002) popular book from 1916, *The Photoplay: A Psychological Study*. And, of course, popular and trade journalism from the period is full of colloquial theories and propositions about the proper place of movies in society (Stromgren 1988). For the most part, however, communication studies happened from the 1920s onward after film was already firmly established as an everyday space for mass gathering, after the struggle to define its place in society had subsided, and bureaucratic regulations or self-imposed norms of production had been well instituted. Studying links between mass culture and the formation of the social self, especially of children, these "media effects" projects involved massive amounts of ethnographic work, especially with the Payne Fund Studies, including (all 1933) Blumer's *Movies and Conduct*, Charters's *Motion Pictures and Youth*, Peterson and Thurstone's *Motion Pictures and the Social Attitudes of Children*, and Cressey and Thrasher's *Boys, Movies and City Streets*. These titles from the series betray the search for the effects of movies on delinquency and socialization, although no significant results could support those claims (Jowett, Jarvie, & Fuller 1996). Other sociologists developed survey methods to study mass audiences at the movies, from Alice Miller Mitchell (1929) to Paul Lazarsfeld (1947; with Merton 1948) and Britain's Jacob Mayer (1946; 1948). These studies of the mass movie audience were key to refining population survey techniques and public opinion research that in turn contributed to sociology's development into a quantitative social science.

These later surveys of moviegoing reflected earlier, stronger links between U.S. urban sociology and forms of social work and moral reform in the Progressive movement. Almost as soon as the picture show took root, Jane Addams wrote about children and movies in relation to her work at Chicago's Hull House, which had briefly operated an educational nickel show of its own (Lindstrom 1999). Addams's *The Spirit of Youth and the City Streets* (1909) included an essay on the influence of movies, "The House of Dreams." The reform imperative of early sociological study of "social forces" led to an interest in studying children at the movies. Especially in urban areas, children were both able to work for some disposable income and also spend significant portions of the day without direct parental supervision. Only in these years were laws written to limit child labor. Even children forced to work, often to support families living in poverty, would still have found some limited version of spatial and fiscal independence from the family and the home. Such independence in modern American childhood brought moving picture shows to the attention of reform movements, which existed alongside and often cooperated with the development of government censorship and regulation. In Chicago, Addams's Hull House and other social work committees were active providing amusements and consulting with city officials (Lindstrom 1999; McCarthy 1976). In New York City, John Collier and the People's Institute took on a burden far beyond their own metropolis when the National Board of Censorship was established to alleviate conflict between city authorities and film showmen (Czitrom 1984; Fisher 1975). Both prominent reformers published their own essays about amusements and public health in important early social work journals such as *Charities and the Commons* (Addams 1907; Collier 1908). Typical metaphors of cleanliness and godliness were used, such as Collier's 1910 essay in *The Survey* that shed "Light on Moving Pictures."

Regional Differences and the Particularity of Toronto

This early sociology of cinema focuses on children's attendance, especially poor children in immigrant and working-class enclaves. The demographics of nickelodeon audiences remain a key debate in the study of early cinema. Very little is actually known about the degree to which nickelodeon audiences comprised women, children, immigrants, or the working classes; but contemporary journalists, reformers, and authorities often associated the cheap amusements with any or all of these socially marginalized groups. Many have tried to verify or dispute the notion that nickelodeon audiences were primarily working-class immigrants (Allen 1979; Jowett 1974; Singer 1995; Sklar 1988). The early audience has also been considered in terms of gender, arguing that young working women could find some lifting of family's restraints while at the show if only for a short time and in commercial ways (E. Ewen 1980; Hansen 1991, 60–89; Mayne 1982). Much of the impetus for regulation and reform was founded upon concerns for the policing or protection of these audiences, which were perceived as prone to deviance. The source of the cheapness of filmgoing was the celluloid film strip, the material basis of its mass production and distribution. The material form also made evident that film could be easily and bureaucratically controlled. Even as regulations were introduced, this cheap amusement was preferable to gambling or drinking, which were thought to be the more traditional forms of working-class leisure. The saloon and the billiard parlor, the race track and the shooting gallery were domains of rowdy and lewd behavior, rarely inclusive of children or women; these places encouraged addictions that could drain a man's nickel faster than any "Idle Hour" or "Happy-Half Hour" picture show. In this respect, sports and recreation, such as parks and playgrounds, were preferable to movies. But, these cornerstones of public education and health were just becoming commonplace, partly in response to the growing significance of commercial amusements.

Showmen, often active participants in their own regulation, tried to elevate the character of their audiences and shows as they sought higher profits. Like amusements before movies, such as theater and vaudeville (Butsch 1994), this can be seen as selling out, both appeasing authorities and abandoning the early audience in favor of upward mobility (Ross 1998; Uricchio and Pearson 1993). Many accounts of the nickelodeon period, especially books providing a wide overview of film history, argue that moral concerns prompting repressive crackdowns hindered the almost natural progress of mass moviegoing. Protests are, in a sense, framed as the middle class walling itself off from a specifically working-class pastime. But then how did movies end up a mass practice inclusive of the middle class? The question is phrased to have an empirical answer—if only we knew the demographics of actual audiences! However, even if the statistics were there to study, it still would not explain how very different types of people came to understand and even appreciate how they were participating in a common pastime with others. Theaters big and small, lavish and drab, in far-flung towns, were charging many prices to see hundreds of different movies—at some point these actually separate audiences became aware that they were part of an apparently mass audience. The answer to the question of how and when the movie audience shifted from class to mass is best answered by describing emergent norms and standards of moviegoing, its conditions, regulations, and promotion. As much as through movie studios and distributors, that process also had to be instituted locally and regionally.

Much discussion occurred surrounding the social problems found at the nickel show, where ages and genders mixed freely at working-class or ethnic-identified spaces. Nickelodeons were, in fact, cast as darkened denizens of vice, and this evidence was key to surveilling not only what was shown, but also the venue (L. Jacobs 1968, 62–66; May 1980, 43–59; Sklar 1975, 18–32). Regulations specific to moving picture shows were first imposed from about 1907 to 1911 as storefront nickel shows introduced a novel, cheap way of viewing films regularly, everyday, all day, in cities and larger towns. If censorship and regulation was meant to protect the juvenile and foreign-born audience and protect society against them, then why would the result be a mass audience mixing in the middle class, too? One answer requires foregrounding how the five-cent show was at first just one place among many to see movies for an initially wide range of purposes. Only over time did entertainment at a movie theater become the recognizable norm. One key factor was that regulation tended to make projecting films outside of licensed, commercial spaces more difficult. Of course, industrial factors were also present: increased costs, more stringent control of who could distribute and exhibit films, and gradually longer, more elaborately produced movies.

Aside from the established place of moving pictures on the vaudeville program, at industrial exhibitions, and amusement parks, numerous sporadic attempts were made at alternative, educational forms of cinema. In a sense small versions of the more professional traveling illustrated lectures, picture shows were set up in churches, schools, and settlement houses, sometimes without profit for civic improvement. Various attempts at such alternatives occurred in Toronto, too, including several of the earliest showmen accommodating religious film shows and social meetings in their auditoriums. Especially for nonfiction attractions, as late as 1913 films such as *Paul J. Rainey's African Hunt*, advertised in *Moving Picture World* how picture theaters were just one suggested location for exhibiting films. Churches, schools, the YMCA, clubs, colleges, resorts, department stores, and natural history societies were equally depicted as possible contexts for such films because these organizations could claim a higher purpose than mere amusement (*MPW* December 13, 1913, 1239). On the other hand, fiction narrative was already the norm; for example, weeks later in the same magazine, an ad promoted a change in format for Melies General Films. The "old style" was depicted with a sparsely attended theater showing "Scenes in Java," while a packed auditorium next door showed the new style "comedy, drama, etc." (*MPW* January 24, 1914, 437). As commercial films became more predictably a matter of fictional narratives, melodramatic and adventurous films, advocates for a more civic form of moviegoing seemed always to fall back on nonfiction "attractions" as the solution to commercial moviegoing as a social problem. An August 1910 editorial in a Toronto paper wrote, "it is most unfortunate that the moving picture entertainments could not rely upon their own best attractions for their audiences" (*World* August 24, 1910, 6). It listed all the wonders of the world that might be caught in moving pictures before claiming this infinite variety of social life "might have been expected to supply an unending series of attractions, both interesting and amusing, instructive as well." The problem with moving picture shows, according to the editorial, was that "whether it be the fault of the audiences or managers," the commercial and fictional emphasis meant the tone of the pictures was steadily falling.

However, a "cinema of attractions" is a concept associated with film before the nickel show, emphasizing the experience of wonderment and surprise of early nonnarrative cinema. Introduced by Tom Gunning and André Gaudreault, the term positions the shorter actuality films of early cinema as a distinct form of spectatorship, against conceiving of early cinema as simply an immature stage in the progress toward fictional, narrative film (Gaudreault 1990; Gunning 1990 and 1993). The term takes on a critical edge on top of aesthetic description when considering how such "attractions" were sanctioned for middle-class educational uplift, a tool in the fight against the affordable amusement of early nickel shows and their new forms of narrative cinema. "Attractions" became associated with noncommercial, refined moviegoing just when narrative film was becoming the norm. The theory of the cinema of attractions does more than distinguish temporally between early nonfiction cinema and the transition to narrative; alternative social practices are also implied, sometimes overtly called into force when certain venues and films competed for audiences by appealing to different class-associated modes of spectatorship. In particular, "attractions" were used briefly to work out how film was to be integrated with everyday routines of family, church, and civic life. Associated with the earlier, more costly, and refined entertainments of variety theaters, exhibitions, and summer parks, the cinema of attractions was subsequently seen as a possible way to ensure respectable, middle-class values counterbalanced the creeping commercialization of leisure at the theatoriums.

Government regulation and police inspection would not restrict films to nonfiction actualities. Quite the opposite. Lee Grieveson's thorough history, *Policing Cinema* (2004), illustrates in detail how governments prohibited nonfiction prizefight pictures and nonfiction "social problem" films depicting the evils of prostitution. American courts in particular supported censorship and local control of problematic moving pictures by legally defining films to be subject to federal interstate law because they were commercial products. The dominant role for film—harmless entertainment—was thus legally mandated as courts denied films the protection of free speech under the First Amendment of the U.S. Constitution (Grieveson 2004, 124–35). That Supreme Court case is just one extreme example, at the national level, of how local particularities were instrumental in making moviegoing a mass practice. The interplay of showmanship and governance in the particular case of Toronto was a careful, iterative process of determining how this novel urban practice was best managed. Management included the organization of finances and of audiences. Both the business people who ran nickel shows and the public officials who monitored them had to compromise to arrive at standards and norms. To some degree, all could agree on safeguarding the people of the city, the mutual source of audiences and public. The measures taken to manage theaters and audiences in Toronto adopted, improved, and sometimes rejected precedents set elsewhere. The terms framing the discussion of film in Toronto were largely set by events in large U.S. cities; for example, when the first Ontario statute of 1908 adapted a recent Massachusetts law. However, care was always taken to adapt measures to suit what was perceived as the particularity of English Canada.

Early municipal measures in Chicago and New York are cited in many social histories of film as influential metropolitan cases. By 1907, middle-class magazines, fascinated with "the poor man's elementary course in the drama," had latched onto "the nickel madness" trying to understand the allure of cheap amusements to the working class on the one hand and the moral crusades against moving pictures on the other (Currie 1907; Patterson 1907). In November 1907, Chicago began requiring every film to obtain a police permit before showing it. This instituted a system of censorship that was vastly more centralized and bureaucratic than the general prohibition of scenes of crime and immorality of a year earlier (Grieveson 1999). In December 1907, a New York court decision temporarily shut down a wide variety of amusements on Sundays. Moving picture shows were shut down as a result, yet taverns and saloons remained open. A compromise was soon instituted where theaters could hold educational or religious shows on Sundays. This was minor compared to what occurred a year later, when New York's mayor unilaterally closed all nickel shows following a public hearing regarding their moral and physical conditions. The mayor's revocation, without notice, of more than 500 business licenses was so drastic that New York's showmen successfully gained a court injunction against the measure (Gunning 1991, 151–55; Uricchio and Pearson 1993, 32–33). Both Chicago and New York saw hundreds of nickelodeons open in the few short years after the electric theater was introduced around 1905. There were simply too many to ignore, especially in light of prominent advice in magazines and from well-known reformers.

In New York and Chicago, nickel shows drew reformers' attention because they were often located in areas populated by the working-class and ethnic groups, places of concern to social workers. Reform surveys of five-cent shows and their audiences could lead to muckraking journalism and in turn regulatory measures. For example, the *Chicago Tribune* printed a sustained profile of the alleged dangers and vices of nickel shows early in 1907, months before the police instituted film censorship (Grieveson 1999). The nickelodeons had drawn scattered attention throughout 1906, but it amounted to nothing at those times (*Chicago Tribune* February 14, March 29 and October 5, 1906). The difference in April 1907 was the recent election of a new mayor whose platform advocated moral reform of petty graft and commercial amusements (Ruble 2001, 155–67). The new mayoralty (and newly appointed police chief) went hand-in-hand with attention paid to cheap entertainments on the part of social reform groups in Chicago. The *Chicago Tribune* then put the five-cent show alongside a wide range of public entertainments that required municipal action, pushing for reform of ticket scalpers, dance halls, slot machines, boxing, roller skating, as well as five-cent theaters. No doubt in those first largely unregulated years of fierce entrepreneurial expansion, ministers, settlement social workers, police patrolmen, even mayors, could easily find enough trouble emanating out of some nickel theaters to justify repressive sanctions against all of them. After all, there were hundreds to search through, and these were most densely visible in poor, ethnic neighborhoods such as Manhattan's Lower East Side, which had been sites of social and moral concern long before the nickel theaters opened, most famously in Jacob Riis's *How the Other Half Lives* (1890). But in April 1907, coinciding with the *Chicago Tribune* articles, the morality of moving pictures and theatoriums in Toronto attracted similar attention. Although the discussion began with many of the same concerns as in Chicago, the debate over moving pictures in Toronto, as already noted, was quickly defused. Existing police supervision and censorship of five-cent theaters had the matter well under control. Chicago had celebrity reformers, an infamously graft-laden police force, a new mayor fulfilling promises, and hundreds rather than a handful of nickel shows. The way concerns about film were handled reflected the particularity of a city, even if there was something generalized about film technology and the entertainments of nickel shows.

Attention to regional differences has found its way into recent social histories of film. Studies of filmgoing in rural areas, small towns, and in cities in the southern United States argue for an entirely distinct character of filmgoing outside New York and large cities such as Chicago (Aronson 2002; Potamianos 2002; Waller 1995). "Manhattan Myopia" was a phrase Robert C. Allen (1996) used responding to a reevaluation of his own revision of the myth of the ethnic working-class character of the early film audience. But of course, more than myopias of geography have been corrected as scholars consider the distinctive viewing situations of, for example, blacks in Chicago, young immigrant women, or Jewish families (Bertellini 1999; Stewart 2005; Thissen 2002). The overtly collective and communicative form of moviegoing makes it almost tautological that cinema acted as an alternative social institution, a school of citizenship, provider of language and cultural lessons, and instructor in the American Dream. But even a handful of cases of ethnic, educational, or racially segregated theaters demonstrates that this process easily varied among neighborhoods and even among theaters. Still, New York's Lower East Side ghettos supplied many mythic, social, and material origins of practices that came to define modern urban American culture, and not just in the movie business (Heinze 1990). The perceived need for institutions of assimilation and regulation of those places of ethnic congregation in New York City certainly provided both example and counterexample of how smaller cities such as Toronto wanted to shape their public spaces and police conduct in neighborhoods.

Between the censuses taken in 1901 and in 1921, Toronto had grown from a population of just more than 200,000 to well in excess of 500,000, and incorporated outlying suburbs into expanding city limits accompanied by massive residential building. This growth came not from any one primary industry but from the general, metropolitan expansion of a wide array of services and small factories, especially for foods, furniture, clothing, and finished consumer goods. Most of the population growth came from immigration, with Toronto's 38 percent foreign-born population in 1910 higher than Chicago or Boston and a close second to New York among the largest cities on the continent. And yet, the official count recorded fewer than 10 percent as "foreign-born," because the vast majority of Toronto's immigrants were "British-born," counted in a separate category (Harris 1996, 23–25). Although Canada became a politically independent "Dominion" in 1867, Toronto was still very much a British colonial city in its character. By 1921, census records show religious affiliation at 11 percent Jewish, 14 percent Roman Catholic, and more than 70 percent Protestant, overwhelmingly the Anglican Church of England and the Presbyterian Church of Scotland. Fully five out of every six people in Toronto claimed "British" as their ethnic origin, a racialized category that included Irish Catholic (Careless 1984, 200–202). Although these numbers provide a container or skeleton to consider its particularity, they only begin to describe the public culture of the city at the time.

Toronto had an enduring concern for moral, social, and civic purity, with the strictest of Protestant, Anglo-Saxon propriety expected from the city's relatively small Jewish, Italian, Chinese, and "Colored" populations, living primarily in the poorest parts of town (Strange 1995; Valverde 1991). A later chapter examines how marginalized people and their amusements received a disproportionate amount of attention. In general, however, amusements were rarely associated with problems of ethnicity and class, the "downtown problem" in the contemporary language of Protestant churches. This was partly because the poorest ethnic district, known as the "Ward," was immediately adjacent to middle-class shopping and leisure downtown just steps from the major department stores. Unlike the rich histories of Yiddish vaudeville in the ethnic ghettoes of Chicago and New York, the Ward in Toronto had only a single theater of its own; the theaters of the Ward were the many downtown small shows. A more significant factor in diffusing the ethnic and class problem of filmgoing in the city was their initial ownership; John Griffin, an older, Toronto-born, Irish Catholic, owned almost all of Toronto's first moving picture shows. Griffin was no upstart entrepreneur prone to pushing the boundaries of propriety. After a career as a traveling circus manager, he used moving pictures as a way to settle down and finally live at home. Overall, in Toronto the five-cent shows became a social problem because the commercial public amusement was restructuring middle-class childhood and family life, as opposed to concerns for the deviant conduct of poor ethnic audiences. In turn, reform was primarily directed at curtailing any tendency to risk unsafe or salacious practices arising from the profit-seeking basis of showmanship.

Toronto and English Canada tentatively upheld a sense of uniqueness in the lack of social evils relative to large cities in both the United States and England (Valverde 1991, 16–17). Although heavily regulated and patrolled, moving pictures were rarely a contentious hotbed of anxiety in Toronto even compared to other amusements such as burlesque and melodrama theatricals at stage theaters (Campbell 1996). Strict regulation of five-cent shows was largely achieved through the collaboration of business, government, reformers, and the public audience itself. On the whole, standards for moviegoing were achieved by "forging a consensus" as did the more official institutions of the city (Russell 1984). Few dissenting voices are found in the documents that inform this study: journalism and advertising, municipal building and assessment records, the police Register of Criminals, letters and reports of the chief constable, minutes of the Board of Control and City Council. Complaints are found on occasion in U.S. film trade journalism, but even there some claimed the strict regulation of filmgoing in Toronto was actually conducive to business. The strongest local protests against any extension of government regulation seem to have lasted only a day in the newspapers, as if following journalistic convention requiring two sides in every debate reported. Taken as a decadelong process, about 1907 to 1916, many more than two sides to the debate surfaced. Indeed, a wide range of people voiced their own vision of the proper place of moving pictures in the city and the role of film in society.

Toronto the Good, or at Least, Toronto the Better

The starkest difference between Toronto and New York or Chicago was that these U.S. cities were then the major production sites for filmmaking and in turn the location of head offices for film distributors. Perhaps a result of safety in numbers, another key difference was the litigious and confrontational independence of theater-owning showmen in these big cities. Toronto showmen's status as importers and renters of other people's film

Figure 1.2. Standard Theatre, "High-Class Moving Pictures." 482 Queen Street West. *ca.* 1909. (Photograph by William James. City of Toronto Archives, Fonds 1244, Item 332.)

product might have predisposed them to cooperation in censorship and theater inspections. However, showmen in other cities such as Cleveland or Philadelphia, even Montreal and Vancouver—none of them film production centers—were also consistently protecting their interests in court. In Toronto even measures that affected finances directly such as license fees and fines for violating bylaws went largely uncontested. It helped that regulatory measures were reasonable compared to those other cities used. The annual license fee in Toronto was minimal and stayed constant, in contrast with smaller Ontario cities such as Hamilton or St. Catharines whose councils cashed in on increased competition by raising license fees and limiting how many were granted. Showmen fought usurious license fees in courts, such as in 1911 when Montreal (*MPW* January 14, 1911, 94) and Pennsylvania (*MPW* December 2, 1911, 701) each raised picture show licenses to $500, fully ten times more than those levied in Toronto.

Some key showmen in Toronto actually invited government inspection, even before the first fire safety law in 1908. In return, the police force was consistent and predictable, famously free of corruption. For five-cent shows, fairness was easy because the city's small number of shows could still be monitored regularly "on the beat." For example, asked to comment on the New York order closing hundreds of nickelodeons at Christmas 1908, the Toronto officer in charge of morality, Staff Inspector Stephen, claimed proudly to the *News*, "there is no lesson for Toronto to learn. . . . The pictures shown in this city are fit for most people to see, and if there were any flagrant violations of good taste, I am sure the police would hear of it within an hour. No; I shall not take action here, as did the Mayor of New York" (*News* December 29, 1908, 3). Stephen was personally sure all shows were already meeting superior standards.

While the directness of such a statement that there was nothing to learn from New York was rare, newspapers reported measures south of the border with a detachment afforded by regional difference. The *World* (December 25, 1908) put a brief recap of the incident in New York on the front page, while the *Toronto Globe* [henceforth *Globe*] picked up an Associated Press dispatch of the subsequent "indignant" protest of "many angry showmen" (December 26, 1908). Finally, the *World* (December 28, 1908) reported New York shows reopened after proprietors were granted an injunction against the mayor. A year earlier, when New York amusements were closed on Sundays while taverns stayed open, the *Star* published an editorial distinguishing Toronto's somber Sunday from New York's amusement habits, linking the difference to problems of police corruption and improper influence. "The fact is that public opinion is stronger against the saloon than against the theater and concert hall, but also that there is a stronger vested interest behind the saloon. Probably the law forbidding amusements could be modified to suit the habits of the New Yorkers; and the same would be done with the liquor laws if they were strenuously enforced" (*Star* December 14, 1905). The political "machine" of U.S. municipal politics could be an essential tool of conflict management within the incredible heterogeneity of cities undergoing unprecedented growth (Boulay and DiGaetano 1985). Unlike New York, Chicago, or Montreal, Toronto was just small enough and homogeneous enough that police could monitor every aspect of civic and commercial life, where even the ban on prostitution was strictly enforced. Policing was severe but fairly administered to the letter of the law, and the police force itself was strictly disciplined to carefully stay within the rule of law.

Police in Toronto followed a British rather than a U.S. model. A municipal Board of Police Commissioners was created in 1858 to act independently of political influence, striving for an impartial force standing outside local networks, circumscribed in its discretionary powers of action through the police chief, closely regulating its activities (Marquis 1991; Rogers 1984). Throughout the late 1880s, Toronto police recruits and officers were systematically pared of secret society affiliations and working-class rowdyism, drunkenness, immorality, and indecency. They were given a gymnasium, a billiard room, a library, and a police Bible class. Unmarried officers were provided a barracks or encouraged to board together and refrain from fraternizing with the public, journalists, and even each other if on duty. Toronto's police force conducted itself as a professional body segregated from class and sectarian interests of the city and submitted officers to the highest standards of discipline and morality with only occasional dispute over the ability to realistically meet these ideals. Such high standards continued into the years of early filmgoing when, for example, racetrack gambling among officers was rooted out at a time when the legality of the issue had been debated (*News* October 1, 1908).

Strict policing made the slogan "Toronto the Good" a reality, at least for a city of its size. But, the city still attracted loud preachers who wanted the whip to come down even harder on "Toronto the Rotten" (*News* October 10, 1908). Against such complaints, the chief constable in these years, H. J. Grasett, always carefully explained that his actions were limited to the letter of the law and that politicians, not police, wrote those laws. The harsh moralism of policing seems conducted with genuine transparency. Far from arcane, this marked the police force as modern and reformed. Many will find this claim of fair policing surprising, even unbelievable; but I propose precisely this trait characterizes the particularity of Toronto. Policing in Toronto was repressive and moralistic, and in retrospect often racist, at least systemically because of the British, Protestant ethnocentrism of regulations (Mosher 1998), but it was fair and consistent, at least insofar as it was largely free from political interference and graft. This was, indeed, precisely the intent of almost every step in the fifty years' previous development of the force. Municipal police forces exercised a dual role. They were, on the one hand, patrollers of the city's public conduct, including printed or pictured conduct. But they were also patrolling the city's built form through inspection and license enforcement, which has since largely become a more bureaucratic matter of planning, zoning, and construction standards. The still-dual character of policing in the early twentieth century partly explains why the supervision of a hazardous, flammable substance such as celluloid film could become so tightly entwined with censorship of the images projected from the film.

Moviegoing soon led to bureaucracies of censorship, inspection, and licensing that largely usurped everyday policing of theaters. Urban planning in these years was just becoming a professional sphere. Reforming and rationalizing bylaws and regulations, however, still fell under the umbrella of the Board of Police Commissioners and the municipal Board of Control, a semipolitical body including the mayor, a few aldermen, the chief constable, and top bureaucrats (Petersen 1984; Rogers 1984). Indeed, the daily correspondence of the chief constable shows his job was primarily concerned with coordinating the actions of the many civic departments that supervised the city: patrolmen in each of the force's divisions, the police magistrate, the city architect, city solicitor, city clerk, city license office, the mayor, and other members of the Board of Police Commissioners and Board of Control; of course, the public had the usual requests and complaints. Journalists and reformers were constantly searching for vice and corruption; failing to find it at home in Toronto, they continually turned to stories of graft in large U.S. cities. That difference was intended when the systems of municipal governance in Ontario were put in place and reformed throughout the nineteenth century. The city's milieu of moral conservatism and motto of Toronto the Good were inseparable from, perhaps even preceded by, municipal offices specifically designed to avoid petty nepotism and corruption. Such policing reflected the primary difference between Canadian and U.S. governance more generally. Most distinct was a relative lack of municipal autonomy in favor of Canadian provincial governments, supposedly structured that way to prevent the recurrence of circumstances leading to the American Revolution (Isin 1992; Taylor 1991).

English Canadian society all but explicitly held up mainstream Protestantism as an informal state religion while church groups in turn treated government as their ally, not their opponent (Valverde 1991, 26). The Toronto police, in particular, took moral reform as its special vocation without resistance from the establishment. A substantial increase in the police budget in the 1870s was granted only on the condition that officers would oversee new liquor licensing laws and enforce observance of Sabbath blue law prohibitions more strictly (Rogers 1984). Their job was to ensure that the conduct of all people in all parts of the city followed the law; at times this meant matching the most austere manners of Methodist prudence. Working-class Catholic or immigrant amusements were held to the utmost Anglo-Saxon Protestant standards; but so was every public aspect of the social and working lives these classes. The Lord's Day Act applied strict Sunday closings equally to Jewish and Chinese merchants, to factory shift workers, to visitors to Toronto, even to traveling American vaudeville performers (*Star* March 27, 1909).

This relatively overt and deliberate religious influence in civic life in Ontario was part of the more consensual development of norms for filmgoing. Several cases indicate how enforcement and regulation in Toronto successfully ensured that showmen followed the spirit as well as the letter of the law. Exploiting loopholes was rare, and often a simple test case set a precedent and reestablished the order of the regulations. Ontario's film statutes could change without parliamentary assent through bureaucratic updates at the discretion of the minister responsible. Ontario Chief Censor G. E. Armstrong recalled in an interview how, within months of the start of provincial censorship in 1911, loopholes that were exploited in the far north of the province were eliminated through simple bureaucratic changes, which had the added benefit of cutting costs (*Star Weekly* June 28, 1913). This contrasted with censorship in Quebec, where a report from 1914 notes the systemic undermining of the Quebec Censor Board right in the city of Montreal. This situation required a rewriting of the cinematograph act to close a loophole (*MPW* June 6, 1914, 1426). Scott MacKenzie (2000) has characterized such resistance in Montreal as evidence of an "alternative public sphere" in francophone filmgoing and showmanship. MacKenzie argues strongly that cinema in Quebec was aligned with the urban working class against the Catholic Church and its tight allegiance with government. In contrast, movie showmen in Toronto and Ontario were more like working partners with Protestant churches and government. Such differences underline how practices of moviegoing and film-showing could vary according to the public culture of a city or region. The local articulation of conditions for moviegoing in Toronto are strongly linked to the general milieu for commercial and public conduct, not least as patrolled by deliberately reformed and professional policing.

Defining the Relation between Film and Society

Articulating a regional version of the definition of film in society was part of embedding film in regional cultures. Despite differences in the tenor of filmgoing and its supervision, the need for oversight was recognized almost everywhere. Toronto's civic institutions may have been modeled to reflect British roots and reject "Yankee-isms," but local institutions were still profoundly shaped by U.S. urban culture insofar as the United States represented a modern model in general. This was true for cultural and commercial novelties, of course, but social scientific discourses crossed the border just as easily. Toronto was headquarters for Canadian social purity groups, and it was the city most influenced by American Progressivism. A sharp contrast was found in both "social gospel" evangelism in the Canadian prairies and strictly parochial Catholicism in Quebec. In her history of reform measures in Toronto, Carolyn Strange (1995) notes, "the civic administration looked for guidance to U.S. cities.... Urban Progressives saw the city as a social problem to be alleviated through rational management and social action" (p. 102). With regard to the entertainments of drama and motion pictures, of amusement park rides and carnival foods, this translated into an open acceptance of American goods and practices, provided always that local standards were given final say.

The annual Toronto Industrial Exhibition, renamed the Canadian National Exhibition by 1904, was the principal site introducing cultural goods and practices to Canada (Walden 1997). Early amusement parks such as Scarboro Beach (from 1907) and Ward's Island (from 1894) provided opportunities for U.S. entrepreneurs to settle in Canada. In Toronto, however, these Yankee hawkers were careful not to bring their habits of Sunday selling with them. Even the circuit of touring commercial dramas and vaudeville was careful to demonstrate some balance between central management in the United States and the local community (see, for example, *News* February 19, 1910). When dramatic reviews listed the latest sensations, they always also played up the local roots of Canadian and Toronto-born players when in town on the circuit (*Star* September 2, 1911). During the development of a code of conduct for censoring plays from 1908 to 1913, the same Saturday dramatic columns detailed the supposedly particular moral respect due Toronto audiences (*News* November 14, 1908). American film trade journals expressed frustration with the inexplicable attraction of Canadian audiences to inferior British films, even as they considered responding to Canadian needs as a way to gain more global export markets for U.S. films (*MPW* December 9, 1911, 795; Steven 2003).

Nonetheless, most people—even authorities and reformers—welcomed moving pictures as a way of connecting Toronto to the continental and world stage of culture and events, as long as local censorship to Torontonians' cultural tastes and needs prevailed. In the months before the Ontario Board of Censors was instituted in 1911, Chief Constable

Grasett of Toronto considered applying the guidance of reviews from the New York–based National Board of Censorship. This branch of the Progressive reform People's Institute facilitated showmen's self-regulation in a compromise to the 1908 dispute with the Mayor (Fisher 1975). Grasett's willingness to apply rather than adapt American ways may have been what finally prompted the higher level of government to take responsibility for the matter. Still, finding a way to assert local influence in film regulation and provide a tone particular to Toronto was an intractable problem. As strictly and ardently as municipal police had enforced early censorship, the chief constable wrote frankly in his annual report in 1913 that he was "glad to be rid of it" when the Ontario Censors took responsibility.

Why did the task of integrating moviegoing into Toronto's civic culture prove so problematic? The contemporary, local perspective was much like remarks on the character of cinema in general. Film was a reproduction of reality that helped establish a strong relation between the city and the world beyond. Since at least the introduction of the technology of moving pictures, cinema prompted the imaginations of commentators and philosophers investigating its character. One of the earliest theoretical uses of film, Henri Bergson's *Creative Evolution* (1911), proposed that thought itself was best understood through the mechanistic illusion of the cinematograph. As an aside, a small newspaper article twists similar ideas into a logic puzzle for the bemusement of the general urban public, "Is There Such a Thing as Motion?" (*Star Weekly* February 21, 1914). More often theories of film conversely borrow conceptions of mind and thought. Analyses of how cinema functions continue to be written, and key phrases in the legacy of this discussion can be listed: mechanical reproduction, the cinematic apparatus, and the democratic art (bowing respectively to Benjamin 1968, Baudry 1974, and Jowett 1976). But long before these theories were written, writers in magazines and newspapers, speakers from pulpits and platforms (and no doubt on factory floors and at department store counters) were in awe of the endless possibilities that were evident in the electric vision of film. Even the occupants of political offices, banking towers, posh salons, and theater boxes took note when the popularity of the movies sprouted nickel shows all over town.

Businesses began using films for commercial promotion, and one of the very first was Toronto's own Massey-Harris farm machinery factories. Government agencies began making and showing films for various forms of propaganda. Again, one of the first was the Canadian government through the Canadian Pacific Railway, making films to encourage European immigrants to become prairie farmers (Morris 1992, 29–39). Even as they aimed to amuse, mainstream films took up social issues from labor and class conflict to women's suffrage and the "white slave" problem (Ross 1998; Stamp 2000). Evangelical preachers used religious films such as *The Passion Play* or *The Life of Christ* to accompany popular sermonizing. In Toronto as elsewhere, the Salvation Army was almost uniquely unafraid of meeting the poor and working class on their own terms and specialized in the use of films in ministry. Even as filmgoing became a major commercial industry, publicity about the varied uses of films proliferated as well, as if to attest to its general social importance as more than harmless amusement. In the Toronto *Star Weekly* alone, frequent articles on the progress of moving picture technology and its social uses noted that the YMCA and other social service clubs used films as part of their programs and healthy leisure (March 16, 1912); that scientists used films in deep sea exploration and in animal psychological experiments (July 19 and November 29, 1913); that university sports teams and journalism students used films for training (November 1, 1913; March 14, 1914); that films were being used for missionary work (December 13, 1913), to teach children about safety (April 11, 1914), and even to reconcile divorcing couples (June 6, 1914). The content and context of film were entirely open. Only gradually did these alternatives become irrevocably marginalized as peripheral to the "harmless entertainment" of commercial amusements. According to Grieveson, in the case of the United States, the emergence of that limited definition can be traced directly to particular racialized and sexualized concerns arising from specific films and consequent regulatory measures (Grieveson 2004).

From either the beginning of the technology in 1896 or the nickel show in 1906, most films were viewed in a commercial context. Film meant cheap amusement. Debates about alternative venues and purposes for film viewing recognized, at least implicitly, that there were alternatives to the profit motive of showmanship. Educational, religious, and scientific films indicate a nascent discussion about reforming filmgoing on a structural level, not simply placing conditions and sanctioning existing content and spaces. There was even the choice of whether there had to be a place for film in society at all. Although film arrived in larger cities such as Toronto before its significance could be debated on these terms, it was later common for suburbs and villages to debate whether to let film showmen in at all. Could a community viably choose to exclude moviegoing? In the United States, attempts to run educational or uplifting picture shows in poor, urban neighborhoods served only to prove that civic-minded alternatives were financially unsustainable (McCarthy 1976, 42–46). More often, especially in rural areas, civic and religious associations willingly shared the profit motive of showmanship by renting their halls for picture shows. This was particularly true of smaller towns, especially in Quebec and the Canadian Prairies. A review of Canadian picture theaters listed in the 1932 *Film Daily Yearbook*, for example, turns up dozens of "Parish Halls" and "Town Halls" as the names of small town theaters. The situation was true even in some small cities, such as St. John's, Newfoundland. Profiled in detail in a later chapter, one case outside Toronto in Weston settled on the compromise of a non-profit show run by the community itself, a rare proposal to include moviegoing but exclude showmanship. The village wanted the benefits of moving pictures to apply equally to all townspeople, in a sense resisting the snob appeal of the Garden Theatre downtown with its slogan of "Rendezvous for Particular People." The debate in Weston was framed as "film or not?" but at times the rhetoric equivocated those concerns into the parallel anxieties of "modern or not?" or "community or not?" Suburbanites who argued against allowing moviegoing were effectively fighting pressures of secularization and urbanization. The city limits were quite literally encroaching on their lives.

2

Socially Combustible

Panicky People and Flammable Films

A fire was caused in the Gem Theatre, corner Northcote Ave. and Queen Street Saturday evening about 11:20, by an electric wire coming into contact with a film of moving pictures. The building was saved and possibly a panic averted by the machine having been properly enclosed in a cabinet, according to regulations.

—"Moving Picture Blaze," *World* August 14, 1911

IN JANUARY 1908 A FIFTEEN-YEAR-OLD projectionist died of burns after the film he was showing caught fire at the Hippodrome Theatorium in St. Catharines, Ontario, a small city between Toronto and Niagara Falls (*World* January 16, 1908). Just a day later came news of another celluloid fire and panicky picture show audience in another Ontario town Ingersoll (*Telegram* January 18, 1908). Both incidents followed on the heels of a theater disaster in Boyertown, Pennsylvania, where 170 people died in a panicked rush to flee a fire reportedly resulting from the explosion of a moving picture projector. Although moving pictures were ultimately cleared of culpability in Boyertown, the tragedy remains associated with the dangers of early moviegoing (Smither 2002, 433). Horrific details from Pennsylvania filled the front pages of newspapers across the continent including Toronto (see, for example, *News* January 14, 1908), but the death in St. Catharines brought close to home the dangers of picture shows as a new type of gathering place.

Reporters drew readers' attention to the long history of theater fires and newspapers reviewed several tragedies of the past, most recently the Chicago Iroquois Theatre fire in 1903, which had led many cities throughout North America to enforce new fire safety bylaws for theaters (Brandt 2003). But this time around, the cinematograph machine, with its electric arc lamp and its combustible reels of cellulose nitrate films, was singled out as the culprit. Justifiably or not, the still-novel technology seemed to escape the bounds of even the most stringent requirements in the construction of theaters. Safety designs for exits, escapes, stairwells, doorways, and asbestos stage curtains could not contain the explosive mix of celluloid, electricity, and hot projection lamps. The chemical combustibility of moving picture technology only reinforced nascent opinions about nickelodeon audiences being excitable and panicky in part because they were disproportionately juvenile, female, foreign-born, and working class.

Within months of the Boyertown incident came a rush of laws specifically addressing the cinematograph and its flammable celluloid films. In Ontario, Massachusetts, and other places throughout North America, legislators gave cinema its first legal definition. Film was identified as a hazardous substance needing careful bureaucratic inspection and licensing. This spate of legislation early in 1908 marked the moment when film technology achieved a broad public persona. In North America, the entrepreneurial boom of nickel show openings around 1906 was followed swiftly by public debates over their social role. Reformers, police, parents, and politicians: each and all together questioned the maturity of nickelodeon audiences and the effects of easy access to filmed depictions of crime and immoral acts. On this cultural and moral plane, plenty of room remained for disagreement and deliberation over the commercial merits of the picture show, the moral effects of its pictures, and the need to censor and supervise audiences. But the 1908 explosion and catastrophe in Boyertown and its many echoes worldwide, such as the death in St. Catharines, finally made one aspect of cinema indisputable: the five-cent show was a hazardous place. The volatile combination of flammable celluloid films and panicky people crowded into nickelodeons meant moviegoing was socially combustible.

A century later, decades after the urgency of the problem dissipated, assuming that fire safety regulations are merely dampers on the energy and potential of exciting, crowded gatherings in public, urban space is easy. Police and government officials, of course, could use safety codes and bylaws to discriminate against supposedly bothersome or indecent activities. Building codes and inspections were indeed introduced largely at the insistence of business interests and insurance companies to prevent property damage and protect land values. But politicized efforts and abuses do not turn fire safety automatically into an ideological tool of urban governance. Following Bruno Latour (2005), celluloid itself can be a social actor, an active part in the networks of film regulation. Respect needs to be paid to the material properties of film technology at the nickelodeon to understand fully the central importance safety played in guiding decisions about the best fit between this novel technology and existing local cultures. Safety measures achieved perhaps the earliest consensus over regulation because of the clear benefits for the public good made stark after disastrous fire panics. Such licensing codes did not tend to ban things outright, but instead policed indirectly by stipulating conditions of consumption—who could take part, when and where things could happen. For public welfare and safety, licensed and inspected businesses such as picture shows became responsible for policing their own customers (Valverde 2003). Characterizing the picture show as a socially combustible place emphasizes how fire safety instigated some of the earliest film-specific laws. These fire safety laws were soon extended into elaborate film bureaucracies encompassing inspection, censorship, taxation, and restricted admissions (for example, barring unaccompanied children from attending films). The frame of social combustibility thus signifies how material safety laws, by defining the technology itself as hazardous, were simply the flashpoint for regulating a range of aspects of moviegoing.

Part of the problem was the indeterminate place of cinema and theatoriums in the hierarchy of municipal responsibilities. In March 1908, two years after the first "theatorium" opened in Toronto, prospective showman David L. Minier met with the city's Mayor Joseph Oliver and Police Chief Constable H. J. Grasett to discuss plans for a new picture show. Minier's initial application to license the picture show was on hold. An earlier letter from Chief Grasett to the city clerk responsible for filing license applications explained that the Board of Police Commissioners had decided to delay issuing licenses for moving picture shows pending a municipal petition to the Ontario Legislature for power to regulate picture shows (Letterbooks of the Chief Constable [henceforth *LCC*] March 11, 1908, 918). Minier would have known about the forthcoming provincial law, but he did not heed the advice to wait. Instead, he visited Mayor Oliver, and the mayor's secretary brought him to see the chief constable, who kept his officially impartial position and said all that could be done was to "re-consider" it at the next meeting of the Board (*LCC* March 17, 1908, 956). Minier had secured a location on Yonge Street just

south of Wilton Avenue (right at the present-day Dundas Square) next to
a hotel and tavern of John Brady, also owner of the site Minier had leased
for the five-cent show.

At that next meeting, the Board of Police Commissioners followed
Mayor Oliver's recommendation and approved the license (*LCC* March
24, 1908, 32). Brady, the land owner, filed a building permit application
the next day for $1,500 in alterations to the store (*Building Permits* March
25, 1908). Soon, in the U.S. show business trade magazine, *Billboard* (May

Figure 2.1. Minier's Comique, 279 Yonge Street. *ca.* 1909. (Photograph by
William James. City of Toronto Archives, Fonds 1244, Item 320.)

9, 1908, 47), Minier was listed as manager of the Comique in Toronto, offering "pictures and songs; satisfactory business," updated to "big business" just a week later. The city assessed the theater for property taxes in July 1908, and Minier's name appeared in the city directory under "Amusements" in 1909. Although Minier never promoted the show with newspaper advertising, and no flyers or programs remain, a couple of photographs still exist, including one dated 1909 that was passed down in the family (Gutteridge 2000, 131).

The meeting between the showman and the mayor, then the police chief, face-to-face with authority, was rare for any business person, but especially for a theatorium owner. This explicit mix of political influence in the regulatory process illustrates how the supervision and authority over cinema in Toronto was not yet well defined. As a still unspecified type of licensed amusement, the theatoriums were not yet singled out as special places of public gathering requiring strictly policed regulation without political interference. Several of the picture shows licensed in the two years previous to this opened without leaving a bureaucratic record. Introducing the apparent influence of the mayor, and possibly Brady as an established merchant, Minier's effort to secure a show license left its trace because it coincided with a moment of uncertainty over whose jurisdiction prevailed. To that extent, visiting the mayor could still change decisions even if the police board had the last word. Approving this and earlier picture shows could still involve informal and interpersonal communication among business people, city politicians, and police.

Minier's maneuver happened just when the chief constable was preparing for the provincial legislature to pass more formal regulations. A fire safety statute, this would be the first measure in Toronto addressed specifically to moving pictures. It passed quickly with little comment outside legislative circles, in contrast to proposals for film censorship in 1897 and 1907, which ultimately reaffirmed the status quo. Once the new 1908 law was passed, the authority of the Board of Police Commissioners was total. On their behalf, Chief Grasett began regular correspondence about picture show licenses only after the Ontario law was introduced in April 1908, while the matter dropped out of the minutes of the Board of Control and those of the City Council. David Minier was the first and only prospective showman to leave a record of a politicized process, negotiating the licensing of his business through personal favors and informal interactions with the authorities. By 1909 lawyers had begun writing letters to Chief Grasett on behalf of prospective showmen. The novelty of cinematographic vision was coming to require a complex rational legal supervision as it took on a place of its own in the range of urban practices of amusement and shopping.

Based on Massachusetts legislation, Provincial Treasurer Matheson introduced his bill in the Ontario legislature April 7, 1908, and it became an Ontario statute a week later. In the end, this first moving picture law was an amendment to the existing regulations for fire safety exits in all public buildings, which had previously meant churches and theaters but now would apply to multistory schools and all places of "amusement" (Ontario 1908). The law also allowed for the possibility of a provincial license for moving picture machines and for local examination and licensing of their operators, not yet called projectionists. It made compulsory, however, the inspection and approval by municipal police of every "cinematograph or similar apparatus" and all locations handling or storing "combustible film more than ten inches in length." Within a few weeks of the Ontario statute being passed, John Griffin, then-owner of a majority of the city's theatoriums, wrote to Chief Grasett applying for licenses under the new regulations. The Chief Constable wrote in turn to the city architect and chief of the fire brigade asking for their prompt opinions (*LCC* May 7, 1908, 447). Minor changes may have been required for safety because Griffin was told the licenses would be granted once the city architect and fire chief confirmed that his five theaters had been "sufficiently provided with the necessary safe-guards for the public attending the performances" (*LCC* May 29, 1908, 678). From this time forward in Toronto, moving picture machines would be strictly regulated as part of urban policing; but the law also applied to all other municipalities in the province, urban and rural alike, including small towns that did not have places to view moving pictures and would not have regular local filmgoing for years to come.

Although no explicit explanation was given, the move to formal regulation was almost certainly a response to the theater fire in Boyertown, Pennsylvania, which had been front-page news in all Toronto newspapers for several days in January 1908. One headline spelled out the social hazard as much as the fire itself: "Theatre panic cost 150 lives—Men lost control of themselves—Fought with women and children" (*News* January 14, 1908, 1). Most of the victims were children and women because the fire occurred during a special Sunday show for families. Unlike previous theater fires, the chain of events in Boyertown began with an explosion at a moving picture machine. By coincidence, the two picture machine fires in Ingersoll and St. Catharines came just days after the Pennsylvania disaster. Although the smaller incidents perhaps drew attention simply as a way to bring the lessons of Boyertown closer to home, the death of the fifteen-year-old projection operator in St. Catharines was without precedent and might alone have merited strong regulatory response.

Reporting about Boyertown noted a long history of theater fires, but this time around the cinematograph machine and its combustible film were singled out as the culprit, seeming to escape the bounds of safer theater construction. Earlier theater fires in Toronto actually had their picture machines cleared of culpability. At Shea's Vaudeville in 1905, the film was actually found intact in its collecting sack under the machine at the back of the burnt-out hall (*MPW* July 15, 1916, 410). Reports of fires at Griffin's Trocadero in 1906 and his Theatorium in 1907 specifically mentioned no films were left in the building overnight when the fire started (*Globe* April 30, 1906; *Star* October 25, 1907). Regardless of such good fortune in Toronto, the two fires in smaller Ontario towns showed moviegoing was by then widespread and that small-time showmen and their employees might be less professional and less careful. Protecting the clean safety record of film in Toronto with further municipal measures was not enough. Regulations needed to apply provincewide.

Why would fire safety become the instigating factor for the articulation of the first law specifically addressing film in Toronto? Authorities needed to consider safety and the material conditions of film and filmgoing during its institutionalization into urban life. First, the city saw a growing awareness early in 1908 of the combustibility of celluloid film. In a sense, earlier moral concerns about film content characterized audiences as immature and needing oversight. The hazardous nature of celluloid, however, led to a more material and mortal problem of spectators panicking as a crowd, the flashpoint of what I will call the "social combustibility" of moving picture shows. This focus diverges from most film history, which lacks concern for the role of fire safety in early film regulation or even dismisses it as an ideological veil for social and moral controls. This absence of attention to fire safety continues a professionalized division of attention a century ago. Safety was an issue primarily, almost exclusively, for those whose job was to guard and reform conditions for building and rebuilding urban space, especially public buildings where people gathered. Ultimately, material safety was the basis for subsequent moral and commercial regulations. The material combustibility of celluloid and social combustibility of audiences led to enduring, bureaucratic oversight of movies, where other problematic novelty pastimes such as billiard halls and peanut vendors instead became innocuous. A few concurrent crises in Toronto over the regulation of amusements distinguish those fleeting problems from the 1908 fire safety law formalizing decisions about moviegoing.

When film was being defined as a special commercial product, hazardous and deserving special treatment, the moralistic rhetoric about film content was curiously absent, albeit temporarily. The concern for fire safety may even have arisen and remained central to theater regulation exactly because it could translate the moral, social, and commercial debates into an agreeable need for safety. In a sense, the fire concern provided specific, quantifiable parameters, so that the apparently value-neutral terms of fire safety provided a way to limit and clarify a regional and municipal jurisdiction over moviegoing. Safety measures instituted a regulatory process and codified a baseline of surveillance and inspection of theatoriums. With this foundation in place, subsequent regulations of more contentious issues could extend existing fire safety measures. This is not to say that subsequent moral surveillance was initially intended. There were, of course, commercial benefits to the wealthy, codified by insurance adjustors and real estate brokers. Nonetheless, fire codes were intended to save lives and not merely to help lower insurance rates and raise land values. The focus on material safety was somehow more immediate than censorship. In place of debates over the boundaries of legally-imposed morality, public safety fell unambiguously under the jurisdiction of municipal government.

Histories of municipal governance in the United States begin with the responsibility to control urban fires. Stipulating conditions for storing and handling hazardous substances are presented as key to understanding how urban commerce and urban space was governed by the turn of the twentieth century. William J. Novak writes about municipal fire safety as key to *The People's Welfare* (1996). He counters the myth that early U.S. government was initially liberal and laissez-faire by looking at the *municipal* level where a panoply of regulations worked to order, discipline, and organize urban space. In Christine Rosen's *The Limits of Power* (1986), municipal authority over everyday life in cities was at its core meant to prevent great city fires that were still frequent until the twentieth century. These fires leveled entire neighborhoods and wide swaths of cities, most infamously the Great Chicago Fire of 1871. In Toronto the last such major fire happened on April 19, 1904, just a few years before theatoriums merited regulation. Moving pictures of that fire are some of the earliest surviving films of the city. Fire safety was not just concurrent with but integral to the general movement toward reform and regulation in late-nineteenth-century America, what Robert Wiebe called *The Search for Order* (1967). As the previous chapter outlined, this reformist era had taken hold in Toronto by the time of the 1908 Boyertown theater fire, which lead to an extension of the Ontario *Egress from Public Buildings Act* (1908) to cover the regulation of film. The Boyertown disaster made it clear that the combustibility of celluloid film was a serious problem of public safety. In response, the 1908 laws in Ontario, New York, Massachusetts, and elsewhere dealt with the specificity of filmgoing. The measures clarified the jurisdictions that would manage and protect the safety of the city against this novel hazard, starting with the material safety of spaces devoted to filmgoing.

Theater Panics and the Social Combustibility of Audiences

Even as fire safety regulations were implemented for moving picture shows throughout North America, the social space of amusements was itself an object of amusement. "The Social Whirl" was an old phrase used for elite society columns, transformed into the title of a minor Broadway hit in 1906 (ads in *New York Times* April 7, 1906; *Chicago Tribune* December 23, 1906). In 1908 a new roller coaster called the Social Whirl was operating in Chicago and being promoted for sale to fairground operators in the show business magazine *Billboard* (April 11, 1908, 13): "This is not a dream, but a real live one; occupying space, 60 × 150 ft." Although as a roller coaster the Social Whirl might have been constrained to occupying just 9,000 square feet, urban space more generally was a type of social whirl, one that authorities saw to require as careful an installation and management as any amusement park ride. Urban life could never be experienced as a pleasurable social whirl as long as the threat of combustibility was imminent whether as a great city fire or a minor blaze. From gunpowder to oil to celluloid, handling combustible materials was adjusted to include routine fire safety measures, although the materials themselves were not banned outright (McSwain 2002; Novak 1996, 56–59). Along with flammable industrial materials, certain practices were inherently combustible as well—crowds of people themselves could collectively burst into panic. Fire safety was as much about managing this social combustibility as it was about securing the explosive materials involved. Put simply, the public required fire safety legislation to learn how to act in orderly ways if a fire actually erupted in a public building.

The sense that the modern city sat on a precipice of danger and destruction did not only depend on sermons invoking moral hellfire and damnation. If a fine line separated amusement from panic, that was equally true of gathering places for education and inspiration. The Ontario law, after all, addressed the cinematograph and its operation as an extension of building codes for all public buildings, including churches, schools, and meeting halls. Amending the Egress from Public Buildings Act in 1908, lawmakers secured the safety of all gathered crowds in confined but semi-public spaces. After a 1904 fire destroyed a swath of downtown Toronto, proper supervision of the material construction of buildings was key to ensuring such a disaster did not recur. The entire well-being and livelihood of the city, in all of its aspects from real estate value to the very life of each person, was seen to depend in no small part on fire safety. The particular form that this concern took in theaters, churches, and public halls addressed the additional prospect of deaths caused not by some material danger but by the more social hazard of a fire panic.

Congregations caught in a burning building died not only from flames and smoke. Equally as dangerous was the chaotic situation of a crowd suddenly experiencing collective fear. The cause of mass death in theater panics was often the particularly social danger that came from the peculiar group behavior of a panicking crowd. Investigations following the Iroquois Theatre fire in Chicago discovered chilling deaths caused by people rushing *together as a crowd* in a confined space. At bottlenecks, bodies were piled ten feet high from the rush of the fire panic. People who were unable to find their own way died from blindly following the rush of the crowd. Still others died because of their inability to avoid that rush of the crowd: people were trampled and crushed (Brandt 2003, 52–58). If the thought of burning to death or dying from smoke inhalation was not bad enough, the specter of death caused by mass panic invoked the fragility of civilized, sociable public conduct on which the modern city ordered its everyday life. The very possibility of this type of irrational social behavior called attention to the need for regulation. A general concern for the particularly modern problem of crowds in urban space, let alone a panicking crowd in a confined urban space, is key to understanding why theater and film audiences would be cast as immature. Indeed, immaturity was literal, not a passing judgment, in the case of the worst theater disasters. As in Boyertown, most of the victims at Chicago's Iroquois Theatre were children, in this case because the fire broke out during a holiday matinee.

The sociological study of theater panics and irrational crowd behavior dates back at least to a minor paper at the first conference of the German Society for Sociology in 1910 (Adair-Toteff 2005, 27–28). Elsewhere, Georg Simmel provided a key sociological theory of the fragility of sociable public conduct in modern civil society. Such an emphasis on the tenuousness of modern, urban sociability among crowds of strangers is entirely distinct from democratic, political concepts of the social contract. Simmel instead characterized urban modernity as reliant on sociability, infused with the danger of overly formal and rationalized, and thus dispiriting, conduct. A mismatch was evident between the formal actions of sociable persons and their subjective sense of being a somewhat passive participant (Simmel 1950, 40–57; also 1990, 228–57). Furthermore, the modern metropolis of his day, as David Frisby (1986) noted, emphasized the fleeting and transitory contingency of everyday experience. Sociable routines and a blasé attitude achieved sensibility in an environment that barraged the senses with constant change. Altogether, the mental life of the metropolis was at odds with its built situation. The juxtaposition of amusement and hazard at the nickelodeon was not exceptional.

The conduct of an audience as a group of strangers in a confined space is a prime example of the tenuous balancing act of sociability. If the norms that made amusement enjoyable were so brittle that, as Simmel (1950) said, alienation could result, a corresponding breaking point in sociability is the easy way it could be abandoned. A fire panic was similar, but contrasted in effect, with a mob spurred to riot by a mass gathering. Without the inciting charismatic speech, a panicking crowd in a theater was even less understandable and ordered than a mob. A common advertising phrase for nickel shows was, "Come when you like. Stay as long as you like." In a fire, however, the urge to abandon the orderly audience could happen all at once in a panic. The flip side of blasé coming and going was the danger of everyone leaving at the same moment. The problem was how to make a safe exit in case of fire, how to replace fire panic with a more rationalized act, as opposed to what happened in Boyertown where men fought women to save their own lives. Aside from prevention, fire safety laws were also aimed at people retaining a sociable, mannered control if a fire required a hasty exit. Norbert Elias (2000) embeds his understanding of state formation in a history of manners, explaining that sociable conduct is rooted in the ideal of continually being in control of bodily functions. Civilized interaction depends on embodied discipline and self-regulation, strongly linked to the ability of social groups to orient to the process of *becoming* civilized and in turn orienting to a process of civilization (Quilley and Loyal 2004). In this sense, one small but vital part of state formation could be fire safety at moving picture shows. Conversely, the possibility of panic in a theater fire could undermine the protective authority of the state. Again, the prospect of losing all sense of mannerism, acting with fear and panic, is the looming shadow of the civilizing process, frighteningly cogent in the prospect of a fire in a crowded, confined space.

Theories of crowd psychology from the late nineteenth and early twentieth centuries proposed how group action could be collective and irrational at the same time, and yet predictable even when reacting to a moment of surprise. Gustave LeBon's *The Crowd*, originally from 1895, soon informed Robert Park's (1972) sociological definition of the crowd as a directed, engaged collective temporarily sharing space, whether or not composed of strangers. Indeed, a collective focus is what distinguished the crowd from the masses, for example of workers and shoppers, which populated U.S. downtowns. Park's description of the crowd is remarkable for how it applies to audiences, perhaps more than any other crowd in fact. An audience made it evident that a crowd could indeed have its attention held by an illusion, even more so once projected moving images replaced staged performance. The focus of a modern, urban crowd did not depend on a charismatic authority figure and no longer needed embodied leadership. Picture shows, after all, were commercial spaces and the congregated friends and families were among strangers, a temporary, voluntary crowd paying to be together. In a sense their commitment was to the show rather than to each other. Add to this the darkness of the auditorium. Heap on top, finally, the electricity used to operate the picture machine, often supplied by a portable gas generator, and finally the chemical instability of celluloid film. The material combustibility of celluloid can thus be seen as only the spark in recognizing the *social combustibility* of filmgoing crowds.

Evident in discussions of cinema during the nickelodeon boom (another, entrepreneurial explosion in the mix) was that the real danger was panic, all too easily spurred by fire. The material part of the fire hazard could be handled through protocols designating jurisdictional responsibility to supervise the handling of film, but the public act of legislating such supervision also worked toward handling theater panic as the social part of the fire hazard. In Toronto, moving picture showmen were already demonstrating their responsibility for the conduct of the audience, claiming high safety standards and inviting inspections by authorities. Their responsibility for audiences' physical health and safety was nonetheless questioned because governments and police forces, charged with stewardship for public conduct in general, had to demonstrate their jurisdiction. Safe conduct was an imperative, not incidental, part of the general good of the city.

Proper policing of fire safety in public buildings, including the expert advice of the city architect and the professional wisdom of the chief of the fire brigade, openly exhibited how action had been taken to make these establishments safe. This exhibition of safety was as important to manage the threat of panic as particular safety measures were in managing the threat of fire itself. Regulation was thus needed for social psychological reasons as well, to inform the public at a theater that smoke did not necessarily mean fire, and furthermore that fire did not require panic. Cleared aisles and exits in visible places were soon required in moving picture theaters as they were in the large playhouses, churches, schools, and office buildings. The regulation of theaters had to ensure that fires did not start and that panic did not result if one did take hold. The years following 1908 tell scattered stories of panics averted while fires confined to the projection booth were quickly doused. With a hint of urban myth, these stories often note how audiences calmly cleared the theater while the piano player provided a marching song (*World* August 14, 1911). Headlines began to report how the "coolness" of a theater crowd averted a panic in Minneapolis (*Billboard* August 13, 1910, 4) and how the "heroism" of a girl playing a march averted a panic while smoke terrified the audience (*Chicago American* March 24, 1913).

Safety Regulations Solve the Instigating Problem of Fire Risk

Histories of film in this period draw on three sets of overlapping issues to help explain the emergence of local regulation responding to the proliferation of nickelodeons. An economic perspective explains the emergence of the nickelodeon as a commercial practice (Abel 1999; Bowser 1990; Musser 1990). A cultural perspective seeks to understand the appeal to audiences (Rosenzweig 1983; Sklar 1975). And a social perspective examines how films became the object of moral supervision in censorship (Grieveson 1999; May 1980; Uricchio and Pearson 1993). Each of these approaches tends to discount and marginalize the instigating matter of fire safety. Reading fire safety through an economic, cultural, and social lens requires a stronger sense of fire as an influence on the way modern urban space was built and rebuilt. At risk of exaggerating the significance of passing comments in otherwise strong analyses, many thorough social histories of the nickelodeon are practically befuddled by the persistence of fire safety as a key concern at the time.

Consider, for example, how Richard Abel (1999) notes with surprise the way the issue was treated with urgency, such as when the first months of *Billboard* magazine's moving picture news in 1906, "continued to stress the alleged dangers of moving picture fires at the same time it reported on the increasing number of new and profitable storefront theaters, in both big cities and small towns" (pp. 32–33). Fire safety issues are elsewhere seen as an ideological mask on the part of authorities wishing to control ethnic or working-class social gatherings. Uricchio and Pearson (1993) grant that "many physical hazards" were part of going to the nickel shows, but they call zoning and safety codes "thinly veiled attempts at suppression" with an "ideological agenda" (p. 31). Such sympathies with marginal audiences can have the unfortunate and unintended consequence of assuming physical safety was of no concern to anyone but the propertied class. The effect is to continue prescribing an oversimplified image of early audiences, dating back to at least Lewis Jacobs's (1968) comment, "the workmen and their families who patronized the movies did not mind the crowded, unsanitary, and hazardous accommodations most of the nickelodeons offered" (p. 56). For England's 1909 fire safety regulations, Marc Jancovich (2003) downplays the explicit goal of fire prevention because "the dangers of fire were often exaggerated. Even when fires did break out, few people were killed by the fires themselves, but rather by the panic which ensued" (p. 38). Fire safety regulations, however, were *intended* to prevent the problem of fire panic as well as fire itself. This is ultimately key to a full understanding of how the regulation of the space and its materials also ordered audiences. Pearson and Uricchio (1999) quote with disapproval an investigation by New York's fire commissioner, "It is a panicky crowd which patronizes the moving-pictures houses of our city—mothers and children in the predominance—many of them foreign born" (p. 66). But it was exactly because the nickelodeon audience was perceived as immature and uncivilized, as feminine, juvenile, and foreign, that the civilizing process of fire safety was a matter of life and death, not just repression. Safety at five-cent shows was essential precisely because the audience was seen as easily panicked.

Recognizing the validity of panic as a genuine modern problem untangles the deceptively rational measures from social and moral concerns without ascribing deceitful intentions to authorities. Panic specifies the logic underlying fire safety as a specifically *municipal* problem of managing publics. Among writers of the day commenting on filmgoing, the fire safety problem is noteworthy especially for professionals responsible for planning public conduct. As with recent film histories, fire or panic was of only passing interest to contemporary cultural commentators. Thus, social workers frame the nickel shows as important for social welfare. Journalists present moving pictures as a subject of interest and curiosity to the general public. Writers in the film trade press emphasize showmanship and quality films. Safeguarding against fire hazard is the prime focus only for insurance adjusters, architects, and municipal governments. Their expertise and professional responsibility was trained to regard these potentially trivial matters as essential.

References to early picture shows in social work journals thus understandably limit their concerns to the mental and physical health of marginalized groups, especially children. Among others, Jane Addams (1907) of Chicago's Hull House and John Collier of New York's People's Institute wrote about nickelodeons and cheap amusements as deserving reform and uplift, not just stricter policing (see also Kingsley 1907; Leupp 1910). Collier (1908) mentions fire safety as the means to the end of lending civic support and legitimacy to nickelodeons as a novel "neighborhood institution" (p. 75). Popular journalism predictably wavers between a general overview and specific issues of public interest. Early surveys of the social scene at the nickelodeon appeared in *Harper's Weekly*

(Currie 1907) and in the *Saturday Evening Post* (Patterson 1907), but neither addressed regulation at all except for some prospect of censorship. In contrast to such writers in social work journals and popular magazines, the economics of making a picture show profitable was more squarely a matter for the newly minted film trade papers. *Moving Picture World* began publication in 1907, and regularly provided showmen across North America with semiprofessional advice about the business of filmgoing. Its discussions of safety are more often framed as unprofitable red tape or as a means to attract a more affluent and profitable audience.

Although writers whose concern was social welfare, public health, general interest, and the film industry do not dwell on fire safety in nickelodeons, the issue was a primary focus among writers interested in the *spatial* regulation and management of cities. Assessing the safety of picture shows was here a matter of expert knowledge translated into standards for licensing, surveillance, and inspection, as tools of municipal governance. *Insurance Engineering* (1909) provided its professional readers a national survey of the extent of regulations for moving picture fire safety across the United States. It concluded with detailed recommendations for fire safety regulations in moving picture shows, useful for cities that did not yet have any. The article ended ominously by addressing the results of these regulations rhetorically to the projectionists: "And now, Mr. Operator, if you have a fire or a panic, you are apt to go to jail." Readers of *Architecture and Building* (1911), on the other hand, in a style more befitting the aesthetic pursuits of architects, presented similarly precise building recommendations with a historic overview of film and a statistical survey of the degree moving pictures had taken hold in society. It included ideas for fire safety such as a second switch for auditorium lights in the picture machine booth. Architectural journals provided a mixture of regulatory detail, historical overviews of theaters from antiquity, and an aesthetic emphasis on ornament and decoration. An entire issue of the *Brickbuilder* was devoted to the design of moving picture theaters but also reprinted the most recent New York City ordinance for moving picture theaters from 1913 (Blackall 1914).

Writers dwelling on municipal bureaucracy were likewise attuned to efficient governance. A report on New York theaters submitted to Mayor Gaynor in 1911 detailed how seven departments of city government had distinct picture show jurisdictions. Overall the report located any fault in the conduct of showmanship with the absence of uniform regulations and the lack of "centrifugal" control (Fosdick 1911). In 1913, the *American City*, a progressive magazine on urban planning and civic issues, called the subsequent centralized responsibility in the license bureau "a model ordinance for the country" (Levien 1913). The same magazine stated a year earlier, "the danger from fire is the one most feared. It is so greatly feared that the danger from panic becomes actually the greatest danger. The lives that have been lost in motion picture theaters have been sacrificed to panic, usually from false alarms." Moral, intellectual, and artistic matters were mentioned only after detailed advice for subduing the risk of "panic deaths" (Fisher 1912).

That fire panic would remain central to this article on progressive urban planning as late as 1912 demonstrates that the physical safety of the audience was vital to integrating theaters into their cities and civic cultures. The fire safety issue could only recede to the background of the discussion after jurisdiction had been securely defined. In the special issue of the *Brickbuilder* from 1914, the law in New York City was introduced with the comment, "whether or not the danger from such houses is more imaginary than real does not alter the fact that this ordinance intends to at least remove any official doubt as to what should be done." The author, an architect, explains in precisely quantified terms the absurdity of requiring only one-quarter of the seats in the gallery, or having a minimum of 30 feet for the combined widths of the exits, let alone how to mop the floors or vacuum the carpets. "It is a pity that a law should be put in force which goes out of its way to impose unnecessary burdens.... The first requisites of the law should be safety and health, and if those are properly safe guarded, other details should not be made to constitute a burden" (Blackall 1914, 47). Without dismissing safety codes in general as ideological, this contemporary professional used the internal logic of the New York regulations to show that regulations specific to small moving picture shows were indeed drastic and unfair.

In New York and larger cities, the concern was especially for audiences comprising immigrant families, while smaller cities and towns shared attention to other vulnerable people such as young working women or children. The wider context is consistently an anxiety and desire to elevate the space of picture shows into a more respectable and mainstream forum for proper, educational moving pictures, at worst "relaxing and innocuous" to return to John Collier's observations from 1908. For showmen, this desire to refine the show translated into increased profits because the audience widened to include the middle class. But understanding how fire regulations and municipal bylaws were a key instrument for ensuring the quality of showmanship and the content of shows themselves is still necessary.

The primary result was a clear delineation of authority and jurisdiction. As Blackall noted for New York in 1914, an ordinance is meant to remove any doubt about what is to be done. A bylaw is, in a sense, an articulation of the orderly conduct in municipal space. It governs by example insofar as bylaws are a public demonstration of the local authority's attention to order and care for the community. It follows that the first regulation in Toronto responded to an apparent crisis over proper jurisdiction, made urgent with the Boyertown disaster and the smaller fires closer to home. The fires made evident that no clear jurisdiction of oversight over the handling and use of film was in place. The loophole of political influence that Minier exploited had to be closed. This required a law from the Ontario legislature, especially if the City Council was unsure about their authority. It singled out the hazard of celluloid as integral to the commerce of nickel shows, opening the door for formal oversight.

Defining Jurisdictions, Film as One of Many Social Problems

Film might have been a richly complex communication between the world and local experience, but this first official regulation of film in the city was restricted with precision to the single matter of fire safety and the chain of authority for ensuring its implementation. The material form of film, its combustibility, helped set protocols for the supervision of film's storage and use. What about all the other possible ways film and moviegoing could have been addressed as social problems? Standards of decency for audiences and the films they watched were still only implicitly a matter of everyday policing of all public conduct. The bylaw against indecency, before the first theatorium even opened, already prohibited the exhibition, sale, or offer for sale of any indecent or lewd book, paper, picture, plate, drawing, "or other thing," and the exhibition within the city of any indecent or immoral show, exhibition, play, "or other representation" (Toronto Bylaw 2449). In practice, however, the police acted mostly in response to complaints, even for burlesque theaters. Play censorship only became a regular police duty late in 1908, and a Toronto play censor did not become a semiprofessional position until 1913 (Campbell 1996; *Star* March 16, 1909; *Star Weekly* November 16, 1912). Within guidelines provided by the Canadian Criminal Code and precedents set by courts (especially Toronto police magistrate, George Denison), cinema in itself did not threaten or change the everyday judgment of what constituted lewdness, indecency, or immorality. Although newspapers reported the judgments of religious reform bodies about the morality of cards, gambling, and theater attendance, any response the church groups might have had about the need for fire safety in moving picture shows went without notice (*News* March 23, 1908). Regulating celluloid still met the audience principally through one word, "Fire!"

Municipal offices began orienting to the new regulations: the mayor, City Council, and Board of Control, but also the police chief, fire chief, city architect, and city license clerk, as well as the many civil servants each directed. The only oppositional voice at this moment came from commercial neighbors of current or prospective showmen such as John Griffin and David Minier. Indeed, while the law was pending in March 1908, officials effectively stifled a petition from Yonge Street merchants, who wanted to cap the number of nickel shows downtown at its current level of six (*News* March 23, 1908). Documents indicate that noise was an issue for some tenants of the area. In the midst of this campaign, Chief Grasett responded to a complaint about loud piano playing at the Crystal Palace, South of Queen on Yonge. Whether such music could be "noise" was not clear because the city bylaw specified the combination of annoyance and "discordance." Grasett recommended the complainant apply for a summons to test the case in court (*LCC* March 19, 1908, 965). Whatever the concern behind the merchants' petition, they did recognize picture shows as a valid commercial enterprise and wished only to limit their number in the downtown shopping area. Thus seeing the first legislation of filmgoing as existing entirely within spheres of economic rationality, as a matter of business regulation and municipal planning is tempting. This reasoning, however, defines showmanship as a commercial matter of provision and consumption—as if watching films were a variation on purchasing anything else. In retrospect, knowing how the mature mass practice emerged alongside regulatory measures such as censorship, knowing that the subject of film maintains today an academic discipline and can support specialty bookshops and publishers, that film was more than just another product for consumption, is all too apparent. Evident differences between amusement and other forms of consumption exist, even at this time when the regulation of moving pictures was primarily restricted to fire safety concerns.

In cities across the continent, reforming civic governance meant a more rational oversight of an increasingly wide range of public practices, those minor in consequence as much as matters of immorality and violence. Modern city planning aimed to order and inspect every aspect of urban life. In Toronto around 1908 when filmgoing was first regulated, similar licensing and inspection crises occurred over ice cream, popcorn, and peanut vendors, and billiard and bowling halls. Compared to moving pictures, several of these were treated in more explicit terms of social and moral purity. These received no less attention than filmgoing in newspaper reports and the letters of the chief constable, although compared to the subsequent social role that movies acquired, they seem relatively trivial. Measures that perhaps seem drastic or trivial now were instrumental to the proper functioning of society at the time. Laws were implemented and strictly enforced to regulate and standardize things such as the purity of milk and the weight of bread, and the Register of Criminals records violations of the milk and bread bylaw. The success of these regulations makes them now seem practically irrelevant because these regulations have become invisible. In exactly the years when picture shows became regulated, buying and selling even basic provisions put consumption at the core of the public good or at least public health. Like imposing censorship, regulating commerce was a matter of social purity, a means of integrating ethnically and economically marginal groups to protect the general health of the city public as a whole (see, for example, *Star Weekly* July 15, 1911). While fire safety was at this moment the cogent issue for five-cent shows, concerns about the conduct of audiences were evident elsewhere, particularly at billiard halls and bowling alleys. The nickel show was sometimes but not right then cast as a commercial exploitation of children; but that problem surfaced at the time in the attempt to control roaming vendors of ice cream, popcorn, and peanuts.

In the 1907 annual report of Toronto's chief constable, submitted to City Council early in 1908, separate categories record the number of licenses and revenue from billiard halls and ice cream parlors as well as other police-patrolled licenses such as for milk vendors, rag collectors, liveries, and secondhand shops. Not until 1913 did theater and picture show licenses become separated from the miscellaneous category in the license office legers. The license schedule specified the need for permits to operate theaters, bagatelles, art exhibits, circus acts, as well as bowling alleys, rifle ranges, billiard tables, roller skating, roller coasters, and toboggan slides. But in the licensing bylaws and civic handbooks, a miscellaneous category for "any amusement or entertainment for which an admission fee is charged" adequately covered picture shows (Toronto Bylaw 2453). This was not changed to specify motion picture theaters until after World War I when the license fee increased to $100 for theaters with more than 600 seats. Some novelty amusements came along that did not quite fit even this general definition and led to amendments to license amusement parks, which did not exactly charge admission (Toronto Bylaw 5319) and "Edison" parlor "slot machines by which pictures are exhibited or musical or other sounds produced" (Toronto Bylaw 4552). Such specific language improved on an earlier, apparently too broad, attempt to license "any instrument or mechanical device for amusement" (Toronto Bylaw 3289). Licensing entertainments was, however, just one part of the quotidian work of policing leisure in the period.

The concern over billiard halls had nothing to do with the game itself. A pool hall encouraged casual loitering, and its rhythms and spaces practically required even active players to just hang out. Presumably, billiard halls were well suited to smoking, swearing, and frank talk among men.

There was gambling on the side, too (*LCC* December 10, 1908, 762). Clearly, their policing and regulation went beyond the game of pool itself and honed in on concern for the interaction and socialization that surrounded the game. Regulating the rules of billiard games could not control what needed attention in the same way that patrolling and censoring theaters and films came to assert authority over the conduct of film audiences. The 1907 annual report of the chief constable recommends that, having increased to eighteen the minimum age to attend a billiard hall, corralling billiard licenses to the city center might make sense. Limited to downtown, the leisure of businessmen and workers could be marked geographically separate from boys' domestic spaces of home, neighborhood, and school. The suggestion to locate pool halls in and near downtown was not enacted, although neighborhood pool halls were opened only in scattered premises on major shopping streets. For example, in the Danforth district a billiard license was issued to C. B. Brewer, a longstanding tavern owner who had lost his liquor license in temperance reduction measures. Responding to a complaining Christian minister, Chief Grasett begged for some compassion, explaining that Brewer was "said to be a very respectable man; that the premises he occupied had held a liquor license for nearly half a century, which was cut off recently, depriving him of his livelihood" (*LCC* June 24, 1909, 342). For the minister, replacing a tavern with a billiard hall continued the problems of immorality and rowdiness prone to be found in any young men's place. For the police, especially in a special case such as Brewer's, billiards could become a more innocuous business within the age limitations and regular patrolling the license mandated.

Such assurances depended on licensing, but private recreational clubs did not need a license to allow their members to play games. Some businesses exploited this loophole and ran "private" halls that were otherwise exactly the same as licensed premises (*LCC* January 30, 1909, 38; March 24, 1909, 501). Regardless whether a private club had a distinct social purpose, police saw the same effect on its neighborhood, but the court decided these "chartered" clubs were not subject to policing or licensing (*Star* July 14, 1909). The law allowed that billiards, bowling, or any other game could be provided by a private club without police oversight, within the limits of the general prohibition against gambling and indecency, of course. This is the key distinction from film because the 1908 Ontario law treated celluloid itself as a hazardous material. That law required the local police to inspect for safety *all* places handling films, removing any possibility of differentiating the social and commercial context of a picture show.

Even more than in theatoriums, what needed policing at a billiard hall was the possibly rowdy, rambunctious conduct of men gathered there, not the formal or commercial apparatus of the game itself. The police had no authority to regulate the normal operation of private billiard and bowling clubs. Billiard and bowling balls, however, were not inherently dangerous or volatile substances such as celluloid film and electric hot-lamped projecting machines. Compared to billiards, then, film's flammability effectively removed the distinction between private and public film shows, and thus between commercial showmanship and alternative uses of film for religion or education. Another key difference between billiard halls and movie theaters follows from the problem of theater panic. Generally having more women and youngsters, show audiences were perceived as immature and irrational. Actual theater fires and the prospect of panic seemed to prove the point. The fact thus becomes important that games such as billiards and bowling are not group activities in the same sense of forming an audience out of a crowd. Eliminating children from billiard halls, and in reality probably not drawing in women either, would have been thought to make the gathering of men at a poolroom less prone to panic.

If cinema was to a degree feminized or rendered juvenile compared to rule-based games, this alone does not explain why fire safety was just the beginning of a drawn-out process articulating its oversight. Other spaces of consumption associated with women and children, such as ice cream parlors, became socially innocuous. These places soon lost their special character and were combined with lunch counters and other "victualling" houses into a newly named license category: "restaurants." Initially, however, whether ice cream was food was not even clear. Hotel victualling houses were always allowed to open on Sundays, but through the Lord's Day Act, the city still prohibited their serving ice cream, cold drinks, and other menu items on the Sabbath. The legal distinction was that only "food" could be sold on Sundays (*Star* May 29, 1911). The starkly Christian basis of the Lord's Day Act in Ontario was still remarkably rational in its implementation. In these years controlling proper Sunday conduct was partly achieved through limiting the sale of novelty confections by claiming they were not food items in legal terms (*Star* July 14, 1909). This prohibition was eliminated in practice when a July 1911 heat wave effectively demonstrated how these items could indeed be essential (*Star* July 8, 1911). An editorial cartoon on "The Ice Cream Vice in Toronto" drove the point home by juxtaposing a little girl with a "Sunday ice cream cone" against a corpulent police officer, "Please sir, I didn't know I was aidin' and abettin' a crime" (*Star Weekly* August 12, 1911, 20). The problem of frivolity linked to ice cream and soft drinks soon fell away as they became indistinct from eating more nourishing and purposeful foods. In a sense, then, confections became a normalized part of everyday eating, and their status as a moral problem, at least in terms of licensing and policing, became diffused into the more general health codes of restaurant and food vendor inspection.

Also of concern were vendors selling "carnival" confections such as peanuts and popcorn, objectionable because they appealed to wasteful appetites, especially of children. With a pushcart, these confections could pop up at a schoolyard, playground, or outside a picture show matinee. The susceptibility of children to their appetites was even lampooned in a *Buster Brown* comic strip in which the characters go out for the day in the city and end up at a picture show and an ice cream parlor before arriving home with tummy aches. The comic ended with a moral about children not giving in to their "dispositions." "The Finish as Usual . . . Birds sing and flowers bloom and happiness is all about, but if you are too

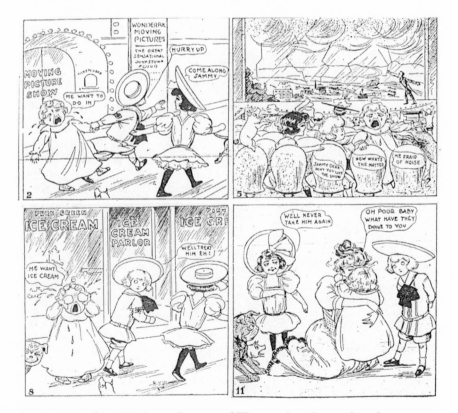

Figure 2.2 In this 1908 Buster Brown and Tige comic strip, moving pictures were equated with ice cream for city children, both preying on children's appetites. (By Richard Outcault, printed in the Toronto *News* on October 5, 1908.)

selfish or mean they are not for you" (*News* October 5, 1908, 23). Chief inspector of the Board of Education, J. L. Hughes, was one of the first to call attention to the novel problem of popcorn and ice cream vendors in a letter to Chief Grasett. The original report is not recorded, but Hughes probably felt responsible for shielding children going to and from school from such preying on their appetites. The first reply thought police might "restrict these people the same way that they do fruit peddlers," but it turned out there was no law to stipulate where and when these vendors could operate (*LCC* May 21, 1908, 601; May 29, 1908, 671; June 2, 1908, 716). Hughes persisted in his complaint, drawing in a principal at a school in the city center that must have been especially prone to vendors. Again, the reply noted simply, "the City Solicitor has advised the Commissioners that they have no power to make such prohibition" (*LCC* March 12, 1909, 430; March 24, 1909, 494). Where the boundaries of the school board's responsibility to protect the interests of children rested was unclear. Hughes, and probably many parents, felt stopping hawkers profiting from children gathered for school was imperative.

Compared to such concerted campaigns against ice cream and popcorn sellers, complaints against peanut vendors are more random and spurious. Their ethnicity, mostly Greek, was often noted in newspaper articles citing the need for interpreters when their tempers or salesmanship ended them in police court, such as when one peanut pushcart seller downtown was somehow whistling in violation of the noise bylaw (*LCC* May 28, 1908: 665; *News* October 22, 1908). Peanut vendors were accused of preying on crowds gathered in parks for band concerts. One city councilor mistakenly advised the park commissioner that the practice was allowed. Chief Grasett firmly corrected the matter. "No one is permitted to sell peanuts or other refreshments in the Parks at any time, much less at Band Concerts" (*LCC* June 22, 1908, 939). The solution was to follow the proper chain of authority rather than rely on the elected officials (*Star* July 10, 1909). A later complaint from the superintendent of the University of Toronto about peanut vendors on a street that crossed the campus was politely addressed, "I beg to inform you that the Inspector of that Division has been instructed to take the necessary steps to suppress as far as possible the nuisance complained of" (*LCC* November 2, 1908, 224; *Star* November 22, 1907). The vendors were permitted to sell on these streets to university students, "but the Police have instructions not to permit them to remain unduly long at any one place," so the complaint could be handled to at least some degree (*LCC* October 19, 1908, 81). By 1911 a municipal committee had recognized that the disparity in the treatment of peanut vendors, compared to ice cream vendors, was indeed because of their ethnicity. One member's expression of sympathy doubles as testimony that confection vendors were becoming an appreciated and normal part of city life. Defending the peanut vendors, he said, "these people though they are foreigners perhaps have a right to make a living. . . . What is a holiday to a child without a few peanuts or an ice-cream cone? I hate to hear people always talking about peanut men. . . . Leave them alone. I think they add to the beauty of the street" (*Star* March 10, 1911, 1).

In exactly the period when the theatorium provided an everyday urban place for moving pictures and illustrated songs, these fairground foods became available everyday, everywhere, because of pushcart vending. A look back at *Billboard* magazine in these years shows that moving pictures were promoted as part of the amusement business at large, not just theater and vaudeville, but circuses, fairs, and carnivals together with a vast array of peripheral supplies, especially of specialty foods. The magazine featured ads for cone ovens, corn poppers, and peanut roasters, coupled with ads for films and theater supplies. Amusement entrepreneurs, at least those reading *Billboard*, would have been familiar with all of these varied activities as integral to the provision of amusement. Ice cream cones, peanuts, popcorn—all these treats were sold alongside moving pictures, and entertainment became a social confection in turn. Not surprising, then, while amusement parks made carnivals a permanent summer attraction in cities, and vaudeville theaters and moving picture shows made theater an ordinary part of urban leisure, the peripheral items of carnival foods found a permanent place in the city. The police were urged to limit the places and times these newly mobile vendors could sell. Such treats were not seen in terms of nourishment but, like entertainment, as the occasion for informal, leisurely gathering.

If cinema became a specifically modern problem because of the electric technology and the chemical character of its celluloid, other practices in Toronto were having their place in society eliminated because their amusement relied, in a sense, on premodern mysticism. Although a topic too complex to address here, one should note that the growing reaction against gambling and alcohol, and the growing legitimacy of the temperance and prohibition movement in these years, can be thought of in these terms, as part of modernization, removing irrational practices from public conduct. A simpler problem was fortune-telling and palmistry. Their commercial basis was a type of fraudulent, dishonest hoax, whatever amusement or social value they might have served. In October 1907 two spiritualists were sent to trial in Toronto. Reverend and Mrs. Clarence Howland were charged with defrauding the public, masquerading illusionist magic tricks within a religious context (*News* October 25, 1907). Fortune-telling and magic were not in themselves illegal, but they had to be presented as commercial amusements and thus required a license, for example, as a conjuring act. Mixing such magic tricks with religion was fraud. The Howlands were caught doing so because they entered the city on the premise of ministering; Mrs. Lowe, who was a self-described student of spiritualism herself, caught them in fakery. When the "materialized" spirits of a dead loved one appeared, she grasped for the ghost and revealed instead Mrs. Howland "who pleaded to be let go" (*Star* October 25, 1907, 1).

The controversy was front-page news in Toronto newspapers throughout November as the Howlands appeared in court. Mayor Coatsworth, who had just announced he would not seek reelection in 1908, added to the topical interest when he had his palms interpreted, a move that was jokingly editorialized as a brave act for a politician. The Howlands took out an ad in the business personals (a category almost exclusively composed of palmists and fortune-tellers). They could now be seen at Broadway Hall for twenty-five cents admission. By the end of the month, they were challenged to a joint show at the establishment's Massey Music Hall, where a Professor Walton would duplicate their "magic." This joint show, "Spiritualism Exposed," was repeated for paying crowds at the Broadway Hall. Walton, at least once beaten, claimed not to be dismayed. Meanwhile, as the case against "spirits and witches" proceeded to Grand Jury early in December, the Howlands finally skipped town.

Note, however, that during these same weeks, Pastor Russell from Pennsylvania defended the Bible at the Grand Opera House in a religious show that promised to take the congregated audience *To Hell and Back* (ad in *News* November 2, 1907). Meanwhile, the Salvation Army presented *The Life of Christ* "by means of between 2000 and 3000 feet of moving pictures." Free tickets were distributed in advance (ad in *Star* November 1, 1907). On the other hand, religious journalist for the *Toronto World* J. M. Wilkinson lectured to Christian-themed films of *The Prodigal Son* and *The Passion Play* for a nickel admission at Griffin's Hippodrome, while an alternative showing of *The Passion Play* was advertised at Applegath's Crystal Palace for a dime (ads in *News* October 5, 1907). With these shows operating in Toronto to great promotion, moving picture showmen in Kingston, Ontario, not surprisingly tried something similar, offering the same religious film shows for free on Sunday (*News* November 25, 1907). This, however, crossed the line and was stopped by police and brought to court as a violation of the Lord's Day Act against commercial activity on Sunday. Whatever the letter of the law, this seems to be a period when the social distinctions between religion and amusement were entirely jumbled. Marginal religious preachers and groups used public halls and theaters to evangelize. Commercial showmen used religious films and themes to reap profits. The point is not that actual audiences at any of these events confused the difference between a film presented by a known religious preacher and a film shown free on Sunday by a showman who showed the same film Saturday for a nickel. The point is that marginal entertainments and evangelists alike were creating a situation that prompted some sorting out through regulation.

The blurring of boundaries between religion and amusement prompted a series of distinctions about which activities could happen where and when, and who could conduct them. The Grand Opera House was a church instead of a theater when it was used for a sermon on Sunday. But the Hippodrome had not become a church when a known religious writer presented religious lectures with moving pictures for a nickel admission on weekdays. The Kingston theatoriums were indisputably violating their amusement licenses when their showmen opened them Sunday for free religious shows. These decisions were not arbitrary. Several factors differentiated sacred from profane. First, a stable professional identity was assumed for showmen because this was the pretext of their commercial license. Furthermore, religious content had to be embodied in a preacher. A film show was religious in purpose only if a charismatic preacher accompanied it, not simply because it had free admission and a religious theme. If a preacher had been called in to lecture to the films in Kingston, maybe they could be permitted; however, the religious films in themselves could not preach and thus remained commercial, even though no tickets were sold. In sum, the character of an activity depended on assuming the character of its presenter was transparent. In a sense, showmen, illusionists, spiritualists, and preachers were all assumed to have a vocation, not just an act. The Howlands' spiritualist pretensions were deemed fraudulent because of misrepresentation, not because the activities themselves were banned. If their clients had known they were seeing a magic show, the spiritual language would be legal. But the use of illusion in a religious context was a hoax.

Motion pictures, although no less illusory an entertainment than fortune-telling or magic shows, could be normalized and permitted because of the technological apparatus of the electric projector. This process relied on clear categories stipulated in bylaws and fire safety legislation. Despite being an escapist distraction, the scientific and technological associations of cinema modernized it and its connection to Edison, to invention, to photography, to scientific observation. Its representative form also made it a potential means of education, thereby making it worthy of reform and regulation. The comparisons of film to other forms of consumption are the converse of similarities between film and matters of public health and public service. Although run for profit by entrepreneurial showmen, moviegoing came to follow social regulations more akin to education, to public health, to moral religious performances. It was integrated on its own terms as part of public planning, as an aspect of civic health.

Instituting Authority and Municipal Problem Solving

Reviewing the regulation of other pastimes alongside film helps establish a more elaborate sense of the particularity of film in society. But in general, what is the character of a social problem that merits regulation? What do these cases all have in common? To start, almost tautologically, each regulation introduced limitations on an existing commercial practice. Safety measures were required. Age limitations were placed on who could participate. Hours of operation were enforced. Selling was either restricted to particular zones or had to stay away from particular sites. As well, the provider of each was subject to changes in policing and inspection and to bureaucratic oversight by applying for a license and keeping it valid. Each case here involved establishing a better match between legal definitions and actual practices. Sometimes the legal definition was changed to reflect how some practices had become commonplace. At other times, a legal definition was repeatedly imposed to maintain the more abstract principle of transparent categories and clear jurisdiction. The variety of regulatory tactics and measures helps illuminate how moviegoing became a mass practice. Altogether the process might be called institutionalization. Leaving this somewhat undefined may be productive, even as it is recognized. Pierre Bourdieu (1991) characterizes the basis of authority as a form of "social magic" in the practice of instituting and categorizing. Calling it magic emphasizes how those involved act *as if* the trick is illusory without insisting that the process of instituting is deceptive for some or all involved. Note this illusion is enacted, an optical illusion rather than a deception in the minds of the actors (pp. 117–26). Bracketing the question of how deeply the authority of regulation is felt, and merely limiting the analysis to the appearance, like magic, of socially meaningful instituting moments, such as the 1908 fire safety law, is thus useful.

Policing billiard halls does not change the rules of the game. Regulating the sale of ice cream does not curb the appetite for a treat. Acknowledging the illusory character of fortune-telling does not change a believer's certainty. If all of these somehow include elements of escapism, their regulation brings them under the jurisdiction and categorizing impulse of managed, administered modernity. The institution of film regulation, too, demonstrates that amusement, including storytelling, needed to be tightly managed once it became urban and modern. In a sense, all institutions are ways of managing and administering people's drives by stipulating the conditions of their practice as social relations, not just individuated affect, harnessing human desires and minimizing the possibility of dangers and losses. For urban commercial practices in particular, this process is instituted through licensing. A licensed provider of escapism still caters to the drives and desires of consumers but must do so within the limitations of also acting responsibly with a sense of the good for the general public. Acting within those conditions defines the boundaries of responsibility.

Inscribing social mandates onto the provision of services is noted in Mariana Valverde's (2003) study of British pub licensing. In particular, she distinguishes municipal licensing from more bureaucratic means of state science and governed surveillance (pp. 141–66). Bureaucracies and surveillance instill regulation at the level of individual citizens, constituted as state subjects holding liberal values. Municipal licensing institutes civic sociability differently. The individual consumer is not constituted as responsible. Instead, the licensed business owner is mandated stewardship for patrons. In a sense, this is not policing through the legitimate use of state violence but an instituted form of repression, a way of managing and limiting individuals' capacity for excess and self-destruction. The first laws regulating filmgoing were concerned almost entirely with the space and safety of the public gathered there. The represented scenes, early films themselves, were incidental during the initial process of regulation, succeeded by problems of public safety and curtailing the entrepreneurial zeal of showmanship in itself. Thus, the law had its first effect on practices of showmanship, internal to the industry on a local level, as showmen became publicly responsible for their theaters. Making the location of film viewing open to public scrutiny and policing did not exactly change the character of showmanship. This paternalistic aspect of showmanship was codified into legal liabilities. Safety became part of putting on a show and a substantive part of its exhibition and promotion. But also, the ideals and ideology of public safety, once extended to the theatorium, implied that the supervision and stewardship for the audience was a shared responsibility of the state and the showman. Showmanship had to give the people what they needed as it sold them what they wanted.

In Toronto by 1908, then, entering into the film business became more explicitly about managing and balancing conflicting constituencies. The industry provided films, and the audience viewed them as a group. But now politicians were included as guardians of the general good of society, including that audience. Police and bureaucratic officials were interpreters of this guardianship in terms of safety measures. Employees and machine operators were now trained and inspected, and responsible for that safety, too. Cinema, unlike other forms of public consumption and amusement (of restaurants, theaters, amusement parks, and even of sports and parks) has practically unique qualities. It has a technological and electrical basis, and also a mobile, distributable, and disembodied content. Any place with electricity could become a cinema house, and portable generators in use at the time effectively made this anywhere. But more important, early in the process of becoming an ordinary part of the urban everyday, becoming a mass medium, moviegoing began a process of becoming *legitimate*. Initially through fire safety regulations, this incorporated urban planning and public safety into showmanship. Subsequent regulations, detailed in the next chapters, incorporated still more aspects of public life into the conditions of filmgoing. Film showmanship thus incorporated perspectives of those speaking on behalf of social institutions. As a variety of authorities came forward, showmanship incorporated often-competing claims while maintaining its "show business" character. What is remarkable is how show business could easily account for the claims made of it and the restraints placed on it.

3

Showmanship in Formation

Incorporating the Civic Work of Competition

The films for moving pictures, used in five cent shows, are not to be had in the city, but by communicating with the Vitagraph Co. of America, New York City; the Chicago Film Exchange, . . . or the Detroit Film Exchange, . . . you may be able to get what you want.

—"Everybody's Column," *Star* April 13, 1907

The picture show business in Toronto is experiencing a "boom," every available plot of ground for miles around is taken up and almost daily we hear of a new one; . . . The butcher, the baker, the candlestick maker are all getting in on the deal, and things are very unsettled.

—"Up in Toronto," *Moving Picture World* August 16, 1913

❧

JULE ALLEN TOURED SOUTHERN ONTARIO in the summer of 1906 looking for a good picture show location. He and brother Jay J., neither yet twenty years old, were sons of a successful shopkeeper in Bradford, Pennsylvania, not so far from the Pittsburgh roots of the nickelodeon craze. After checking out Hamilton, Jule picked Brantford, a smaller city a bit closer to Niagara Falls. Allen's Theatorium opened November 10,

1906, a storefront site with 150 borrowed kitchen chairs. The family remembers it as an instant success (Cox 2000, 45–46). Even with the smaller population, being the first to open in Brantford would be a more secure step than the original plan for Hamilton. Jay J. joined his brother and they established a more elaborate theatorium, Wonderland; people paid to stand for the first days until new chairs arrived. The early lead in Brantford allowed the Allens to expand to other small cities, now against competition, in Berlin (renamed Kitchener during World War I) in May 1907, and later that year in Kingston and Chatham. The Allens even created a film exchange, the Canadian Film Company, to rent films to other showmen.

One of those Kingston competitors against Jay J. Allen's Princess Theatre was Ainsley Burrowes's Bijou. Burrowes had most recently been an editor at the *Detroit Sunday News-Tribune*, but established a nickel show in his Ontario hometown after spending six months studying the moving picture markets in Pittsburgh, Toronto, Detroit, and smaller places in the United States. Over the years, he had been "a labor agitator, a surveyor, a commercial traveler, a book agent, a telegraph operator, a farm laborer, but chiefly and most of the time a journalist" (*MPW* September 7, 1907, 420). Despite local roots, his agitating past and American experience seemed to rub Loyalist Kingston authority the wrong way. Burrowes tried showing religious pictures without charging admission on Sunday, November 24, 1907; his actions led to criminal charges. A reporter for the *Kingston British Whig* (November 25, 1907) wondered if Ontario might have a "United States Sunday" before long, pointing to Burrowes's most recent connection to Detroit (see also *News* and *Star* November 25, 1907). Other early Ontario showmen left similar, if less detailed, accounts of entering the picture business only after surveying the market over a wide area. The stories of Burrowes, told as he set himself up in business, and the Allens, told after their "rise and fall," share some important aspects. Both early showmen took advantage of an open border between Canada and the United States. The Allens' youth and Burrowes's wanderlust betray different backgrounds, but both saw the moving picture business as an opportunity to settle down. Both scouted the territory broadly looking to open with a favorable start. Both had a keen awareness that success depended on finding an unexploited market. And both avoided Toronto, where a single showman, John Griffin, ran all of the shows in town. Late in 1906 and early in 1907, the picture show market there was already locked up.

Chapter 2 showed how the first step toward regulated standards for moviegoing defined film as a combustible, hazardous substance. Chapter 4 outlines the subsequent development of film bureaucracies and censorship. This chapter considers how the commercial character of movies was remade locally in Toronto. Between the first theatorium and full vertical integration of the movie business by 1920, movie showmanship took on a sense of civic responsibility. At times, this chapter might seem to be a mere chronology of the film business in Toronto. The intention is more focused: to demonstrate how showmanship confronted the problem of taking root in particular places, balancing the interests of the city with the distinct interests of a transnational industry. A successful film showman was a permanent local merchant who represented a global product and who created a space particular to the city by projecting images distributed from around the world. Early showmen perhaps showed their craft was a service to the city and its people, while later theater managers might instead boast about links to corporate chains; but their showmanship was at all points defined by the tenuous character of being resident in the city while trading in imported films. That balance rested on the coexisting efforts of competing showmen.

This chapter develops a typology of showmanship and uses those ideal types to consider in detail the early dominance of John Griffin and the growth of competition in Toronto within the wider context of changes in the U.S. film industry. Although corporate mechanisms to control and reorganize showmanship were not uniformly successful, staying inside the system as it conglomerated required modern management. An intermediate step, however, was voluntary showmen's groups, exhibitors' protective associations, that instituted pseudo-professional self-regulation, lobbied government, and promoted filmgoing in general for the mutual benefit of competing showmen. By 1920 theaters were fully vertically integrated with distributors and studios. The chapter concludes with a brief look at the ballooning salaries of key national managers, many times larger than John Griffin's had ever been. At least by that measure of big business wages, this showman whose early dominance in 1906 had fended off the Allens and Burrowes was reduced to just one minor, local figure among many.

What about Griffin's early showmanship made clear to eager entrepreneurs that they had best avoid Toronto? In 1907 the city had a large, increasing population and a relative lack of theatoriums compared to elsewhere. Perhaps real estate prices and rents downtown were excessive in the Ontario capital city. Perhaps it seemed Torontonians, on the whole, would snub cheap amusements because respectable and expensive entertainments were packing houses at six major theaters with two more under construction plus a new suburban amusement park at Scarboro Beach. Perhaps outdoor amusements were especially popular in Toronto year-round, precluding cramped indoor nickel shows. Aside from many small, free ice rinks and some well-designed toboggan chutes, in the winter people could enjoy small orchestra concerts at one of over a dozen commercial skating rinks, and at several roller skating rinks and park bandstands in the summer. Unlike in smaller cities and towns, moving pictures were also showing daily on the Keith's Vaudeville bill at Shea's Yonge Street Theatre, plus burlesque films at the Star Theatre, for example, called the "Girligraph" the week of November 19, 1907. The Star also showed the occasional film of a high-profile prizefight, for example, of Burns–Moir the week of December 23, 1907. Toronto saw plenty of investment in theater in exactly these years. The cheaper, smaller shows of the moving picture market, however, were relatively slow to take hold in the city. As late as February 19, 1908, a query to "Everybody's Column" in the *Star* claimed Toronto had only eight moving picture shows, still lower than the number of theater stages. At that time in Chicago, five-cent shows outnumbered theaters at least tenfold, judging from the 1909 city directory.

The nickelodeon myth tells of an upstart, almost rogue, lack of established norms and standards, of miniscule start-up funds needed for small-time entrepreneurs such as the Allens or Burrowes. Most nickelodeons were supposedly nothing more than converted stores with benches and unfinished furnishings, almost deliberately temporary. Nickel shows came and went, many with no record. And yet in Toronto, a single showman, John Griffin, quickly opened the first four theatoriums by August 1906. Although three of the four were built in converted storefront spaces, no other aspect of Griffin's early dominance follows the stereotyped account of the nickelodeon era. Griffin's early control was based on substantial personal investment and rapid expansion. His entry into the moving picture business was not a tentative, risky move. All of his first four picture shows were relatively large auditoriums of several hundred seats each. Reportedly from the start, all of them were well appointed with fireproof projection booths at safety standards that were still far from standard, although perhaps the result of one of his theatoriums burning down soon after opening and needing to be rebuilt (*Globe* April 30, 1906). Unlike many of the first theatoriums in other cities, all of his were on the ground floor and had proper fire exits right from the start. His earliest shows were still lucrative ventures when sold to other showmen after 1910. Under various managers, all four of them stayed open at least fifteen years, and one of them nearly forty years.

Why would these four moving picture shows prevent Allens' and Burrowes's competition? Why did they instead pick smaller cities? Neither their business dealings nor John Griffin's are known. They and Griffin certainly seemed to rely on family or personal bankrolls rather than outside investment. All rented retail space rather than starting from land ownership to build anew. They all rented films from film exchanges in the United States until Canadian film exchanges opened late in 1907. The question demands a general look at salesmanship at the turn of the twentieth century to sketch what alternative forms of film showmanship might have been open to fledgling entrepreneurs.

Ideal Types of Showmanship

Put plainly, film showmanship imported and reproduced images for local audiences. But, even that simplification betrays an irreconcilable problem, as showmanship at its core was caught between responsibility for the locality and representing external commercial interests. In purely economic terms, picture showmen were retail merchants selling ready-made products for consumption. Many elements were produced locally, such as piano accompaniment, small-time stage acts, sing-alongs and lectures, plus promotion and decoration, sidewalk barking, and ballyhoo (Altman 2005; Lacasse 2000). The importance of these can be thought of as cultural, as the context that marked the difference between showmanship and salesmanship. Without the industrial product of films as the focus, all of these attributes together would have remained a crass dime museum rather than a moving picture theatorium. Some early film showmen in Toronto, those who could demonstrate their local roots, had more leeway to act as if their practice was a craft independent of its mass distributed products. Other early film exhibitors, coming from outside Ontario, young, perhaps Jewish, instead had to promote their transnational product as a modern phenomenon connecting the town to the world outside. Those with strong local ties to Toronto were initially successful and grew fastest. But those showmen who embraced the transnational character of movies defined how film showmanship differed from management of the amusements that came before it. Later still came another type of showman in control of corporate boardrooms, in a sense abdicating showmanship altogether in favor of rational management.

Despite key classical sociological texts on the character of bureaucracy and the division of labor, the problem of modern management was most cogently described only with the maturity of corporate culture following World War II (Mills 1951; Reisman 1960). Social histories of early corporate middlemen note that management at first denoted social status rather than codified routines. Managers ascribed methodical duties to underlings well before management itself followed routine procedures. Even efficiency was a value partly enforced by court order (Haber 1964, 54–80; Zunz 1990, 33–66). Too few descriptions of the day-to-day work of Toronto's film showmen exist to verify such observations. Instead, abstract distinctions among possible forms of showmanship can help develop ideal types that reflect the available details. Although the term has an unwieldy pluralism in its usage within sociology, the method of articulating *ideal types* is in line with the move to reclaim Max Weber's work as an interpretive, historical method, a reassertion that ideal types are "heuristic constructs [that] aim to conceptualize *patterned orientations of social action*. Moreover, Weber's ideal types aim neither to provide an exhaustive description of empirical reality nor to formulate the 'laws' of society" (Kalberg 1997, 216). An ideal typology conceptualizes the struggle evident in case studies. The ideal types are thus imaginary entities having explanatory value, conceptualized from the case to make evident what is at stake (Weber 1949, 72). Fleshing out competing forms of ideal types of film showmanship will contribute to making sense of Griffin's quick rise to dominance and the subsequent development of a highly competitive field of film showmanship in Toronto.

Only in the last decade of the nineteenth century did retail sales of mass distributed goods become a prevalent part of local everyday life with the possibilities opened through railroad distribution, standardized packaging, patent protection, national advertising, and electric refrigeration. Retailing anchored in city stores was a vivid part of the managerial revolution, "the visible hand," and thus distinctly modern (Chandler 1977). Mass distribution through wholesale jobbers allowed retail "stores" to become entirely distinct from small local "shops." In terms of permanent stores in cities and towns, the changes that mass distribution allowed through economies of scale were most evident in department and chain stores (Monod 1996, 195–229). As part of a general industrialization under way, the changes were gradually applied to many small independent types of shops. The fine-tuned division of labor facilitated by mass distribution allowed local selling to be temporally and spatially apart from prior parts of the chain of production and preparation. Of course, a transnational market for standardized products allowed economies of scale in promotion as well, providing standardized advertising that did not have to be typeset or engraved at local newspaper offices (Laird 1998; Strasser 1989). By 1895, daily pages advertised the large department stores alongside elaborately illustrated display ads for still-familiar brand-name products such as Sunlight Soap and Salada Tea. If those brands are more specific to Canada, soon came products also familiar to Americans: Grape Nuts, Jell-O, Wrigley's, Sunkist, Gillette, and, of course, Coca-Cola. These packaged products could be found at almost any corner store but were most likely cheaper sold in quantity at chain stores. Ads for chain stores first appeared in Toronto newspapers around the time filmgoing was taking shape. Most are now defunct or long past their prime, but they spearheaded the mass market a century ago. By 1905, United Cigar Stores and

St. Leger Shoes already had five locations each. By 1910, the first four Tamblyn's drugstores were open. Still-dominant Toronto grocery stores, Dominion and Loblaw's, both began advertising in 1921 and grew quickly. The names may betray regional rather than global roots of chain stores, but those stores' shelves were filled with transnational brands, just as film showmanship worked to represent the continental and global brands of novelty prepackaged products.

Conceptually, the origins of chain stores and branded packaging go back to traveling salesmen, especially those peddling patent medicines, setting up temporary medicine shows with great claims of healing powers, moving on to the next town before ineffectiveness was evident (Johnston 2001, 23–25; Laird 1998, 16–23). Having a shop owner resell goods produced elsewhere maintained a trace of disparaging accusations against snake oil sellers. But this also illustrates a strong link to the negative connotations of showmanship, especially in the American use of the word, associated more narrowly with medicine shows and carnivals compared to the more generic British meaning. *Moving Picture World* constantly prompted U.S. "exhibitors" to abandon old-fashioned showmen's bally-hoo (see, for example, July 20, 1912, 238; and September 14, 1912, 1053). In general, retail salesmanship shook off the shady meanings of itinerancy by demonstrating managerial rationality alongside strict adherence to municipal regulations. Standardized in this way, urban retailing became a localized performance of the very networks of mass production, distribution, and communication that allowed the mass market to include local shops initially.

Two ideal types of showmanship are in opposition here between snake oil seller and modern, efficient manager. The former is akin to the traditional treatment of traders as outsiders to city markets. In typologies of the traditional urban marketplace, the roots of legal oversight of commerce, accounting, and investment have been traced to the need to set conditions for foreign exchange within local markets (Sjoberg 1960, 182–217; Weber 1958, 65–89). But in these classical, urban sociologies, suspicion of trading foreigners is cast against the local craft guild rather than modern management (Braudel 1982, 314–17; Sjoberg 1960, 187–196). In the traditional market, goods produced locally through artisans and trades were produced through a strictly monitored guild system, which had a monopoly over the local conduct of arts, crafts, and labor. Intercity trade was still important, in fact, it has been theorized as precisely the source of the spread of knowledge, creativity, and innovation (J. Jacobs 1969; Soja 2000, 19–49). But, a traditional, and most often legal, distinction was made between craft labor that was of the city and commercial trading that was from outside the city. This is true even of the roots of amusement and entertainment, in the differences between religious festivals and holiday parades, often the responsibility of guilds and local societies, and the marginalized status of traveling minstrels and troubadours (Braudel 1982, 81–94; Hanawalt and Reyerson 1994). The monopoly within the city was supported through a firm integration with local religious and political leadership, through what was supposed to be a deeply ethical responsibility for the everyday life of the citizens (Braudel 1982, 412–16). In contrast, many acknowledged, specifically in legal judgments, that commercial trade with outsiders had no such ethical relationship to the city: caveat emptor, buyer beware (Preston 1975).

Adding the possibility of traditional craftsman to the snake oil seller and the modern manager makes three ideal types of salesmanship that film showmanship could use as its paradigms. The traditional craftsman combines monopoly control, strictly kept membership, artisan production, and a committed, often religious, relation to the city and its citizens. This carries forward into modernity as an ideal, an ethic of responsibility to the community. The next form of salesmanship, also rooted historically, combines impermanence, deceit, mistrust, and imported goods in the figure of the medicine man selling snake oil. This type of salesmanship has historical roots in foreign trade in city markets but continues into the modern age as a suspicion of hucksterist advertising and generally of mass-produced goods. The third type of salesmanship combines rational management, standardization, and professional accountability into the figure of the manager—an embodiment of the modern means of industrial production and distribution. This type of business is associated with all that was novel in the early twentieth century: mass distribution and advertising for prepackaged products, the scientific management of continental markets.

Management may not yet have been the most prevalent form of salesmanship at the turn of the twentieth century, but it was recognized as gaining influence, as the style of "progress." Not only scholars such as Max Weber recognized this tendency; it was valorized by figures in mass production and merchandizing such as Henry Ford, Frederick W. Taylor, and Boston retailer Edward Filene (S. Ewen 1976, 23–48; *World* March 14, 1915; Zunz 1990, 34–36). Rational management bridged the divide between local and foreign trade by anchoring trade routes with resident, representative sales agents. In the shadows, of course, another modern form of salesmanship negated the progressive claims of the managerial form. Mass consumption could be cast negatively because it was based on depersonalized selling and conspicuous consumption, catering to the irrational, and implicitly feminine, values of taste and fashion (Huyssen 1986; Sombart 1967; Veblen 1998). This form of salesmanship implies a dose of cynicism, or at least deliberate pragmatism, but it is evident in the famous dictum the customer is never wrong, specific to Chicago's Marshall Fields department store, "give the lady what she wants" (Wendt 1952), and other tropes that professed to know how to turn mass tastes into fortunes. This sentiment was later borrowed by Paramount Pictures' Adolph Zukor for his 1953 autobiography, *The Public Is Never Wrong*. Among the documented practices and claims of Toronto film showmen, it is most plain in the snob appeal of advertised claims that picture shows were "high-class," "refined," or were, in the Garden Theatre's phrase, "a rendezvous for particular people." Showmanship could also, then, take the form of an exploitative relation to community.

Novelty was key to exploiting curiosity; it was not just introducing a new product to purchase but new ways and places of consuming, perhaps reworking into everyday form something known from special occasions or only available in big cities. Novelty, being first, was cheaper than advertising and easier than getting the word out through handbills and ballyhoo. While fair-sized towns with no moving picture shows were still to be found, novelty was a factor that could lead prospective showmen away from competing against Griffin in Toronto. At this early point, few managerial mechanisms existed for film showmen to connect their businesses to local communities. Moving picture shows were not yet attracting venture capital from established investors, either locally or continentally. During the first years of the nickelodeon, local picture shows were opportunities for independent entrepreneurs to risk opening locations without formal conglomerations or licensed commitments with film producers or distributors.

Beyond the electric technology of film projection, early film showmen relied on more traditional forms of salesmanship because they were independent entrepreneurs who either had to demonstrate a commitment to the traditions of the locality or to exploit the modern novelty of film itself. Young, Jewish, and American, Jules and Jay J. Allen would probably have begun with a relation to their community based on the mistrust of the snake oil seller, unless they could find a town where the fascination with the novelty they provided would overcome those biases. Something similar was perhaps true for Ainsley Burrowes, whose adventures led him far and wide, arriving from his most recent assignment in Detroit. In Kingston, his hometown, he had a chance to package moving pictures as a discovery from abroad brought home. In both cases, moviegoing was introduced as an imported product within trading relations crossing borders. In contrast, Griffin's theatoriums in Toronto seem to have gained an early dominance not just because he was first but because he was able to propose that his special craft was film showmanship, molding an imported commodity into a local product with the skill of an artisan. It seems Griffin's edge came from being able to demonstrate, like a monopoly guild, that his business was something of Toronto, that he was committed to the city.

The Rise and Fall of the Griffin Amusement Company

A Toronto-born Irish-Catholic, John Griffin was said to be nearly six feet tall, immensely broad and with the build of an athlete. In 1906 Griffin was relatively old, age fifty-two, compared to the teenaged Allens, and he had lived on the same street in Toronto since 1901 after years working as an agent for traveling amusements and circuses (*Globe* August 14, 1931). Prior accounts of his business, however, can barely expand on this scanty overview provided reporters for his 1931 obituaries. Interviews and testimonies provided decades after the fact force his efforts into the mold of the ramshackle nickelodeon myth, but his first theatoriums do not really fit the on-the-fly model. Griffin's early shows took substantial investment, probably a combination of deep personal coffers, formal or informal connections to film distribution exchanges, and a hefty dose of luck—the right place at the right time. He leased prime sites downtown for his first four theatoriums. Relatively large, built at the start to high standards, each stayed open at least fifteen years.

The first four Toronto theatoriums in 1906 were near places where women worked and shopped. Three were downtown close to the large department stores and their factory shops, and the fourth was near garment factories west of downtown. First to open in March was the Theatorium across Yonge Street from Eaton's growing department store (Bossin 1951). The Lyceum was farther south on Yonge across from Simpson's department store, also expanding in these years. Both these department stores, since renamed Sears and the Hudson's Bay Company, respectively, continue to anchor downtown shopping at Yonge and Queen a century later. Griffin's third was the Trocadero on Queen Street just west of Eaton's and City Hall, on the site of present-day Nathan Phillips Square and New City Hall. This place was destroyed by fire and quickly rebuilt (*Building Permits* May 1, 1906). In the next municipal ward to the west, the Auditorium was the largest of the four at Queen and Spadina Avenue in a working-class area near the garment district. No source cites any other theatoriums in Toronto until the following year.

Griffin's advantage might have been his advanced age, experience, and local family ties. One result of his early dominance was a relatively slow start to the picture show business in Toronto. After an earlier start than other Ontario cities, by the end of 1907 the city still had only eight theatoriums (five of them Griffin's) for a population in excess of 350,000.

At the same time, four picture shows were advertised in Ottawa (in other words at least that many) for a population of about 80,000, and also four open in Hamilton (population 56,000), whereas Kingston and Brantford each had three shows with populations of just 20,000. Working-class Hamilton with its massive steel mills provides a good contrast. On January 18, 1908, the *Herald* reviewed the city's history and current entertainment scene. The article claimed commercial amusement was an important part of the growth of the city and painted moviegoing as a special site that acted as a carnival where everyone was included. Men, women, and children of all classes enjoyed "the imaginary outing" before returning to their respective homes in different neighborhoods. Film in particular turned men "back into children," something the writer thought only a cynic would object to. Such ringing endorsements were never recorded in Toronto newspapers, which were slow and cautious about moviegoing. What was the difference and how much could it be rooted in the particular way John Griffin operated his shows?

Discrepancies in theaters per capita demonstrate early picture show competition cannot be reduced to some single quantity. The openness of the market to an entrepreneur depended on the field of competition, and thus not the number but the relative strength of competitors. Explanations using numbers per capita, implied in my previous list of other Ontario cities, fail to consider the degree to which Griffin's early control in Toronto proceeded to shape moviegoing (as well as regulation and theater building) for years to come. A list of electric theaters and nickelodeons, published on December 15, 1906, in *Billboard*, provides a measure of just how exceptional Griffin's position in Toronto was. Compiled unevenly, specifically lacking all but a few entries from Chicago and New York, the *Billboard* list is nonetheless a neglected source for comparative analysis of early nickelodeons. Seating capacity and the number of shows per week at each site were reported, allowing a good sense of how relatively substantial or makeshift Griffin's theatoriums were. In these terms, Griffin's four theaters in Toronto stand out for their uniformly large size. Each seated audiences of 300 to 400 people. Although far from the largest (one theater in Philadelphia could hold 1,000 people), almost every other listed city had many much smaller theaters.

A seating capacity of 300 was far larger than the smallest picture shows in other cities, which was as few as 60 people. None was larger than 250 seats in Pittsburgh, Detroit, Milwaukee, Baltimore, Cincinnati, or Cleveland. When the number of weekly shows is factored in, the average Griffin theatorium in Toronto could sell in excess of 11,000 tickets weekly, about three times the average nickelodeon in all of those cities, except Cleveland at about 8,500. Aside from size and capacity, not a single other place, small town or big city, lists more than two shows in town with a single showman running all of them. Griffin's early control and relatively large theatoriums shows the nickelodeon and its filmgoing culture was highly variable from place to place. And yet within a decade a continental network of norms managed film distribution, theater building and management style. Once competition opened up, Toronto became more like other cities of its size. By 1910 the city had three dozen picture shows. Yet even this late, just a few small shows operated against Griffin downtown because new theatoriums were mostly scattered in neighborhoods. The market in Toronto began on a different path from other cities, where competition was perhaps fiercest at the beginning.

Part of Griffin's business plan was carefully publicizing and demonstrating responsibility for the needs of the community. But then, newspapers note these demonstrations of social service only following transgressions on Griffin's part, one accidental and one personal. The accident came with an early-morning fire in the Theatorium on Yonge Street in October 1907 (*News* October 25, 1907). A few weeks later, the *Star* noted the Griffin Amusement Company sent a $25 donation to the Firemen's Benefit Fund, expressing thanks for responding within three minutes of the alarm and saving his theatorium (*Star* November 14, 1907). Note the donation came from Griffin's company, not from him personally, and of course Griffin must have been the one who let the *Star* know about it. The special show of sincerity might also have been in response to personal trouble earlier in the fall. On September 27, 1907, John Griffin was sent to jail for fifteen days, with no option of a fine, for beating his wife. A row over finances and property had escalated to blows. Worse, for a showman, the incident was on the public record and the court report ran in the daily newspapers. As an almost literal penance, while in jail Roman Catholic Griffin turned his largest show house over to J. M. Wilkinson, prominent religious features editor for the Sunday *World*. Throughout October, Wilkinson lectured to *The Passion Play*, the first theatorium advertising in the city.

Griffin's age, experience, and apparently deep pockets allowed him to operate a small chain of theaters right from the beginning. In June 1907 the Griffin Amusement Company was registered with the Ontario government, an official partnership with son, Peter. Employees and wages are listed with property tax assessments of head office beginning in 1907. A year later John Griffin, president, was assessed a wage of $1,000, a figure that fluctuated each year, but was never again that high. Although wages do not tell the whole story, simply defining the president's position as a waged employee of the company shows a certain degree of modern management and detached rationality in the operation of Griffin's company.

Figure 3.1. Toronto-born theatorium pioneer, John Griffin, and his twin the-aters—the sixth and seventh in his chain and in the city. (Left: *Billboard* June 27, 1908. Right: *Star* August 14, 1931.)

Griffin worked to integrate his theatoriums into Toronto's leisure traditions, rather than boast and exaggerate moviegoing as a break from the past. This was partly achieved by developing an increasingly stronger relation between Griffin and vaudeville, moving film to the sidelines of the show, in contrast to being the focus at the start. As a career showman, Griffin perhaps saw film as part of traditional amusements, rather than something entirely novel. Correspondence about Griffin appeared regu-larly in *Billboard* and *Variety*, trade journals gathering film under a wide umbrella spanning from Broadway stage to rural minstrel. In contrast, news about Griffin in the specialty trade paper *Moving Picture World* is almost nonexistent until 1913. Continuing in the circus showman tradi-tion, now adapted for films, Griffin could present his shows as the prod-uct of his own craftsmanship, as if even the filmed entertainment was something he took ownership of. Shortly after Griffin's new Hippodrome and Casino opened in 1907, portraits of Canadian lieutenant governors, representatives of the King, but also a "splendid," and "life-like" portrait of Griffin himself, were painted for its lobby (*Billboard* February 1, 1908, 43 and May 9, 1908, 28). "Griffin's," the branded name of each theater, hung out publicly on an electric sign and was blocked out in letters across the façade instead of the specific name of each place. The crafts, as

Table 3.1. Known Griffin's Theaters

	Name	City	Open as Griffin's	Griffin's Until
1	Theatorium (storefront)	183 Yonge, Toronto	In March 1906	1913
2	Trocadero (storefront)	96 Queen W, Toronto	In April 1906	1913
3	Lyceum (storefront)	141 Yonge, Toronto	By July 1906	1907
4	Trocadero (rebuilt after fire)	96 Queen W, Toronto	By July 1906	1913
4	Auditorium (storefront)	380 Queen W, Toronto	By Aug. 1906	1913
5	Vaudevite (storefront)	248 Yonge, Toronto	By April 1907	1908
6	Hippodrome (storefront)	219 Yonge, Toronto	By June 1907	1915
7	Casino (storefront)	221 Yonge, Toronto	By June 1907	1915
8	Vaudette (summer show)	Lakeshore, suburban Toronto	July 11, 1908	1910
9	Griffin's Family (purpose-built)	St. Catharines	Nov. 30, 1908	1916
10	Variety (purpose-built)	8 Queen E, Toronto	April 9, 1909	1920
11	Agnes Street (was Lyric Jewish)	72 Agnes (Dundas), Toronto	Aug. 30, 1909	1910
12	Griffin's (was Albert Opera House)	Stratford	May 9, 1910	1914
13	Griffin's (was Orpheum)	Kingston	May 9, 1910	1920
14	Griffin's (was Carman Opera House)	Belleville	May 10, 1910	1927*
15	Griffin's (was Royal Opera House)	Guelph	May 16, 1910	1922
16	Majestic (was melodramas)	25 Adelaide W, Toronto	Aug. 29, 1910	1915
17	Griffin's (was Opera House)	Woodstock	Sept. 10, 1912	1922
18	Griffin's (was Opera House)	Welland	Sept. 23, 1912	1922
19	Griffin's (was Savoy Opera House)	Owen Sound	Feb. 3, 1913	1920
20	Griffin's (was Royal Opera House)	North Bay	In April 1913	1920
21	Griffin's (was New Theatre)	Brockville	Aug. 29, 1913	1915
22	Griffin's Hippodrome (purpose-built)	Hamilton	Nov. 3, 1913	1915
23	Griffin's (purpose-built)	Chatham	Nov. 24, 1913	1929*
24	Griffin's (was local opera house)	Thorold	Feb. 12, 1914	1922

continued on next page

Table 3.1. Known Griffin's Theaters (*continued*)

	Name	City	Open as Griffin's	Griffin's Until
25	Griffin's (was Kilbourne Theatre)	Owen Sound	Nov. 16, 1914	1922
26	Griffin's Yonge Street (remodeled)	219 Yonge, Toronto	May 2, 1915	1916
27	Griffin's (purpose-built)	St. Catharines	May 6, 1915	1927*
28	Griffin's Ford City (purpose-built)	Windsor	April 5, 1918	1920
29	Griffin's (was Auditorium)	Sarnia	Nov. 21, 1918	1925*
30	Griffin's (was King's Theatre)	Sault Ste Marie	May 28, 1919	1925*
31	Griffin's (was Corona Theatre)	Fort William	Oct. 6, 1919	1920
32	Griffin's (was Victoria Opera House)	Goderich	Nov. 3, 1919	1920
33	Griffin's (was Grand Opera House)	Cobalt	Dec. 11, 1919	1920
34	Griffin's (was Lyceum)	Port Arthur	By 1920	1922
	Error or Summer Airdome	1806 Queen West, Toronto	1910 Directory	

* Griffin's in name only in final years.

opposed to sales, orientation of the Griffin Amusement Company seems to present the appeal of film shows as a reflection of the showman himself, but it was a stance only a monopoly could afford. It lent itself to pretensions and flamboyance, and ambition for expansion rather than improvement and strengthening of the foundation. Ultimately, it was fundamentally at odds with the particular characteristics of the technology and commercial practices of the film business.

The Griffin Amusement Company expanded rapidly and became the preeminent chain of moving picture shows throughout Ontario with business arrangements linking to chains of theaters in Michigan, Quebec, New England, and the Maritime Provinces. In Toronto, Griffin ran a maximum of eight theatoriums at a time, a total of eleven theaters at some point. Expansion outside the city began in St. Catharines and continued until at least thirty-four Griffin theaters straddled the province. On May 14, 1910, the *Toronto News* reported that Peter Griffin was traveling throughout the United States, "picking up a score of desirable leases. . . . When this great chain is completed Griffin's, Limited, will probably control about 150 houses" (see also *Billboard* February 12, 1910, 5; April 16, 1910, 16). Griffin leased the Majestic vaudeville playhouse downtown in 1910, marking a turn away from moving pictures (*Telegram* August 23, 1910). Whether his supply of moving pictures was tenuous or whether he simply did not believe moving pictures were the source of further growth is not clear.

As early as the 1909 opening of Griffin's 1,400-seat Agnes Street Theatre daily advertising promoted "refined" vaudeville rather than films, offering five, then six, seven, and finally eight "big" vaudeville acts. The Majestic advertising listed stage acts by name, "and the Majesticograph." Leasing four older playhouses in a big expansion in May 1910 made Griffin's Vaudeville, not moving pictures, the leading theater in the smaller Ontario cities of Stratford, Kingston, Belleville, and Guelph. A dubious notice in November inflates the extent of Griffin-controlled picture houses to 300, including the start of a new chain across the Maritimes and a new office established in Seattle (*News* November 5, 1910; *Billboard* November 19, 1910, 14). Expansion stopped around 1911, just after the moving picture show business in Toronto had undergone a boom period and was about to enter a lull for a few seasons. At this time, the Yonge Street real estate of the leased Hippodrome and Casino was reportedly purchased to build a movie palace (*Billboard* November 25, 1911, 20). Ownership of the property did not change hands on city assessment rolls, however, meaning *all* the reports of expansion need to be treated skeptically. When movie theater building resumed in Toronto at the end of 1912, the Griffin Amusement Company was not part of it.

The source of the early rapid expansion was precisely its weakness. Griffin chose to become a small-time vaudeville circuit booker, turning toward what was still a more prestigious form of amusement, but one that was dramatically more expensive and less profitable. Jones, Linick, and Schaefer did much the same thing in Chicago, shifting to small-time vaudeville after holding a near-monopoly in Loop nickelodeons. It led to short-term success but in the end shut them out of the movie market. Small-time vaudeville, still profitable around 1910, was responsible for the growth of Marcus Loew's circuit in New York, except that Loew began in vaudeville and shifted to film, not the other way around. Vaudeville allowed Griffin to create a regional chain rapidly, but it seems also to have been a somewhat stubborn decision to ignore the accounting sheets at the end of each week. Consider, in contrast, a letter to *Moving Picture World* from a new leaseholder at the Nickel in Quebec City, who calculated to the penny the cost of running vaudeville against simpler musical songs and accompaniment:

> All we know are what the facts and figures say. Vaudeville in a moving picture house does not pay. I would suggest that proprietors should go over their statements and work out their average weekly or daily receipts. . . . If they cannot do it themselves, a few dollars for a bookkeeper will be well spent, and the sooner the better (*MPW* July 9, 1910, 93–94).

Here in detail was a professional film showman. He has kept track of every penny and calculated the balance of receipts versus expenses of the effects of introducing vaudeville, showing the supposed respectability of vaudeville did not pay. Of course, it was a letter to a major *film* trade paper, not to *Billboard* or *Variety* with their reports about Griffin. At the time, *Moving Picture World* made frequent calls to distinguish moving pictures from crass, cheap vaudeville, although there was tentative excitement when pictures were added to classy, big-time vaudeville bills. (*MPW* January 8, 1910, 13; January 22, 1910, 81; February 26, 1910, 288).

Recent scholarship has carefully differentiated early film showmanship from what later became mainstream moviegoing. Studies of early film shows in Toronto strongly argue that a uniquely Canadian, local context was explicitly part of the entertainment despite references to imported images and songs (Keil and Braun 2001; Steven 2003). This describes, however, only extraordinary shows rather than the everyday routine of the theatoriums. For the nickelodeon program, popular music and sing-along illustrated songs were mass-produced and imported locally just like the accompanying films. The small-time vaudeville acts

Griffin offered were also advertised available through ads in U.S. trade papers. Although care was taken to make shows homey and locally understood, Griffin's shows had nothing particularly Canadian or nationalist.

Financially, Griffin operated his company as a family-run firm and circulated available cash into expansion rather than reorganizing to rebuild and strengthen existing locations. Griffin did not purchase real estate, and with just a couple of exceptions to prove the rule, the Griffin Amusement Company leased older, existing playhouses rather than build new theaters. This left plenty of room for competitors to take advantage of eager investors and stay up-to-date with newer, more palatial theaters. If rent was a drain on Griffin's expenses, then the wages of vaudeville acts proved even worse. By 1913, he even sold off or lost the lease on most of his Toronto theaters, focusing almost entirely on big-time vaudeville at the Majestic. Griffin's leases were signed and expired frequently. Of thirty-four confirmed Griffin's theaters, no more than twenty operated simultaneously. The number of theaters remained steady from 1913 into the early 1920s, but in those last years many were in the farthest outposts of Northern Ontario and none remained in Toronto.

Small storefronts and leased old playhouses continued to be Griffin's business plan instead of buying real estate and building against the onslaught of bigger, brand-new picture theaters opening throughout the metropolis of Toronto. Of course, many of these paths not taken would have required investment capital and partnerships outside the family-run company; this applies especially to building new theaters on purchased prime real estate. Rule number one for Griffin's family-run firm was proudly avoiding outside investment. Overall, Griffin's decline appears to be exactly the source of his original dominance, a tendency to trust in traditional rather than innovative forms of business management, which had a compound effect in providing traditional rather than innovative forms of moviegoing. He moved into vaudeville and away from feature films, leasing old-fashioned opera houses rather than building new theaters, and in Toronto he remained squarely downtown when dozens of competitors were building all over the city. News about Griffin finally appears around 1913 in *Moving Picture World*, but the company was by then focused on theaters in smaller Ontario cities (see, for example, *MPW* July 12, 1913, 214). Griffin continued to operate, as late as 1924 and after, but one by one the original shows were given up and taken over by competitors.

Griffin's Early Competitors and the Civic Duty of Showmanship

One of the original four Griffin's theatoriums had already passed to a competitor by October 1907, when the Hippodrome showcased J. M.

Wilkinson and the *The Passion Play* in apparent restitution for John Griffin's domestic assault. Prominent Yonge Street milliners Llewellyn J. Applegath and Sons purchased the Lyceum, next door to their hat store. Griffin responded swiftly to the prospect of competition by opening three more picture shows: a pair side-by-side at Yonge Street and Shuter Street, the Hippodrome and Casino, and another right across the street, the Vaudevite. (All were just steps away from the establishment's Massey Music Hall). Applegath renamed his Lyceum site the Crystal Palace and advertised its own show of *The Passion Play* exactly the same day Wilkinson began lecturing at Griffin's nearby theater. "Nickel" show was already a misnomer as the Crystal Palace called itself a "High-Class Moving Picture Theatre" charging a dime instead. A small announcement in the *News* explained, "If at any time our prices are higher than those of other moving picture theaters, it will only be on account of the very select and high-grade nature of the pictures. This will also have a tendency to make our audience more select" (ad in *News* October 2, 1907). The Crystal Palace boasted that the superior pictures and more refined crowd were worth the extra nickel, whereas Griffin countered by renting out several of his theatoriums for moral and religious education and amusement.

Figure 3.2. L. J. Applegath purchased the real estate under Griffin's Lyceum and renamed the site the Crystal Palace. 141 Yonge Street. *ca.* 1914. (Photograph by Ernest Hoch, Archives of Ontario, William H. Hammond Fonds, Image 21973.)

Other ventures were making moves into West end neighborhoods. Just a block away from Griffin's Auditorium, John Long opened the Rex storefront theater on Queen Street (*Building Permits* May 3, 1907). In November 1907, for the first time in Toronto, a theatorium advertised its grand opening: Dreamland, "Full Orchestra, Moving Pictures and Singers. Clean, bright attractive show. Adults 10¢ Children 5¢ Performance 7:30 p.m. to 11 p.m. daily" (ad in *Telegram* November 15, 1907; *Building Permits* October 28, 1907). Griffin and Applegath downtown rarely bought ads—the religious shows in October 1907 are exceptions until years later. Whether the ads for the Dreamland reflected ambition, necessity, or foolish pride, they were not enough to make the show an enduring success. Maybe the venture was intended to be short term, or its quick passing might be connected to a Greek showman Harry Manglan being cited for operating a theater without a license, the first picture show violation in the *Register of Criminals* ([henceforth *ROC*] November 22, 1907, line 1134). Would a showman open his theater with high-profile newspaper ads without knowing to obtain a permit? At this early stage, perhaps it was possible. After all, police still had no jurisdiction except against indecent performances, and the $50 show license was the only regulation.

These small moves toward competition were all taken by independent showmen. Even Applegath branching into the moving pictures from his hat shop was a significant competitor more because he owned the real estate rather than due to the size of his theatorium. The more substantial threat to Griffin's early dominance was the prospect of U.S.–affiliated chains opening a branch in Toronto. Several chains of nickel shows were strong elsewhere in Canada. In small-town Ontario eastward to the Maritime Provinces, C. W. Bennett operated a chain of Unique five-cent shows from 1907 to 1909 to complement his expanding chain of Keith-affiliated vaudeville theaters. Out of Winnipeg, through the Prairies and down into the midwestern United States, Paul LeMarquand was the president of a chain of Starland theaters from 1909 for several years. Neither of these chains operated in Toronto. The most important early chain of nickel shows was the Nickel shows run by Keith vaudeville interests out of Boston. Throughout 1907, the chain opened Nickel Theatres across eastern Canada; the first in Saint John had actually been named Keith's in 1906. Next was Halifax, then Sydney, and out to St. John's, Newfoundland. The chain then doubled back to Quebec City, Ottawa, and finally opened two shows in Montreal. Keith's Nickel shows invariably leased large community halls, often owned by religious-affiliated groups. At the end of December 1907, Toronto newspapers reported its Montreal managers had arranged something similar in Toronto. The YMCA's Association Hall, just North of downtown on Yonge Street, was leased for "the coming season." Ads began days later in all city papers, leading up to an opening on January 6, 1908. The "Picture Hall 5¢" would offer "magnificent moving pictures with illustrated songs by notable artists, continuous performance from 12 noon to 10 p.m." Their ads repeated a version of the slogan used elsewhere, "Come when you like. Stay as long as you like." Although the name "Nickel" was not used in Toronto, the 5¢ icon was prominent, and many ads included the phrase, "The Nickel Programme." Unlike any other picture theater until almost a decade later, the Picture Hall advertised in all six daily newspapers. Proposing moving pictures as a legitimate amusement among established theaters was key to Nickel promotion across the entire chain.

Toronto proved a stumbling block, although newspaper reviews of the shows claim it was well attended. Unlike the community meeting rooms that the company rented in Ottawa, Montreal, Halifax, and St. John's, the Association Hall in Toronto was in constant use. Almost immediately, the Picture Hall had to adjust its schedule to fit other meetings, including several days in January for a large Bible study conference. This must have frustrated the management, upsetting their already standardized promotional routine of continuous shows day in, day out. The final ad for a Picture Hall show came just a month after opening. The chain's experiment in Toronto failed, despite success everywhere else. It might have been the lack of available space because the chain was reluctant to own land or build from scratch. With Toronto's public halls in constant use, the company would have had to buy real estate and erect a new structure. It might have been the competition from Griffin's theaters, already well-founded and more centrally located, where in other cities the chain was first to open. It might have been pressure from Shea's big-time vaudeville not to have two Keith-affiliated entertainments in town despite price and program differences. Unlike Bennett and Keith's affiliates in other cities, brothers Jerry and Michael Shea, managers in Toronto and Buffalo respectively, were particularly skeptical of moving pictures and stuck to only the biggest of big-time vaudeville until relatively late in the game (Lenton-Young 1990, 204–6).

On February 19, 1908, a query to "Everybody's Column" in the *Star* (a public forum for reference information) noted that the city had eight picture shows: five run by John Griffin, plus L. J. Applegath's, John Long's, and just one other run by Edward Manning, most likely the Picture Hall. Toronto had the same number of theatrical stages, as well as numerous public halls and churches used for meetings. Compared to already hundreds of nickel shows in New York and Chicago, moving pictures were no runaway success in Toronto. Even within Canada, the city had about the same number of picture shows as Winnipeg, Vancouver,

Ottawa, and Hamilton, despite their significantly smaller populations. These months of modest expansion show the filmgoing market in Toronto was still rather modest, well over a year after Jule Allen came to Ontario looking for a place to begin cranking the projector. Delayed a couple of years, the market eventually opened. By the end of 1908, four more were open, and the number almost doubled in 1909. In the midst of that flurry of activity, the *Star* published an article giving a social, economic, political, and geographic survey of the film business in Toronto; it was phrased as a debate over whether the picture show was a fad. One city councilor was even so sure it was a fashionable craze that he proposed the best way to regulate its demise was to let it run wild and burn out (*Star* May 22, 1909). The article is a good indication that theatoriums drew attention to themselves as an emerging part of neighborhood shopping streets and everyday life early in 1909.

Moving pictures were now running daily except Sunday in seven neighborhoods, with four more shows planned in another three areas of town. Two of the new competitors were constructing purpose-built picture shows from their foundations, including Walter K. Hill's Colonial opposite City Hall, perhaps the first luxury picture theater in Toronto. Another phenomenon had begun: small-time showmen who owned their show's real estate. Charles Welsman on the East side and Robert Burke on the West converted their small shops to storefront shows, which they managed themselves. From the initial Elysian, Welsman went on to expand this site and also operate a large theater across the street. Burke's story is more humble. Fifty years old and living in his carpentry shop on Dundas Street (now Ossington Avenue), he converted the space to show moving pictures and ran the show himself. Burke named his show "Fairyland" and ran it until he died in 1914.

Here, finally, better than Griffin, Applegath, or Minier, Robert Burke's is the mythologized story of the nickelodeon boom, differentiated from the big business conglomerations that followed. While holding up Burke's Fairyland as a symbol of the intensely local, independent scale of theatoriums might be tempting, it is the *only* clear case in Toronto of humble and modest beginnings. Burke is really the only one who personifies the ideal type of showmanship as a local craftsman who was not in any sense a trade representative. As Griffin's early chain demonstrates, balancing traditional and modern management, showmanship had always included attention to corporate management, which did not simply arrive without precedent when formal incorporation began. Showmanship, especially film showmanship because of the international trade involved, had always tenuously enacted the tension between the local and the global. The overall process might have headed toward professionalized management and away from a more traditional entrepreneurism. However, the particular circumstances of nearly everyone, Burke excepted, shows conglomeration was embedded from the start in the problem of making showmanship more civic-minded.

Promotion and Circulation: Film Exchanges and Local Competition

The key to opening the film market in Toronto and throughout Ontario was film exchanges providing a steady supply to local exhibitors. Griffin's first competitor, Applegath, was a local merchant with the resources to purchase the real estate out from under the Lyceum, renovate it, and repackage it as an improvement of Griffin's model. But, both were still locally responsible, established businessmen. At this early stage, at least in Toronto, a mechanism did not yet exist to allow showmen without local roots to open a show with minimal expense. Only after local film exchanges opened, such as the Allens' Canadian Film Company out of Brantford, did small-time entrepreneurs establish neighborhood picture shows as an alternative to the expense and risk of leasing a place downtown. Exchanges opened in Toronto in the summer of 1907 and the first two advertised in city newspapers (before any picture show itself had done so). First came ads in August for a branch of Montrealer Léo Ouimet's Ouimetoscope Film Exchange, which had listed itself as a film supplier in the *Moving Picture World* (May 18, 1907, 173). Within a run-on sentence that explained the need for Ouimet's service, the words, "Everything Is Moving on Earth," were highlighted in large bold letters (ad in *News* August 10, 1907). A few weeks later, ads began for the Dominion Film Exchange, headquartered in Toronto. It was first listed in the *Moving Picture World* directory in July with a display ad "Canada Headquarters" (ad in *News* August 31, 1907; *MPW* July 20, 1907, 319). These ads were an indication of more competition and a growing regional market for picture shows all over Southern Ontario. Several other companies supplied films to the Ontario market, such as a classified ad for the British-American Kinematograph (*Star* January 18, 1908, 15) and a Windsor branch of the Detroit Film Exchange (*MPW* July 20, 1907, 311).

In Toronto, Charles Thompson was the first manager of the Dominion Film Exchange. Thompson, "the well known adjuster and circus man," had been manager of the Palace Theatre on St. Lawrence Street in Montreal until early in 1907. When he sold this theater, he simply said his plans were to take the summer off (*MPW* April 13, 1907, 86). By September 1907, the Dominion Film Exchange was operating in Toronto with Thompson as manager. At the production and technological end of the film industry, however, events that had been in the works for a decade finally precipitated with a March 1907 court decision. In the United States, the result was that the Thomas Edison Company held clear patent rights for almost all cameras, projectors, and films in use on the continent. By the first months of 1908, an Edison-led patents trust was established through which all manufacturers, producers, distributors, and exhibitors of films submitted licensing fees. Later in 1908, this process was consolidated formally through the Motion Picture Patents Company, or the Patents Trust, a license trust Edison designed to control competition. The industry saw strong and swift antitrust opposition, but the effect bifurcated all branches of the film industry in the United States into "licensed" and "independent" factions (Staiger 1983). When the *Moving Picture World* trade directory first split the two groups of licensed and independent films suppliers, Ouimet in Montreal was the only Canadian exchange siding with the Patents Trust. This changed in a few weeks, and *all* Canadian companies were listed as independent possibly by default because U.S. patent law did not extend across the border. Even in the United States, the Patents Trust could not suppress the self-proclaimed independent movement spearheaded out of Chicago by Carl Laemmle, an important early exhibitor who would eventually turn this independent distributors' network into Universal Pictures. In Canada, even if not by force of law, the film trade split into a mirror of these two affiliations. By 1909, Applegath was operating the Crystal Palace Film Exchange out of his theater on Yonge Street, soon the Toronto representative of the independent faction, now formally organized into the Motion Picture Distributing and Sales Company, or simply the Sales Company. Ouimet's exchange seems to have become a branch of a new Gaumont Film Company of Canada in October 1909 (*MPW* August 14, 1909, 233; October 9, 1909, 506).

By 1909, the Dominion Film Exchange was clearly and formally part of the Patents Trust. A major player in the Patents Trust and head of the Kinetograph Company in New York, Percy L. Waters was listed on assessment rolls as president of the Toronto company from 1909. The legal status of the Patents Trust did not cross the border, so Canadian film companies had to be bought outright to fall under the control of the trust. The success of direct ownership of the Dominion Film Exchange in Canada, in a sense, set the precedent for the model of conglomeration followed in the United States. Formal conglomeration of film distribution in North America appears to have first happened in Toronto. Not until April 1910 did the Patents Trust formally create a distribution branch, buying outright regional exchanges and renaming them all branches of the General Film Company, with Waters as its general manager. As this happened in the United States, Waters followed suit and reorganized the Dominion Film Exchange in Toronto as an autonomous branch of the General Film Company with new offices on Front Street. The old offices on Queen Street East were taken over by the Allens' Canadian Film Company, by then headquartered in Calgary but becoming a nationally-dominant Sales Company film supplier. Soon after the Allens opened their Toronto branch, Applegath closed his Crystal Palace Film Exchange, the previous local Sales Company representative.

Local film exchanges spawned more than picture show competition. They also prompted the first regular journalism about the film industry in Toronto from 1908 to 1911 in the Saturday drama and music page of the *News*. Content and quotations for occasional articles came from George F. Law, local manager of the Dominion Film Exchange, and Peter Griffin, manager of Ontario's dominant chain. "The Left Box" was a theater column in the *News* penned by "Thespis," perhaps *Billboard*'s Toronto correspondent Joseph Gimson because many local articles were copied there. The column began in October 1908 as part of a revamped weekend amusement page, which now included more photographs of performers and an illustrated banner. The page was unique among Toronto newspapers at the time because it presented serious journalism about the local entertainment business instead of just promotional reviews of upcoming shows.

In April 1909, an article described the film industry's growth as "a matter for general marvel" and quoted Law's estimate of 150 theaters in Ontario and 65 in Montreal alone. The manager of the Dominion Film Exchange said, "the Canadian theatoriums are in most cases owned by individuals. No trust exists here, either in the ownership of buildings or film supplies" (*News* April 3, 1909, 25). He made no mention of Toronto or Griffin. Instead, the film exchange manager provided a national perspective. A September article once again quoted George Law emphasizing the general well-being of the business throughout Ontario. In May 1910, articles about Griffin's began appearing once the chain shifted to focus on vaudeville and widened into a regional circuit. This dispersion away from Toronto left open the possibility of a move into the city for picture theater chains affiliated with U.S. distributors. This is how the Buffalo-based Mark–Brock chain entered Toronto, obtaining the lease to the old Shea's Yonge Street theater after Shea's opened a new vaudeville palace in 1910. After heated gossip and heavy bidding for the lease, in April 1911 it was confirmed that Buffalo's Mitchell Mark and H. G. Brock had secured an agreement to renovate the site. In Toronto, their Strand opened in August 1911, the first downtown movie palace focusing on films instead of performance and the first to advertise film titles with large display ads in the two weekend papers.

Figure 3.3. Buffalo's Mitchell Mark and Henry Brock opened the Strand on August 21, 1911, three years before they opened the Broadway Strand at Times Square. 91 Yonge Street. *ca.* 1914. (Photograph by Ernest Hoch, Archives of Ontario, William H. Hammond Fonds, Image 21958.)

The Mark–Brock chain was no small competition. Its origins in Buffalo had already spread throughout New England and to Ottawa and Montreal, operating the Français and Family Theatres in each city. After the Toronto Strand opened in 1911, the chain expanded with Strands and Regents throughout the northeastern United States, culminating with their 3,000 seat Strand in Times Square in 1914. Managed by the most famous and successful showman in the United States, S. L. "Roxy" Rothaphel, the Broadway Strand was treated as a turning point signaling the undeniable presence of film in the mainstream with theater and vaudeville (Hall 1966, 36–43). In Toronto, the Strand continued as the premiere place for first-run films even after 1914 when new Loew's and Shea's Vaudeville palaces opened. George Schlesinger came to manage the Strand after working for Mark–Brock at the Français in Montreal. He renovated the theater lobby, installed a costly organ, and even tested the waters in Toronto for sensational "social problem" films and frank advertising—this lasted only a few weeks (*Star Weekly* May 9, 1914; June 27, 1914). Within a few months, Schlesinger's brother Leon replaced him in Toronto, moving up from the Academy Theater in Buffalo (*Star Weekly* September 5, 1914). The *Star Weekly* printed a review of Leon Schlesinger, whose "interesting career" had begun as an usher in Buffalo when he was just thirteen. Since then he had been an actor, press agent, ticket seller, treasurer, and manager for theaters in Philadelphia, Chicago, and then manager of picture theaters in New Jersey and New York, in Calgary and Regina, earning a reputation as a "doctor for sickly houses." His pithy slogans summed up his philosophy of showmanship: "quick action," and "give the people what they want" (*Star Weekly* May 15, 1915). After a slow start with Griffin's low-key traditionalism, modern showmanship had truly come to Toronto.

This brief profile of Leon Schlesinger's career contrasted with John Griffin's apparent presentation of grounded, locally committed showmanship, even more so if Schlesinger's long career as a professional manager in show business was written with a dose of self-promotion and puffery. The American, stopping in Toronto to secure an established advantage among new competition, boasted of making a midmanagerial career out of giving people what they wanted. He had no fear that in Toronto he would be accused of exploiting the local public on behalf of U.S. corporate interests. He was helping heal a sick theater in their midst, and it was an operation he was specially trained to do. Similarly illustrated and boosterist profiles were printed in Toronto newspapers at this time for Phil Kauffman, regional manager for the Allen's Famous Players Film Service (the successor to the Canadian Film Company when they switched from representing Laemmle's Universal Pictures through the Sales Company to the newer Paramount film franchise). In 1915 with Famous-Lasky feature films growing in importance, Kauffman himself became the subject of promotion as he made promises in advertising, such as "I am going to make Paramount a household word" (*Star Weekly* March 6, 1915; June 12, 1915). It was a more crassly commercial boast than Schlesinger's, but it was made equally with the assurance of a corporate manager sure he had the fix for what the public craved. Noting the Jewish names of this new generation of showmen hints at a corresponding change in the public role of showmanship in Toronto. Now that the Allens were established in Toronto, if their ethnicity had been a problem in 1906, it clearly was not by 1914. Griffin's early advantage might have because he was older, Toronto-born, and Christian, but there are now no indications that Jewish, American, or foreign-born status was considered a liability. Applegath might have had fewer problems as an established Jewish merchant and landowner; but now the Schlesingers, Kauffman, and the Allen brothers were demonstrating that modern movie showmanship could be a valuable and respectable service to the community, whether or not done by Jewish showmen born, raised, and trained elsewhere. Nonetheless, the corporate and openly persuasive approach, especially on newspaper pages, was built on the early work Griffin had done to demonstrate that filmgoing could be an integral part of city life.

Corporate Mechanisms of Film Showmanship in Toronto

In 1914, Mark–Brock conglomerated its Canadian and some Buffalo hold-ings, offering shares for $300,000 in stock in United Motion Picture Theatres Limited, including part interest in the Strand on Yonge Street. These ads claimed that the movies were "probably the most profitable industry in the world to-day" (ad in *Globe* January 3, 1914). The big business structure of Mark–Brock was not exceptional, although its suc-cess was. A handful more Toronto-based picture theater chains left traces, although their influence has disappeared with their long-past failures. As early as December 1909, building permits were filed under corporate names rather than the names of showmen. An early corporation selling shares was Canada Moving Pictures, Limited. Advertising $40,000 worth of shares, the company had "options in five of the most lucrative earning playhouses" and already owned and operated a leading Yonge Street show (ad in *Globe* July 18, 1912, also in *Star Weekly* and *Jack Canuck* July 20, 1912). The July 1912 ads selling shares claim that "the general public has made the Moving Picture Industry what it is to-day, and for the first time the public is offered an opportunity of reaping the financial benefits." None of the listed board of directors seems to have any other involve-ment in the local film business. Instead, all were merchants and financiers whose primary interests lay elsewhere, including directors of another small chain, the Montreal Moving Pictures, Ltd., which sold shares for $100,000 several weeks later (ad in *Montreal Star* September 6, 1912; *Montreal Standard* September 7, 1912). In Toronto their plans were hardly ambi-tious, although they renovated an older show and installed a Wurlitzer "orchestra" organ (*Star* November 16, 1912). They offered a modest sale of shares to buy out smaller, older picture shows rather than make the move of building new, larger theaters. Their existing picture shows down-town such as the St. Denis, Standard, Cosmopolitan, and Comique were all closed by 1915 after a chill in the economy came with World War I and new fire codes stipulated theater-quality escape routes.

Selling ambitious plans for picture show chains had happened ear-lier or was more common elsewhere. An exceptionally early example is an invitation to invest in Jones, Linick, and Schaefer's Orpheum Theater in

Chicago's Loop (*Chicago Tribune* October 11, 1908; ads on October 14, 1908; October 15, 1908). Detroit showmen stand out for unusual promotional zeal, getting newspaper coverage of building plans and in return running ads for shares in dozens of theaters from 1912 to 1914. In contrast, early owners in Toronto such as Applegath and Griffin probably relied on their own pockets. Remaining family-run was a safe and secure business practice, but Peter Griffin later explained that his family's company never went public as a matter of old-fashioned responsibility for taking business chances. "Dad never sold stock in any of his ventures. He could have done so with big results on many occasions, but he staunchly refused to do so. He took the chance and if failure was his reward, then he took the blow and no one else" (*Mail & Empire* August 14, 1931, 2). Again, Griffin acted consistently and deliberately in traditional terms, rather than taking advantage of modern techniques of expansion and corporate organization. Again, this was at odds with the direction of the film business over these years, rooted as it was in the industrial and transnational character of film as a commercial product. Following a traditional attitude on management and corporate structure was actually at odds with the ambitious plans to expand the company into a regional, perhaps continental, chain with branches far from its headquarters in Toronto. Such networks of distribution, especially in moments of rapid expansion, practically *required* modern corporate organization, a key aspect of which is going public with a shares offer.

Selling shares, however, was no guarantee of success. Just as Canada Moving Pictures failed, the small Motion Plays chain folded, too, although its theaters stayed open under new owners. In 1913 and 1914, Albert J. Bentley was president of the small chain of new theaters, his name listed in weekly advertising and on several municipal documents. The names of Bentley's theaters indicate an Anglican, not American, patriotic bias: the King George, the Royal George, the Prince George, and the Queen's Royal (*Telegram* May 15, 1913; also ads in *World* June 8, 1913). What regal variations were planned as names for two more theaters, one left unfinished and another never built? The Amalgamated Moving Picture Shows Ltd. placed several ads for $500,000 worth of shares in daily newspapers, more than ten times the amount offered just a year earlier by the Canada Moving Pictures. Ads for Amalgamated described plans to found a chain starting with an older theater on suburban Bloor Street and a new storefront theater on Yonge Street downtown, as well as other interests and plans (ad in *Globe* June 5, 1913; *Star Weekly* June 7, 1913). These two Amalgamated theaters in Toronto had closed by the middle of the war, just like the storefront holdings of Canada Moving Pictures. Yet another failed chain, the National Amusement Co. publicized ambitious plans during the war for a major national chain using a rebuilt Sunnyside Theatre in the West end as its flagship; but the theater was soon sold (*MPW* January 8, 1916, 283). Whether by coincidence or simply sharing the same ill fate, a company with the same name tried to get off the ground in both Ottawa and Vancouver around the same time (*MPW* July 17, 1915, 532; August 7, 1915, 1036).

The more successful cases come from local showmen who could raise enough capital to turn an existing successful small show into a single, but impressive, neighborhood movie palace. In 1913, Sam Lester, Harry

Figure 3.4. The Madison Picture Palace in the Annex neighborhood opened December 23, 1913. (Architect: J.A. MacKenzie.) At the time, it was one of the largest theaters in the entire city. Renovated many times, it remains open in 2007 as the Bloor Cinema. 506 Bloor Street West. *ca.* 1919. (Photograph by J. V. Salmon, City of Toronto Archives, Fonds 1231, Item 800.)

Alexander, and Maurice Mentel built the Doric on Bloor Street near the small show they had taken over in 1911. They soon also bought D. A. Lochiel's $40,000 Park Theatre nearby. William Joy's Beaver Theatre, which held more than 1,100 people, opened late in 1913 in suburban West Toronto. It was on the same block as his Wonderland picture show, built late in 1907. Another independent able to build big and maintain success was John Brady, the property owner for Minier's Comique downtown in 1908. He built the Madison Theatre at Bloor Street and Bathurst Street, a neighborhood palace with 1,000 seats. These independents found a niche with early suburban movie palaces. By the time the Park, Beaver, and Madison opened, Toronto was in the middle of a theater building boom that would continue until about 90 picture theaters were open just after World War I began in 1914. By then about half were purpose-built movie theaters, and several older storefront shows had just closed. George Perry, manager of the U-Kum Theatre on College Street, described this building boom as it was happening, "The days of the small house of 200 to 300 are numbered, and, while there are a number such going up, the builders had better spend the money in farm lands from which the returns would be much greater" (*MPW* August 16, 1913, 737).

Authorities in Toronto, at least from a regulatory perspective, supported an open, competitive market among theaters. At no point did the City Council act to limit the number of show licenses as a matter of policy, as had been done in such places as Hamilton and Brantford (*World* June 8, 1913). The bureaucratic process of licensing became a transparent extension of the notoriously by-the-book police commission. None of this is to claim that regulation was absent or slack; quite the opposite, legal and social regulation of Toronto's and Ontario's picture shows steadily extended its jurisdiction each year. In 1909, a provincial license was instituted, police mandated censorship of films and posters, and projectionists were formally licensed and examined. In 1910, Ontario Provincial Police began to centralize censorship for the province through the film exchanges, leading the Toronto police to begin plans for a police board of film censors. In 1911, the province preempted those plans, created an Ontario Board of Censors, and barred children younger than fifteen from attending unless accompanied by an adult. Also in 1911, the city prohibited vaudeville and stage performances in picture shows unless the building had an additional $100 theater license and could pass the fire codes expected of theaters.

Through all of this ramped-up regulation, only minimal protest, lobbying, or even comment is recorded on the part of the showmen of Toronto. This changed in 1913, partly because the number of theaters was doubling from about forty-five to niney in just two years, but also because the provincial regulations for that year introduced a new system of theater licenses, graded according to the population of the municipality of the theater (*Mail & Empire* May 17, 1913). This was immediately recognized as particularly problematic for the older, small shows in Toronto because it treated small and large theaters, corporate and independent showmen, as equals simply because they shared the same market. Showmen in Toronto organized a Moving Picture Association of Ontario, at first led by Noel Mandell of the Criterion, one of the oldest and smallest shows in the West end.

In the largest U.S. cities, collective "protective" associations among picture show managers and owners formed in response to the first unilateral edicts closing shows. When government regulations treated competing showmen as a class of equivalent people, protective associations turned that collective swipe into a collective voice. *Moving Picture World* notes the formation of exhibitors' collectives in 1908 in cities such as St. Louis and Philadelphia (March 7, 1908, 183; December 19, 1908, 504). The new trade magazine *Nickelodeon* reported how "unfair" government actions in 1909 were being fought collectively in places such as Cincinnati and Detroit (January 1909, 18; August 1909, 57). Collective organization in New York went back to early in 1907 when the Board of Electricity ordered dozens of picture theaters shut (*MPW* March 16, 1907, 20). When New York's Mayor McClelland revoked more than 500 common show licenses in December 1908, the motion picture league in the city was able to quickly and successfully obtain a court injunction and have their theaters open again within a few weeks (*MPW* January 9, 1909, 32; May 22, 1909, 670). Shortly afterward in Montreal, in response to high municipal licenses, moves to close picture shows on Sunday, and growing competition, a league was organized among the city's film showmen (*MPW* February 20, 1909, 200). By 1911, the Motion Picture Exhibitors' League of America (MPELA) was organized in Ohio as a national association (*MPW* July 22, 1911, 111). City, region, and state subassociations formed in an ever-greater number of places with each annual convention. There was a section of the *Moving Picture World* devoted to MPELA's constant discussion of local censorship, Sunday blue laws, prohibitions against children's attendance, as well as overly stringent policing and licensing (*MPW* June 8, 1912, 916; weekly thereafter).

The film business responded to pressures for social reform by internally adopting a collective approach and isolating unhindered competition as a problem (*MPW* June 29, 1907, 259; June 20, 1908, 525). "Cooperation versus competition" was the argument. Elevating the character of the show went hand-in-hand with elevating the business and its financial security (*Nickelodeon* March 1909, 63). Especially in *Moving Picture*

World, a more collective and professional showmanship was proposed to offset calls for censorship. Political and legal lobbying against official regulations could be successful only if owners demonstrated that self-regulation within the film industry was not just possible but already evident. Of course, a simultaneous development was the standardization of the films themselves (now with recognizable "picture personalities" such as Florence Turner, the Vitagraph Girl), diminishing the importance of the local context provided by the exhibitor (DeCordova 1990). This movement toward collective showmanship was delayed in Toronto where municipal regulation, while strict, was careful to act with fairness and transparency. Licensing could not be accused of being taxation in disguise. The Lord's Day Act prevented any other commercial competition on Sunday anyway, so lobbying on that issue was not needed. Censorship problems were lessened rather than exacerbated because police could deal directly with a small number of film exchanges that imported films produced elsewhere. By 1913, however, competition was saturating all parts of the city with movie shows. Unionized machine operators had for a few years been meeting collectively. Now, partly political and partly social—like their employees' union meetings—the showmen of Toronto would act collectively.

The 1913 Moving Picture Association of Ontario was short-lived. Another 1915 group was organized, the Motion Picture Protective Association of Toronto (later of Ontario). Perhaps because this time exchange men and distributors were included, this second group endured. Its impetus was the 1914 city regulations for fire safety (*MPW* December 12, 1914, 1503). Many of the oldest, smallest theatoriums were forced to close. Leon Brick at the Garden, for example, had to remove more than thirty seats for new safety codes only a year after renovating for previous regulations. Protests are not mentioned in the daily newspapers, perhaps due to World War I coverage, but in the *Moving Picture World* the fallout from these regulations was big news from Toronto (*MPW* February 6, 1915, 862). Soon after, the Protective Association was formed, electing Brick as its first president (*MPW* February 20, 1915, 1170; March 13, 1915, 1639). Within months successful lobbying reduced provincial license fees (*MPW* June 19, 1915, 1966). Their most effective moment of collective lobbying came in 1916 during World War I, reducing the proposed rate of an amusement tax on every ticket (*Telegram* and *Globe* May 6, 1916; *Globe* May 16, 1916). Social events were just as important, some with great public promotion. There was also a supposedly patriotic offer to train returning soldiers to be projection operators. Of course, it was an association of managers, not employees, and the training school was probably as much an effort to break the union as help out disabled veterans

(*News* April 29, 1916). The most high-profile effort of the Protective Association was a "movie ball" in 1916, shortly after the wartime amusement tax began. The affair brought movie stars Francis X. Bushman and Beverly Bayne to town as special guests (*World* March 26, 1916; April 6, 1916). By 1917, more than 100 members inaugurated the expansion of the group to all of Ontario (*World* January 25, 1917).

Other aspects of the film industry were contributing to the collective organization, even in these years before formal vertical integration. First to organize transnationally were unionized projection operators. Late in 1909 in Vancouver and Toronto, perhaps elsewhere, locals were formed as part of international unions. One essay describes the labor of machine operators in their fireproof boxes hand-cranking the reels of flammable celluloid as the deus ex machina of the storefront cinema (Barnard 2002). The Toronto picture machine operators held annual banquets years before the managers' exhibitors' league held regular dances. A photo of the Toronto operator union's first annual banquet, printed in the *Moving Picture World*, plays up their classy attire and composure, so different from the normally oppressive sweat from the heat of the projection booth. "Truly it is a credit to the operators as a whole. The men here assembled will compare favorably in looks with those seen at any similar affair given by the manufacturers, exhibitors, or film men. The faces of those alert, clean-cut, intelligent men who could grace any walk in life" (*MPW* February 11, 1911, 301). The Toronto union of picture machine operators was organized in November 1909 and first listed notice of a monthly meeting in the *Star* labor column mid-May 1910. A small notice of their executive in 1914 listed Clarence McMahn as president of Local 173 (*MPW* February 14, 1914, 804). Associated with the introduction of Ontario censorship in 1911, the operators' union in Toronto voluntarily proposed a new safety policy for government regulation of their trade (*Globe* May 8, 1911). The union began an advertising campaign in the *World* in 1915 about the importance of trained employees, "Safety First: This Theatre Employs a Union Operator." Toronto seems never to have been the site of a strike, but at least once the union came close (*MPW* March 11, 1916, 1677).

Although unionized employees were the first aspect of the film industry to organize, another important element in forming a collective out of the Canadian film industry was a national film trade journal. The *Canadian Moving Picture Digest* started out small in Montreal in 1915 and grew to incorporate film exchange newsletters before moving its headquarters to Toronto in 1918. Again, all of these efforts and practices standardizing the film industry in Canada, most through head offices in Toronto, were established before vertical integration with U.S. studios.

Central organization was largely a local effort to demonstrate that the competitive field of showmanship was a responsible part of the community.

Famous Players: Transnational Vertical Integration

Demonstrating that movie showmanship could be a responsible part of the urban fabric was most overt during World War I, an aspect of moviegoing reviewed in detail in this book's conclusion. The war effort provided a display of moviegoing as "practical patriotism" and demonstrated that Toronto showmen could play an important part in the war effort. This does not disguise how the local organization of the film business depended on increasingly formal links with U.S. film producers and distributors. Nathan L. Nathanson had a near unique role in the Canadian film industry entrenching the predominance of national theater chains vertically integrated with Hollywood studios (Moore 2003). Nathanson began a direct involvement with the cinema business in 1916, when his former boss E. L. Ruddy partnered with millionaire broker J. P. Bickell to open a downtown movie palace, the Regent, on the site of Griffin's Majestic. It was first managed by Leon Brick from the Garden Theatre (*World* August 26, 1916). The company before long acquired the downtown Strand, the Garden, and a few other Toronto neighborhood houses, as well as newly built theaters in Toronto and several smaller cities in Ontario. As it grew into a group of theaters, it was renamed Paramount Theatres; but it was not yet connected to Paramount in the United States (White 1931, 16–20).

The Canadian franchise for Paramount–Artcraft pictures was held since 1914 by Nathanson's next door neighbor Jay J. Allen through the Allen family's Famous Players Film Service, begun when the Allens severed their connection to Universal Pictures. The arrangement allowed their theater chain to expand rapidly from roots in Calgary to a Toronto headquarters and flagship theater by 1917 (*MPW* February 19, 1916, 1159). Following World War I, the Allens refused part ownership to Paramount's Adolph Zukor and the Famous–Lasky parent company in New York. Meanwhile, Nathanson's Canadian Paramount was positioning itself in direct competition against Allen Theatres through major expansion plans (*Canadian Moving Picture Digest [CMPD]* May 10, 1919; May 31, 1919). By July 1919, the Allens' franchise was officially reneged and Famous–Lasky established their own Canadian distributors. Nathanson continued to build theaters (*CMPD* September 15, 1919; October 18, 1919). Finally, in February 1920 Canadian Paramount became officially linked to Zukor's Paramount and Famous–Lasky. Nathanson became the first president of Famous Players Canadian Corporation exhibitors.

Investment came from Canadian big business (*CMPD* February 20, 1920). By May 1923, the Allens were bankrupt and Nathanson bought dozens of their best theater assets for about the cost of just one movie palace.

A concrete measure of the movies becoming a mass medium and a big business are the wages of top corporate managers. By 1921, the Allens were taking wages of $30,000 each, about ten times greater than the salary paid to their theater managers, and a combined amount that makes even Nathanson's 1924 wages of $23,622 seem modest. These incomes were vast sums. John Griffin had recorded in 1908 a wage of just $1,000 as president of his own company. Perhaps relying on money in the bank, he never again earned even that much and usually reported the same or just more than he paid his key managers. With their vaudeville circuit in decline, by 1918 John and Peter Griffin reported wages of next to nothing, only $60 each. Criminal charges are another measure of the difference between the early showman and later executives. Whereas John Griffin's name appears in Toronto's Register of Criminals three times for Breaches of the Theatres Law, imagining Nathanson or the Allens showing up in front of the police magistrate is difficult (*ROC* January 30, 1912, line 2061; August 29, 1912, line 2848; September 13, 1912, line 1607).

In February 1914, just as filmgoing was becoming a big business and an everyday practice in cities, the comic strip *Dream of the Rarebit Fiend* depicted being an entrepreneur and purchasing a moving picture show as a nightmare. At first the dreamer sees long lines and thinks "I'll make a fortune with it." Soon the business drops off, and the people disappear, first from the line up and then from the city altogether. The buildings and stores surrounding the picture show fall away, too, leaving nothing but the picture show in a fallow field before the dreamer wakes up thankful not to have been an entrepreneurial showman after all (*Star Weekly* February 28, 1914). Perhaps this same frightful vision led John Griffin toward costly vaudeville and away from the films that made him famous. This fear was unfounded. An ad boosting Toronto real estate noted compiled figures for building permits between 1907 and 1913, when the city nearly doubled in population to 500,000. Aside from housing, the ad gave categories for factories, warehouses, offices, schools, and "theatres and moving picture shows." More than $1 million had been spent building sixty theaters and picture shows (and at least forty more were yet to be built.) The same figure was spent on warehouses, and it was more than half the amount for factories or offices (*Star Weekly* March 21, 1914). Moving picture companies soon held generous amounts of real estate in all major cities and most towns in the country, incredibly valuable because much of it was downtown. The city was, in a sense, being shaped and changed by moving picture theaters, not the other way around.

The final steps building a national movie theater chain were selling shares and "going public." As recounted earlier, Canada Moving Pictures offered $40,000 worth of shares in 1912, increased tenfold in the next years as Amalgamated Moving Picture Shows offered $300,000 in 1913, and the United Motion Picture Theatres offered $400,000 in 1914. Those figures increased tenfold again when Famous Players Canadian Corporation advertised the sale of $4,000,000 in shares in 1920 (ad in *Globe* April 28, 1920). In an effort to counter this sale, in August and September 1920 Allen Theatre Enterprises ran a series of ads in newspapers in Toronto and across the country, culminating in a prospectus for $2,500,000 worth of shares. The illustrated ad campaign leading up to the offer explained how the company carefully selected only the most refined and entertaining films and how motion pictures were an industry bringing the nation into maturity through progress, with a picture palace box office flanked by scenes from power generation, agriculture, mining, pulp and paper, and grain elevators. Two ads gave the details of film selection and censorship, and a managers' meeting was shown testifying to proper corporate responsibility. One ad illustrated how far the movie theater industry had come, as a prospective investor peers through a looking glass at an old-fashioned "nickelodeon" (perhaps the first time that particular word was ever used in Toronto) and sees into the future of massive ornamental movie palaces. It was quite starkly the difference between the theaters Griffin opened in 1906, and those Famous Players and the Allen chain built in 1920. Film showmanship was now a rationalized, centralized matter of management. The novelty was now a mass medium, thoroughly integrated into the everyday life of the city and the nation.

4

Senseless Censors and Startling Deeds

From Police Beat to Bureaucracy

> It is most unfortunate that the moving picture entertainments could not rely upon their own best attractions for their audiences. . . . But whether it be the fault of audiences or managers, the tone of the moving picture business has been steadily falling, until one is by no means safe in going to see one of the so-called entertainments.
>
> —Editorial, *World* August 24, 1910

⚘

U NTIL THE LAST WEEK OF AUGUST 1910, police in Toronto had merely confiscated and destroyed objectionable films without criminal charges. But then they "started a crusade against the proprietors of moving picture shows where scenes of startling deeds, bloody and otherwise, are put on" (*Telegram* August 26, 1910). For the first time, film showmen were brought to court and sentenced for showing indecent moving pictures. In two cases, a showman was fined $50 or thirty days in jail for "exhibiting pictures illegally" (*Globe* August 27, 1910, 13; *World* September 1, 1910, 11; *ROC* August 26, 1910, line 1878; and September

1, 1910, line 11). The shift from confiscating films to laying criminal charges happened at a point when the content of film was supposedly regulated by the Ontario Provincial Police. Yet, Toronto policemen continued to stake out their right to pass judgment over the morality of public acts. The parallel government tactics of censorship were now in conflict, levying $50 municipal fines against independent showmen following provincial policy. The problem prompted Staff Inspector Kennedy of the city police's morality squad to propose some form of centralized censorship before films were sent out to theaters (*News* August 27, 1910, 7). Under the pseudonym Thespis, the drama editor of the *News* sided with the police, although his column, "The Left Box," had earlier ridiculed police censorship decisions when films based on Shakespearean plays were banned (*News* September 3, 1910; February 26, 1910).

The criminal charges and censorship problems took place amidst a spate of controversies over moving pictures in the city and society. In 1910, harsh rebukes were still common following any acknowledgment of social benefit in moving pictures. Even as the Methodist General Conference finally lifted their ban on amusements (*Star* August 26, 1910), they also urged a ban on moving pictures of prizefights for the entire country (*Telegram* August 31, 1910). The *Star* printed an editorial citing Chicago's Jane Addams supporting the integration of "the stage and life" (*Star* August 31, 1910); just a week later came another editorial connecting boys' delinquency to Wild West movies (*Star* September 7, 1910). That news was reported the same day an article about educational moving pictures in Detroit schools ran, but that measure was designed specifically to limit the immoral and harmful effects of commercial picture shows on children (*Telegram* August 27, 1910). The harmful effects of moving pictures took an even more literal form that week in Toronto, as the logic of child-labor laws was turned against theatoriums employing juvenile performers on stage (*Globe* August 26, 1910). Editorials endorsed the idea under the headlines, "Exploiting Childhood" and "Debasing Moving Picture Shows" (*World* August 24, 1910; *Star* August 27, 1910).

Filmgoing in late August 1910 was evidently in a period of upheaval as new theatoriums continued to open all over the city. The 1908 fire safety law had not made filmgoing innocuous but merely laid a foundation to extend regulations further. Assumptions about the influence of moving pictures on children became a limit case for deciding how best to regulate not just the material safety of the auditorium, but also the commercial character of the practice of moviegoing and the moral character of the depicted scenes. Not all measures were prohibitive or imposed limitations on showmen. Churches, schools, and settlement houses recognized the appeal and educational value of moving pictures and moved to establish their own alternative noncommercial sites of filmgoing.

As film showmanship became more civic minded, it both presented itself as a locally rooted practice and represented transnationally distributed products. Various forms of film regulation, detailed in this chapter, proceeded to grapple with a different but equally delicate balance. Overall, disputes and mediations faced a choice between *dispersing* regulation to the daily practice of police, showmen, families, and church groups, or *centralizing* decisions more efficiently into a standardized bureaucracy. Just as showmanship had balanced modern management with situated craftsmanship, so too did the governance of film rest on having to both respond to the social context of moviegoing and yet, in practice, act consistently with expressed standards.

The push for localized measures always ran counterpoint to the pull of bureaucratic centralization. Between the growing place of film in everyday life and corresponding attempts to resist its influence, a compromise established government bureaucracies as well-organized systems of regulation. This chapter details the installation of a bureaucratic censor board but starts with an exceptional case that highlights the norms. Relatively late, in 1912 and 1913, a proposed municipal film show in suburban Weston provides a rare case of a community debating whether to have any movies at all. That nonprofit theatorium was planned at a moment when westerns and crime pictures were linked to a high-profile manslaughter and thus to juvenile delinquency in general. This case delineates the social debate over regulation, noting the special importance of the limit case of children's moral corruption and commercial exploitation. From there, legal regulation escalates from case-by-case licensing through to all-encompassing bureaucracies.

Theatoriums in Toronto were initially subject to two forms of regulation. The first was the process of getting a license to operate, and the second was policing for decency. Indecency was regulated by municipal police according to the Canadian Criminal Code, but a city bylaw stipulated the chain of command and procedure for patrolling. Specified spaces and conduct requiring attention were defined broadly enough to include any commercial amusement. By the time theatoriums arrived, prohibitions against lewd public conduct had long been extended to patrolling for the exhibition, sale, or even offering for sale of "any indecent or lewd book, paper, picture, plate, drawing, or other thing," including any "indecent, immoral or lewd play or other representation." Aside from prohibitions against selling indecent items, bylaws also allowed police to enter "any place of public amusement or entertainment" and request a stop to indecent acts and depictions (Toronto Bylaw 2449). When moving pictures attracted attention in 1907, these existing measures put the suspicions on hold. The municipal police force claimed to have the matter well under control, an explanation that was accepted until competitive showmanship began to flourish and picture shows began to open on neighborhood shopping streets. For all of Ontario, in 1909 policing the *moral* character of film shows was explicitly allowed by the Ontario parliament as an amendment to the 1908 law that first required fire safety inspections (Ontario 1909; *Globe* March 16, 1909). By 1911 film censorship became centralized in a Theatres Branch of the Ontario Treasury and was entirely severed from municipal police duties (Ontario 1911).

Even after the Ontario Board of Censors was created in 1911, the prospect of a picture show opening where none had been before prompted debate about the character of filmgoing and its relation to community. Not just regulating but reforming the commercial aspect of showmanship prompted alternatives from volunteer associations such as the suburban Weston Town Improvement Society. Such proposals actually opposed government's role in the equation, at least implicitly claiming formal regulations only worked to support the profit-seeking character of showmanship. In practice, however, the conflict rarely spurred reformers to oppose government measures because monitoring for safety and indecency was acceptable even if commercial amusement in general was not. Thus, the capitalist basis of moviegoing was, in a sense, protected by regulation well before the film industry consolidated into a big business.

The predominance of commercial amusement marginalized the alternative educational, scientific, and artistic purposes of film. In the United States, the Supreme Court ultimately sanctioned this when it denied film the protection of free speech afforded to journalists and public speakers and instead classified even newsreels as commercial goods legally restricted to providing "harmless entertainment" (Grieveson 2004). The same distinction was even more sacrosanct in Canada, where provincial censorship policies were instituted early with little room to object in court (Dean 1981, 135–38). In rendering entertainment harmless, regulation had the unintended consequence, at least implicitly, of defining nonprofit, nonfiction film as harmful. Educational motives were held up to special scrutiny in the case of films about "social evils" and "social diseases," which used nonfiction forms to document the problems of prostitution, unwanted pregnancy, and venereal disease (Dean 1981, 19–25; Grieveson 2004, 151–54 and 172–86). The early nonprofit picture shows planned and practiced in Toronto did not employ such subjects of public health and moral instruction. Their plans for healthy, moral amusement differed only on commercial terms from mainstream picture shows. The source of elevation and uplift for the picture show was simply the context of the community providing it directly.

Film-Going as Town Improvement
in the Suburb of Weston

In cities, of course, nickelodeons and theatoriums opened before efforts to reform filmgoing. After all, something had to exist already if rules were going to regulate it. The order was reversed in most smaller municipalities. Suburbs, especially, saw a chance to differentiate themselves from cities by considering what form local moviegoing should have before it even arrived. Outside Chicago, for example, suburban councils routinely denied licenses to prospective showmen until the movies were undeniably mainstream. Proposals to allow Sunday movies were continually defeated until the late 1920s. Larger suburbs of Chicago even had their own censor boards rather than blindly accept decisions from the Loop (*Oak Park Oak Leaves* March 7, 1914; *Evanston News-Index* October 28, 1915). Even after an Oak Park censorship attempt failed, the local newspaper continued to advocate that a distinctly suburban cinema could be a point of pride (*Oak Leaves* July 10, 1915).

Another example of this type of debate happened in 1911 and 1912 in Weston about ten miles northwest of Toronto. The official city limits were still expanding to incorporate adjacent suburbs. Culturally, the city limits reached even further. Weston was becoming more of a suburb, less of a village. Its people were keen to rearticulate its relation to the city by considering what differences village life in the outskirts could offer. For example, the best of modern reforms were incorporated locally by the women of Weston's Town Improvement Society (TIS), whose activities are well-documented in the local weekly *Times & Guide* and in the village council minutes from their frequent formal proposals. The group debated the merits of women's suffrage and organized improvements in health care, parenting, public safety, and simple aesthetic matters such as planting flowers around the Town Hall. Late in 1912, in response to a showman's request for a permit, TIS proposed to the Weston Council to deny the license and instead establish a moving picture show three nights weekly in the Town Hall.

They believed running a municipally-owned show, like all its activities, would be a form of town improvement. Under local supervision, the amusement would demonstrate a willingness of the village to modernize its cultural and social life. Local control over motion pictures could be a distinctive quality of the suburban neighborhood, which had learned from downtown's excesses and mistakes. A letter to the *Weston Times & Guide* asked, "Surely we will not deny ourselves the use and enjoyment of the most wonderful development of electrical science simply because many of the Queen Street shows have a bad name" (November 22, 1912, 4). The TIS would show the same movies and charge the same admission as the showman who was turned away. The difference was that the suburban women would take stewardship for the quality of the show and its audience. The issue was hotly debated in the letters to the editor of the *Weston Times & Guide*. One response to TIS thought the picture show scheme was a threat to the welfare of the town's children and the poor; the writer questioned the commercial aspect of movies as leisure. "I sincerely hope the better thinking class of the town will rise up in righteous indignation and say we will not allow this evil in our midst, no matter by whom introduced. Just think of it, sapping the pockets of the poor to help the poor" (November 22, 1912, 4). The entire column of letters to the editor took up the issue in the next week's paper. One naysayer noted simply that the council and TIS should stick to more pressing concerns of "the interests of the ratepayers of this town by doing something toward securing better fire protection" (November 29, 1912, 8). Another letter, signed Progress, supported the cinema because it would be controlled by the town's responsible adults and was meant for them. "What is there in Weston for diversion, when a business man or workmen and their wives have done their strenuous days work, why nothing. . . . What could be more beneficial and pleasing for a man than to take his wife or his young lady to a clean, educational, healthy Picture Show?" (November 29, 1912, 8).

The debate starkly contrasted two views about how regulation worked within the wider culture of the day. On the one hand, TIS and its supporters saw an opportunity to provide a modern, secular public space. This stood against a conservative caution that recognized little opportunity for a moral and social form of showgoing, that moving picture shows in the suburbs would all too similar to those already existing in the city. The newspaper itself sided with the TIS liberal agenda, reprinting an article from the *Ladies Home Journal*, perhaps clipped out and sent in by a TIS member, about how "Moving Pictures Make Travel Possible" (*Weston Times & Guide* December 27, 1912). The article espoused a belief in the importance of affordable and uplifting amusement. A suburban village such as Weston had the chance to introduce moving pictures in a supposedly proper context. For a show run by a community group, regulation would be informal but management, hands-on; this stood in contrast to the more typical laissez-faire approach to showmanship that ironically relied on regulation to limit harmful social effects.

By the time the newspaper printed this article, however, the village council had already rejected the proposal (Weston 1912). While that moment was a relatively slow year for building new picture theaters in Toronto, the next year was the busiest ever. A full year later, early in November 1913, TIS became convinced a movie entrepreneur would soon come to town and again applied to council for a picture show in the

Town Hall. Reported in the *Weston Times & Guide* and in the council minutes, TIS was prescient or knew something, because by the end of November a showman had actually requested a commercial license in town. The debate resumed. Once again, writers sent in letters to the editor of the local newspaper, the first printed November 21, was signed Pro Bono Publico. During this second year considering the proposed town picture show, the council agreed to write a bylaw for TIS to operate a theater. But at the next meeting to approve it, the TIS picture show measure followed the request from entrepreneurial showmen for a commercial show license. The council minutes record the license was not granted (Weston 1913). Once the showmen had been turned away, TIS voluntarily withdrew their request for their own plans. Apparently, the need for their social work in amusements evaporated along with the threat of a showman coming up from downtown. Maybe it was one of these prospective showmen who wrote to the newspaper the following week, signed Burnt. The writer sarcastically suggested that perhaps now that the women of Weston had given up on the movies, they could turn their attention to fire protection because "If the TIS wants to still have the old town to 'improve' they had better hurry before a big fire comes along and wipes this burg off the face of the map" (December 12, 1913, 4).

While any business could be subjected to this type of action on the part of a town improvement society, the issues were more explicit for moviegoing in community, especially for the gendered labor of social work like that of TIS. Would TIS ever think to open its own town grocery, shoe store, or five-and-dime? Not likely, although a secondhand shop or thrift store might serve poor families. That they would have thought to open a tavern, billiard hall, or poker den is unlikely, although these activities were often provided by branches of religious and social clubs. The Town Improvement Society held a vision of amusement in particular as a modern need that could be integrated properly into a reformed suburban life. They held other social gatherings besides their own meetings, organizing lectures, classes, and small shows in the Town Hall. Moving pictures were seen as an outgrowth of these community events. Because picture shows relied on forming an audience, the market was explicitly communal. Although preferable to the rowdy crowd at a tavern, racetrack, or billiard hall, moving picture shows were nonetheless seen as a problematic place.

Moviegoing could be seen as exploitative and corrupt because they were commercial and a threat to the lessons of churches and schoolrooms. On the other hand, the idea of a community-run picture show recognized the chance for a modern space of gathering and socialization, entirely different in quality from other amusements and especially other

mass-produced goods. As the reprinted *Ladies Home Journal* article demonstrates, the idea was not peculiar to Weston. The TIS dealt with public
issues that required communal stewardship that were more obviously
connected to civic interests. They thought of filmgoing, leisure, and
amusement as part of that domain of responsibility, as related to health,
in need of rules for safety, and connected to political involvement; in
short filmgoing was something done by the community, not by individuals. As one TIS member wrote back in 1912, "Shall we not have the
pleasure, too, and put it within reach of the working man and his wife,
and let us enjoy it together?" (*Weston Times & Guide* November 29, 1912,
8). Their form of moral reform included pleasure, and their tactics for
town improvement included collective enjoyment. By the time of the
Weston TIS proposal in 1912, a more bureaucratic and centralized form
of provincial film censorship had begun and outright indecency was not
likely a concern. Such matters had largely been taken care of by higher
levels of governments than the village council. Instead, the problem for
the Weston council was an either-or situation: the municipal decision
whether to license a business. In this case, it amounted to whether Weston
would be a place with movies at all.

Since 1909 all moving picture machines as well as all persons operating them needed a provincial license to handle film as well as a local
amusement license. In 1916 municipalities could no longer refuse a license to a show already holding a provincial license (Ontario 1909, 1916).
In the intervening years, including the time of the Weston proposals for
a town show, local councils still had to deliberate the matter of a municipal license. The Weston TIS, however, did not see mere municipal licensing as an adequate assurance that an entrepreneurial showman would
provide the right type of moving pictures to the village. A licensed picture
show would still be profit-seeking and still cater to the lowest common
denominator rather than take on the additional mandates of acting on
behalf of parenting, churchgoing, and education. Licensing might ensure
limitations on the exploitative commercial character of a local moving
picture show just as censorship would, but it would actually institution-
alize the commercial character of the provision of amusement and leisure.
The TIS understood the question of whether to accept film into their
community as an opportunity for progress and modernization. The educational, informative, and pleasurable aspects of filmgoing were taken as
the elements of its modernity, as the means by which the village would
become a town. Welcoming film into their community would make Weston
modern by connecting it to the city and the world beyond. They assumed
managing the show themselves would allow those desirable aspects of film
to be severed from those aspects considered dangerous, namely the com-

mercial and entrepreneurial basis of showmanship. In a sense, TIS refused to accept the modern tools of censorship and licensing as the necessary means to modernize their town with moviegoing. In the end, this
refusal to recognize formal film regulation as applicable to their suburban
lives delayed a film show from being established in Weston until 1925. In
the meantime, the option of suburban commuting to commercial amusements was an alternative form of modernization.

The Weston TIS believed they needed ownership, not just oversight, of the everyday running of the show and its showmanship. Perhaps
they even felt empowered to such actions because of the existence of the
central bureaucracy of the Censor Board because they would not risk
renting immoral or indecent pictures, even by mistake or misunderstand-
ing. They had a suspicion of showmen rather than film itself. But everyone did not share such trust in moving pictures for town improvement.
There was a coincident recognition that movies corrupted young minds
and led them astray. For example, the advice from Pro Bono Publico
noted urgently an accidental shooting linked to western movies. "May I
be permitted to draw the attention of the readers of this paper and others
to another instance—there is hardly a week without one—of the evil
effects of the Moving Pictures" (*Weston Times & Guide* November 21,
1913, 4). The letter goes on to detail how the Toronto coroner had
condemned the influence of westerns at moving picture theaters at an
inquest into the shooting death of a boy in another suburb. High-profile
associations between moving pictures and children's delinquency under-
lined the argument over showmanship in Weston.

Mimic Battles: Children, Film, and Delinquency

The "fatal mimic battle" leading to the death of Thomas Crisp of Toronto
in November 1913 was sensational front-page news (*Star* and *World*
November 17, 1913). Although the young men involved in the suburban
shooting were referred to as "boys" and the pictures published in the
newspapers show fresh-faced innocence, they were actually aged 16 to 18.
Thomas Crisp, alias Price, was boarding downtown in Toronto where he
worked. Still, his photos in the newspapers played up his youth, such as
the ironic picture of him in a western cowboy hat on the front page of the
Star or the playful shot of him riding a bicycle on the front page of the
World. Although murder charges resulted against Crisp's mischievous friends,
Cecil Babcock and William Sherman, the papers did not imply that they
were malevolent or guilty. The guilt, then, lay with their influence: westerns. Their countryside hunting trip turned fatal when the boys started
a mock western gunplay battle with their loaded rifles. Exactly this form

of play was often taken as charming, such as earlier in the year when the *Star Weekly* (January 11, 1913) ran a photo of boys in mock gunplay. Somehow in Crisp's death the movies were objectified as the cause of stupidity and carelessness on the part of otherwise-innocent boys (*Globe* November 18, 1913).

Two years earlier, when the Ontario Board of Censors was created, children were prohibited from attending movies without an adult. The young men involved in the shooting death, however, were all old enough to purchase their own movie tickets. Regardless, the paper extended coverage of Crisp's death, looking at children's movie attendance through reports from a lecture by Chief Censor G. E. Armstrong (*Star* November 18, 1913). The chief censor might have been on the defensive because of the shooting incident because Armstrong pointed the finger at the inability of the city police force to enforce the spirit of the law. The difficulty was that children needed only have their tickets purchased by an adult, not by their own guardian or parent. He thus implicitly defended the decency of the films he had passed. Armstrong is quoted: "Flagrant violations go on daily. . . . The children themselves invented the evasion, and have grown really expert at getting away with it. . . . It is now a common sight to see children approach adults and plead with them to buy the tickets and see them inside, and it takes a man of strong will or natural antipathy to children to refuse the request" (*Star* November 19, 1913, 7). The article hints that the problem was really children's scheming, that the innocence of youth could be used to deceive sympathetic adults to help break the spirit of the law. Earlier debates in Toronto and elsewhere framed "nickel madness" among children as almost an illness (Currie 1907; *Star* April 27, 1907). The Ontario censor in 1913 skewed this somewhat to deflect criticism of the movies onto children themselves.

In the modern city, spare change afforded children a great deal of mobility and freedom. This distance from family supervision, and the source of nickels spent on movies, typically came from working, often to contribute to the family's income (Nasaw 1985). In an article meant to expose the scandal of child labor and the reckless independence that came with money-in-the-hand, the *Star Weekly* (March 30, 1912) calculated that Toronto's school children collectively earned $4,533 each week! The freedom of spare change and spare time, or rather how these were organized as personal resources for leisure outside the family, has been theorized part of modern rational authority and related to the expanded role of money as the basis of modern interaction (Simmel 1990, 285–303). While I believe the problem of modern financial independence remains intractable when discussing children's filmgoing, this contrasts with research on working and immigrant women's leisure in this period, which understandably casts women's labor and growing financial independence in positive terms (Balides 1993; Mayne 1982; Peiss 1986). This stance in support of modern independence is more difficult to sustain when it concerns children's nickels. For young women, a few pennies allowed a few moments respite from responsibility; but from the point of view of parents, the problem was precisely how just a few pennies could afford children independence.

Activities such as movies trespassed on the authority of the family, especially of mothers charged with character development, those same TIS women trying to counteract entrepreneurial showmanship. Such concerns were antithetical even to the chief censor of Ontario who was not concerned about children's financial and social freedom when they went to the movies; instead, he took it as a sign of adults' weakness when they could not say "no" to children. Unlike what was taking place among the reformist mothers of Weston, the commercial basis of filmgoing was not questioned at the highest level of moral oversight for the film industry in Ontario. Along with Armstrong, the first censor board included two picture showmen, Otto Elliott (who became full-time theater inspector) and Robert Wilson (who managed the Onoka Theatre on Danforth Avenue, used during the daytime by the censor board). In charge of regulating the film industry, the members of the Ontario Board of Censors had incorporated sympathy for the economic and industrial organization of the industry but still fully trusted that their guardian role in regulation was perfectly able to limit any harmful effects if administered properly (*Star Weekly* June 28, 1913). While a muckraking paper such as *Jack Canuck* (October 28, 1911) could be viciously skeptical of the "Senseless Censors," the Ontario board gained begrudging respect south of the border as "a sincere and conscientious friend of the picture and disposed to be liberal and friendly to manufacturers" (*MPW* October 7, 1911, 25).

The women of Weston may have thought that they, too, would not be able to deny their children once a show came to town. In its own way, reform was about controlling the means of providing amusement, not about questioning entertainment, let alone leisure, as a problematic matter altogether. Feature stories in the *Star Weekly* about other social service clubs and settlement houses in 1912 frequently mentioned using or owning moving picture machines and films (see, for example, *Star Weekly* March 16, 1912; *World* May 16, 1913). In particular, the Salvation Army was well known for its early adoption of moving pictures as a means of urban proselytizing, for example, playing *The Life of Christ in Motion Pictures* in Toronto in November and December 1907. Groups working with children recognized the appeal of the moving picture show and used it to encourage a healthy imagination among the poor city children, perhaps unable to read or afford

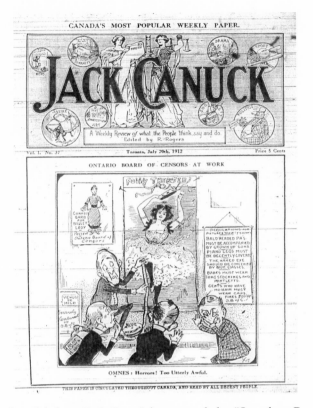

Figure 4.1. Scandal sheet *Jack Canuck* lampooned the "Senseless Censors." July 20, 1912.

books. An editorial in the *Star Weekly* (June 8, 1912), taking a cue from a sermon by the city's Rev. J. E. Reid, even advised clergy to go to the theaters and ball games themselves to see "what kind of attraction it holds for young people" (p. 20). Jane Addams of Hull House in Chicago embraced modern amusements, including scenes of violence and romance. According to J. A. Lindstrom (1999), it set Addams's sympathetic approach, for example, her take on moving pictures in *The Spirit of Youth and the City Streets* (1909), apart from the moralism of many censorship calls for stricter policing. Addams specifically notes that even the crudest melodramas and western pictures could be the source of a healthy escapism, especially for poor or immigrant children of the worst sections of U.S. cities such as Chicago where she had initiated her settlement house. The spring of 1907 saw the advent of a short-lived Hull House nickelodeon. It was a successful, if temporary, early version of what was planned for Weston several years later. But, commercial showmen were particularly irked when churches and social groups took their business away by turning to the same mainstream pictures that regular profit-seeking theaters relied on. The opinion of a proprietor of several five- and ten-cent theaters claimed with confidence that the institution of the new Ontario Board of Censors would have "all the correcting effect necessary" to stop the competition of churches. "The Churches have no call to become rivals of the picture show managers. Legislation has been placed in force which plentifully guarantees the morality of the shows from now onward" (*News* April 22, 1911, 23). Such checks and balances were negotiated through the police force and by extension the act of legislation.

School Board Inspector J. L. Hughes was more stridently taking charge of the welfare of children in relation to moving pictures. He kept his opinions within official duties, corresponding directly with Chief Constable Grasett instead of taking his concerns to the newspapers or the public. In 1908 Hughes failed to push Chief Grasett to find a way to prohibit ice cream and popcorn vendors from selling their treats too close to schools. In later years when he suggested limitations on showmanship and the zoning of picture shows away from schools, the chief offered some accommodation. In March 1911, some theater managers were soliciting school children directly, either with flyers, by selling tickets away from the box office, or both. Hughes and Grasett refer to them as "tickets of invitation" but also mention the "sale of tickets on streets" (*LCC* March 11, 1911, 746). The prospect of flyers becoming litter allowed Chief Grasett a bylaw to clamp down on this form of showmanship (*LCC* March 15, 1911, 761). The next correspondence with Hughes early in 1912 concerns a permit for a theater backing onto a school yard, enough of a concern for the secretary-treasurer of the Board of Education also to write complaining. Hughes's suggestion was more specific: no picture shows should be permitted within 1,000 feet of schools. Both replies from Chief Grasett simply note that the matter will be considered at the next meeting of the Commissioners (*LCC* January 23, 1912, 885). In this case, the Board of Police Commissioners permitted the license, although they often later considered protests from the community surrounding a theater. Another example of the school inspector corresponding with the chief constable came in January 1913 when allegations that theaters on Queen Street West were admitting unaccompanied children led to a summons and charges against the theaters' owners (*LCC* January 29, 1913, 748; *ROC* February 6, 1913, lines 516, 528).

While educators, churchmen, and parents were working to prevent immoral influences from the movies, picture shows continued to be named part of delinquency: by children themselves. In several reported cases a young criminal tried to pin the blame on moving pictures. The letterbooks of the chief constable compile constant allegations against nuisance boys, and the role of moving pictures in the bad public conduct of children was only a peripheral concern. In fact, the newspaper just as commonly reported how the public character of filmgoing was *helping* to fight crime with two incredible local cases of wanted men on the run caught, one in the audience and another on screen (*Star* April 6, 1911; *Mail & Empire* November 22, 1913). Moving pictures were fingered as leading children astray. However, at least in newspaper articles, seeing the problem as imitating dangerous or immoral actions, not exactly corrupting innocent minds, was more common. In a sense, some doubted the apparent influence of movies as they became socially prevalent, and the assumption that children were impressionable was tenuous. As early as 1908, in the middle of the negotiations leading to the first regulations specific to films, the *Mail & Empire* (March 23, 1908) picked up a story from Montreal for its front page, "Imitated Moving Picture and Nearly Hanged Himself." Already here in this early record of a child imitating a feat seen in a moving picture, a nuanced reading could note the tension between the assumed influence on young minds and acknowledging that children were complicit by blaming the pictures after they got in trouble. In other words, the movies were already an excuse adventurous young boys offered when their plans went wrong and they were caught. Although newspaper accounts, parents, and authorities might have been willing to blame the influence of moving pictures, one must also acknowledge that children, too, were learning a novel excuse when required to explain offensive behavior.

Even newspaper editors were not equivocally disdainful of pictures, such as when the *Star* (September 7, 1910) seemed to mock a *Montreal Herald* (August 27, 1910) exposé of the "state of anarchy" of the picture show business there. Still, compiling a list of the disastrous consequences for some young viewers was all too easy. The effects included suicide, gunplay, and theft in a 1911 magazine story from the United States (R. Barry 1911). But the context of the supposed influence of moving pictures is the social and legal requirement of eliciting a confession and an explanation. The willingness of such journalists and magazine editors to list the dire consequences of children's filmgoing also highlights how young viewers could recognize that the movies were a good explanation when they found themselves required to supply an excuse.

At the time of the incident in Montreal in 1908 Toronto still had only eight picture shows. When fingerpointing at the movies came up again in 1911, most parts of the city now had several dozen picture shows. The papers picked up an item from the police court. Charlie Bradley was charged with burglary and arson after trying to break into the safe at the lithograph shop where he worked. He said he got the idea from a nickel show. Such delusions of sophisticated robbery led the *World* (March 20, 1911) to note almost sarcastically, "it wasn't any wonder Charlie Bradley failed. No one can deny that he is the 'champion' burglar of the 90-pound class. . . . His performance is the top notch of kid crookery" (p. 8). Adding a touch of editorial judgment of the situation, with echoes of "nickel madness" from 1907, the *World* added that Charlie said "that he got his burglarious ideas at the nickel shows, and carried them out in order that he might secure the funds to go to more nickel shows, presumably to get more ideas." The *Telegram* (March 20, 1911) kept more to the facts, explaining how Bradley had "told a wrong story at first, but afterwards admitted that he had done it. He said that he had been to some nickel shows, and thought it would be easy to burgle a place" (p. 7). The social context of the picture shows, the need to have nickels to go to the pictures, was noted alongside depictions of crime in the films. Exactly this sort of criminal juvenile stunt could be worked up into evidence of the social danger of the picture shows. But the papers' coverage is more complex than that. The threat of picture shows was by now not simply that they taught children deviant behavior or instructed them how to be criminals. Both newspaper reports in this case imply that the problem of picture shows was that they tricked children like Charlie into thinking it was easy to be a successful criminal.

Baneful to Our Canadian Life: Nationalizing Toronto's Exemplary Situation

Just as the first law for handling combustible celluloid was introduced in 1908, moral reform committees of the Canadian Methodist and Presbyterian churches, headquartered in Toronto, were turning their national lobby for good governance toward commercial theaters. Beginning with instructions for churchgoers to beware of idle leisure, clergy made calls for more stringent censorship of plays and against publicly displayed posters depicting immoral scenes (*News* March 23, 1908; September 22, 1908). The Methodist Board of Temperance, Prohibition, and Moral Reform soon suggested a specific regulation: eliminating theatrical acts that depicted risky behavior "dangerous to life and limb" (*News* September 12, 1908). Staff Inspector Stephen of the Toronto morality squad accepted the suggestion and began more stringent judgment against theater posters lining sidewalks (*News* October 9, 1908).

Headquartered in urban, English-speaking Toronto, models from the Progressive movement in the United States influenced Protestant religious moral reform in Canada. Some still sought a distinctly national solution. Since 1894 the Methodist General Council had heard annual reports from the Committee on Sociological Questions; and in 1902 a separate Department of Temperance, Prohibition, and Moral Reform was created primarily to study, lobby, and work toward temperance and absti- nence in alcohol consumption. The Baptist Church in Canada formed a similar body in 1906 and the Presbyterian Church in 1907. Despite alcohol reform as the central plank, the approach was broad and holistic. Other social problems in Canadian cities were studied, including how they were policed, and translated into suggested laws to administer efficient, fair, and transparent moral codes for all parts of the country. Reformers analyzed the forms of policing in Canada and elsewhere, selecting an optimal system and lobbying for it. This often meant suggesting the entire country follow the example of how things were already done in Toronto. Still, the simplified solutions of prohibition and censorship were elements of a more general- ized reform movement. In their national networks, church groups studied issues sociologically and economically and also based decisions on eco- nomic and social understandings of the causes and contexts of immorality.

The inaugural meeting of the Presbyterian moral and social reform body in 1907 discussed all of the obvious moral problems—graft and the need for electoral reform, alcohol, gambling, prostitution, Sabbath laws and habits, and legal protection of juveniles. Brief mention is also made of other minor matters such as control of billiard halls and police censor- ship of "nickel in the slot" amusements (Presbyterian *Minutes* 1907, 5–6). Moving picture shows had not yet come to the attention of the nascent reform body. In 1909 there was still only a miscellaneous discussion of five-cent shows at the close of its meeting, this time about prohibiting the attendance of children unless accompanied by a parent or guardian (Pres- byterian *Minutes* 1909, 23). The content of films went without comment, and there was still no call for concerted film censorship. By 1910 the limitations of discussing such matters only at an annual meeting were becoming evident, as well as its blinkered esteem of Toronto. Even on key issues of liquor licensing and prostitution, the practical recommendation was to nationalize the system of rigorous policing and strict moral gov- ernance already hard at work in Toronto. When the committee turned briefly to recreation and amusements, the nationalization of a Toronto- centric reform policy was the discussion in its entirety. The final motion merely sent formal congratulations to the government of Ontario for doing such a good job regulating the picture shows of Toronto and the province (Presbyterian *Minutes* 1910, 11–12).

Admiration for the leadership of the Ontario and Toronto authori- ties is equally evident for the Methodist reform committee. One of their earliest archived reports in May 1907 consulted with Toronto's Legislation and Reception Committee about establishing censorship of theaters. The phrase "five-cent shows" is on a concluding impromptu list of possible further work, although no follow-up seems to have occurred (Methodist *Report* 1907). By 1914, when the Methodist General Conference met, film censorship had been established in all provinces except Prince Edward Island. This government action and jurisdiction had been approved, but censorship concerns were on the wane among mainstream church groups. The commercial, profit-seeking basis of modern amusements remained a problem; but the focus was by then on suggesting alternatives, such as playgrounds and sports. A report from the Committee on Commercialized Amusements was part of the 1913 meeting of Methodist reform board. Heading a list of eleven items was a statement deploring "the fact that many forms of public amusement are so commercialized as to become mere money-making institutions" and urging efforts to "secure the elimination of the element of private profit from public amusements." Although the theater might be a means of education and recreation, "Canadian theatres, however, do not appear to be conducted according to the high ideals which should govern an institution claiming to educate and uplift the people. . . . We are convinced that under present conditions the influence of the stage is baneful to our Canadian life" (Methodist *Minutes* 1913). Diligent censorship was the recommended policy. Other items considered pool rooms, prizefights, and gambling. Unlike the earlier concerns in Toronto over commercialized amusements and carnival foods in relation to children, at the Weston Council, among the Toronto Board of Education, and with the chief constable of the police force, this report makes the commercial basis of modern amusements a matter of urgency for the morality of Canadian *adults* generally, implicitly the theater for women and gambling for men. And yet, movie theaters in particular were deferred entirely to a separate report from the Committee on Child Welfare. The lower cost and everyday qualities of moviegoing, compared to playgoing, continued to cast cinema as a juvenile matter, as a concern of family life and parenting, not the moral life of mature adults.

In a similar vein, the Presbyterian Church of Canada at its 1910 General Assembly articulated a strong, sociological explanation of the importance of regulating picture shows:

> The People's play and particularly the children's play, are and ought to be, in a special sense, the concern of the Church. It often happens that on the street, in the public park, in the one-cent, and five-cent show, or in even the better class of theater, demoralizing work

is done in a single hour that the Church, the Sunday School and the home, combined, will not undo in a month, or in some cases a lifetime. (Presbyterian *Acts and Proceedings* 1910, 286)

Some sort of censorship and control of public amusements was imperative. On the other hand, the committee recognized that "it is still more important to provide clean substitutes, and this is no easy matter" (Presbyterian *Acts and Proceedings* 1910, 287). The committee pointed to the need to expand on experiments in supervised playgrounds . In the reasoning of even mainstream churches, secular amusements were always on the verge of immorality because of their commercial form.

Then, why was not police and government oversight seen to make amusements legitimate, or as contributing to the underlying problem? The key seems to be the distinct moral situations of mature if errant adult leisure and showmanship's exploitation of children's immature appetites. Once adult accompaniment laws were in place from 1911, the responsibility shifted away from showmanship to parents and adults buying tickets for children. Similarly, greater availability of playgrounds, sports, and noncommercial leisure shifted the responsibility away from showmen to the individual conscience of parents. In general, once adequate regulation was in place, the highest bodies of mainstream religions were more likely to accept the secular character of mainstream amusements as harmless and turned their attention to developing alternative forms of educational and healthful recreation. Lee Grieveson (2004) argues strongly that a series of scandals and court decisions in the United States restricted film to commercial, harmless entertainment. Changes in the overall place of film in Canadian society clearly dovetail with this process, although the legal framework and immediate issues of race and sexuality are arguably absent.

Mainstream Protestant churches adopted Toronto-centrism as a nationalist policy, which is not to say it sought an umbrella to accommodate differences with French Catholic Quebec. Toronto-based Protestant churches sought reform and improvement, in contrast with the well-documented antagonism toward cinema on the part of the Catholic Church in Quebec (Gaudreault et al. 1996, 105–12; MacKenzie 2000, 194–200). Altogether, at least judging from newspaper reporting, police records, and minutes of Protestant church moral reform committees, it seems that far from remaining a contentious firebrand social problem, a consensus had been forged in Toronto in the few years following the first safety regulations in 1908. By 1911, prominent educational film lecturer Lyman Howe was given the forum of a newspaper article in the *News* to explain that it was important to "Give Pictures Proper Place" (*News* May 20, 1911; see also Musser and Nelson 1991). Because of proper regulation and oversight plus the occasional educational film lecture by upstanding showmen such as Howe, Toronto's picture shows were rarely a cause of concern. Rather than criticize the laxity of policing, censorship, and government in general, the churches used their national scope to suggest Toronto's governance was exemplary. And indeed, if the goal was tight censorship and policing, the conditions placed on Toronto's picture shows were in fact exemplary.

Licensing before Censorship:
Toronto's Primary Regulatory Device

After the 1908 fire safety regulations, moving picture shows continued spreading throughout larger towns and smaller cities all over Ontario as well as encroaching on the neighborhoods of everyday family life in Toronto. In 1909, the Ontario legislature extended the scope of municipal policing in the Egress from Public Buildings Act of 1908 to require local police forces to censor film shows as they inspected for fire safety (Ontario 1909). The Ontario government also instituted at this time a provincial license for picture machine operators and a $100 provincial license fee for each moving picture machine; this was a relatively low cost and was most likely meant to cover the cost of supervision rather than to generate revenue as a tax. There was little notice of protest on the part of the film showmen, although at least one Ontario paper included muted grumbling from local picture show managers; they objected more to the increased stringency of fire codes than the license fee (*Ottawa Journal* March 19, 1909).

Within weeks of the new clear-cut power to censor, the Saturday drama column of the *Toronto Star* reported the results. The article provides a rare, detailed description of the relation between the city police force and the moving picture shows:

Staff Inspector Stephen is devoting some time of late to the numerous moving picture shows which have sprung up all over the city like mushrooms on a summer morn. These places are censored now, just like the seven big theatres. Policeman Bloodworth, who happened with an accident at the jail a couple of years ago and has since been minus the use of one arm, is looking after the picture shows. One place has been practically forced out of business by the vigilance of the police. It was situated in the center of the city, and it displayed prominently a number of very suggestive and indecent poster pictures, indicating the nature of the show within. It caught the crowd, which is always on the lookout for salacious entertainment, and it also caught the eye of Mr. Stephen. Consequently, he seized the posters, prohibited the exhibition of that class of pictures, and the moving picture place didn't last long after the official house-cleaning was completed. It no longer exists now. (*Star* April 10, 1909, 8)

The quick stomping out of a singular egregious show seems the exception proving the rule that Toronto picture shows were well-policed, respectable places. The mark of mainstream respectability might have come at the expense of the city's only Jewish theater because it was the only show to close around this time and thus most likely bore the brunt of this crackdown. On the whole, Staff Inspector Stephen noted that he received few complaints about Toronto's picture shows, none at all in the first three months that year. Implicitly, the good state of filmgoing was a result of police vigilance.

Unlike journalism's focus on censorship, the day-to-day focus of policing was squarely on doling out licenses for new shows and patrolling nickel shows for mundane code infractions. This was the moment when the Toronto film market finally opened to significant competition against Griffin. The procedure of obtaining a picture show license from the Board of Police Commissioners was of vital concern to prospective showmen. Beginning in 1909, the board required all applicants for show licenses to prove that the neighborhood did not object to the proposed location. The April 1909 *Star* article about police censorship of picture shows also noted that the very same week a license application was denied for a show uptown on Bloor Street. Both clergy and laity gave deputations to the Board of Commissioners, at first opposed by Mayor Oliver, who asked them to prove their objections. The discussion was recapped in the article:

> "Have you seen a moving picture show?" demanded the Mayor. "No," said the deputation. Then his Worship told them a few plain truths about the wisdom of getting some first-hand knowledge of the subject before they came in to kick. "I've gone around to see those shows just to be in a position to know what I'm talking about," said the Mayor to the *Star* man. "I've found them pretty decent, and it makes me sick to hear people putting up a kick against something they never saw." (*Star* April 10, 1909, 8)

The mayor's political willingness to undercut the complaints had more swagger than sway, and the board denied the license. Subsequent depositions voicing complaints about prospective shows almost always won out against showmen's lawyers. The letterbooks of Chief Constable Grasett contain ample correspondence dealing with picture show licenses that were denied. Would the character of Toronto film shows have steadily improved without such a firm regulatory hand? Such a rhetorical question takes for granted that a market for filmgoing could exist outside of its licensing and policing, its inspection and claims made by authorities for the city's public. Although police censorship might be more vivid and licensing is easily dismissed as merely a tax, they are impossible to separate from the legitimate market functioning of the picture shows business in Toronto as anywhere else. A show without a license would operate outside the authority of the state, in a sense constituting a black market if run for-profit. A market for moving pictures requires licensing to provide the apparatus for maintaining standards, especially in the earliest stages of a novelty practice becoming legitimate.

Granting someone license to operate involved more than a simple political decision over who was permitted to open a business in town. Mariana Valverde (2003), unpacking the "police science" of regulating British pubs, notes that licensing extends state responsibility to the proprietors of businesses. According to Valverde, city bylaws and municipal policing demanded that "spaces and persons conform not only to law but to community norms" (p. 142). The Toronto bylaw against indecency betrays this impulse to ensure all public conduct happened within limitations at penalty of police powers. Licensing and laws against indecent public conduct worked to instill self-censorship and a sense of civic duty among business people and their customers. More formal, bureaucratic surveillance of picture shows emerged only as the loose relations of policing and commerce were taken as inadequate or at least inefficient. Local licensing is a way of tempering the harshness of patrolling public conduct because police powers are dissipated throughout the many establishments in the city. The license is a governing tool that indirectly polices businesses, especially those providing services and spaces of interaction that may become problematic. A tool of urban problem solving and discretionary policing, licenses operate relatively informally and without direct state surveillance. Instead, they constitute decentralized authority ensuring people's conduct in certain spaces is under constant surveillance and discipline, not because state officials and bureaucracies are micromanaging, but because business proprietors take on the responsibilities of government. Relieved of responsibility for maintaining standards, showmen's competitive playing field is leveled within the market, assuming everyone adheres to the prescribed standards. Even if these limits are stretched, even in the extreme case of graft, no competitor openly flaunts violating public safety standards. Licensing and policing, in a sense, free showmen to concern themselves entirely with profit obtained through proper rational management rather than through tactics that might be disastrous such as overcrowding, cheaper equipment, or untrained machine operators.

From 1909 to 1914 at least thirty proposed show licenses never opened as theaters. Although a few must have had trouble with financing, most of these cases were simply not permitted. Altogether, at least one-quarter of all license applications were turned down. The refused licenses in Weston might have been exceptional for the village; in the context of the entire area of Toronto, however, it was just one of many similar cases. The licensing decisions of the police commissioners in effect implemented a zoning policy over the location of picture shows throughout Toronto. Importantly, however, rules zoning theaters appear to be unwritten. This policy was allowed to remain informal, varying widely depending on the neighborhood and surroundings of the proposed show location. For example, the suggestion from the Board of Education to forbid picture shows within 1,000 feet of school yards never became policy, although the social concerns were incorporated into the licensing process on a case-by-case basis. Similarly, although some licenses were denied because they were too close to churches, others were near churches. The policy depended on the neighborhood, on the particular church, on the particular response to the particular license application. The board considered the proposed theater in relation to the existing area of its location, assessing resistance to the picture show, and usually granting the license if there was none. Toronto picture shows were thus never restricted in number or in zoning, although a reasonably strict de facto zoning was in effect that ensured picture shows remained on commercial strips, never too close to churches or schools run by sensitive ministers or principals.

A refused application to open a show on Bloor Street, mentioned in the *Star* article in April 1909, is the first such case with traces in Chief Grasett's letterbooks. Early in January 1909, George W. Woods had written to appeal his unsuccessful first application. The reply explained that it was "considered undesirable that a Show should be introduced into that locality, and also on grounds of a large petition signed by many people in the neighborhood against the application." Woods was told his letter appealing the decision would be brought to the next commissioners' meeting, but "it is not likely that they will alter their decision" (*LCC* January 8, 1909, 819). More than a dozen licenses were approved in many neighborhoods in the first months of 1909, and a concerted effort to limit or discriminate against moving pictures in general does not in any way appear to have been made. Quite the contrary, without an explicit policy as a guide, the Board of Police Commissioners was allowing picture shows to open all over the city.

The peculiarity of the large petition against Woods's show demonstrates the approval process considered the fit between the existing neighborhoods and the prospective showman, taking protests and petitions as a sign of future trouble that could be preempted on a case-by-case basis. Yet later in 1909 in the same neighborhood as Woods's application, a show was approved on nearby secondary street Dovercourt Avenue. Perhaps a theater off the main street, a block or two away, avoided the immediate problem that had earlier raised concern. Or perhaps Woods himself was the concern because he seems not to have found an alternative location, unlike some other failed applicants who simply changed plans. The round-the-corner show on Dovercourt was one of the few theaters permitted off the main shopping streets. Other shows just off of shopping streets were refused permits because they were adjacent to residential lots and houses. These cases provoked some protest from neighbors, keenly protecting the boundary between commercial and residential property. License applications were denied in all parts of the city for proposed locations on the East side, West side, uptown, and in neighborhoods of all socio-economic classes. Applications appear to have been considered case by case. Even sites for prospective shows downtown were considered in terms of the community fit of the show's "neighborhood." Two white-collar investors wrote about a proposed show right in the city center on Yonge Street, just steps from existing Griffin picture shows and David Minier's Comique (*LCC* March 3, 1909, 348). This show was not permitted.

Because most correspondence is with lawyers and not addressed personally to prospective showmen, assessing from the Chief Constable's letters exactly what legal recourse if any was available when a license application was turned down is difficult. In practical terms, several options were available. An alternative location could be found so the licensing procedure primarily cost time by delaying plans. Another option was to open a different type of shop or obtain another type of commercial license for the location. However, a couple of curious cases demonstrate a persistent, obstinate inability to pursue an alternative plan for a picture show location, despite the setback of failing to obtain a municipal license. After some theaters were refused licenses, the premises remained empty for years, apparently until the neighborhood found the option of a picture show more palatable than a vacant shop. One such place on College Street did not open until seven years after the first failed application for the site (*LCC* September 30, 1909, 316). The New Theatre at 928 College is noted as finally opening after "lying fallow for three years because of inability to secure a license" (*MPW* April 22, 1916, 661). By then plans were underway for an Allen's movie palace only a block away. As the independent showman recognized nearly a decade earlier, it was a good location for a high-class picture show—so much so that the high-class neighborhood surrounding the site seems to have refused to admit it.

Just a bit farther east on College was a similar struggle on the part of Mrs. Lena Herman whose family had already built the Monarch (*Building Permits* April 19, 1912; September 3, 1912). The building was complete by the time Herman applied for a license in spite of the objection of a local Presbyterian minister (*LCC* October 1, 1912, 106). In a surprising case of sympathy, the board eventually granted the license instead of accusing her of trying to circumvent the process (*LCC* April 23, 1913, 301). The loophole was promptly closed, as Chief Grasett advised the city architect that all future show licenses had to be granted before building permits were issued (*LCC* March 27, 1913, 133). Herman's loophole resulted from careful attention to independent jurisdictions. Police decided on licensing, which was an entirely separate matter from building code inspection and building permits, itself entirely separate from provincial licensing of cinematograph projecting machines and their operators. In retrospect, streamlining the procedure was an obvious move toward efficiency and fairness to investors, entrepreneurs, reformers, and neighbors alike. It nonetheless took over four years to emerge in such terms. Before this exceptional case—which laid bare the possibilities for trouble—the less formal process avoided problems through a general consensus over the chain of authority over filmgoing in the city. The Board of Police Commissioners had always invited, in fact insisted on, the active involvement of a variety of concerned actors to assess the social place of each licensed picture show location. In return for simply being included, those involved offered little debate about the validity of the procedure. With just one exceptional case of actively soliciting Christian ministers' opinions, Chief Grasett's correspondence betrays no organized effort to favor any particular type of constituent—religious leaders, educators, parents, residents, business people, film industry representatives, prospective showmen, or their lawyers (*LCC* April 2, 1913, 166–68). Rather, each of these voices spoke in relation to specific proposed picture shows, when each had a direct concern for the particular impending decision. It was almost as likely for a minister to write asking permission for a temporary religious exhibition of moving pictures. For example, Brigadier Bond of the Salvation Army successfully asked for a license exemption to show films of Booth's funeral in September 1912 (*LCC* September 14, 1912, 940). A month earlier Rev. J. L. Keith-MacLeod was sent instructions on how to get a picture show licensed, apparently for his own church hall (*LCC* August 28, 1912, 818). Except for discussions about legislation with other civil servants and the mayors, in only a single case does Grasett address a citizen about the general regulation of filmgoing in Toronto, and that advice was meant to rebuff a notoriously overzealous evangelical group calling itself the Vigilance Association (*LCC* May 22, 1912, 161; see also Campbell 1996). Almost without fail, Grasett upheld his office's integrity and kept his duties strictly to pragmatic and administrative matters.

The Melancholy Dane Is Muzzled:
Bureaucratic versus Police Censorship

While the Board of Police Commissioners attended to licensing, the morality squad had long been cutting film scenes in response to complaints and informal inspection. Despite the morality squad's consistent claim to have a firm grasp on things, the possibility of censorship by a central bureau reviewing film before it was distributed was first mentioned early in 1909. That was when the *Toronto Star* informed Mayor Oliver that New York City had installed such a system. The mayor said it sounded like a good idea. Censorship took two more years to come to fruition in an Ontario statute. In the interim, the Toronto municipal police and the Ontario Provincial Police issued concurrent and at times conflicting mandates over film censorship. The Theatres Branch of the Ontario Treasury, including the Board of Censors, eventually usurped any formal jurisdiction city police exercised over moving pictures. In fact, the role of the city police force was never fully eliminated because they retained jurisdiction over criminal matters, but the Provincial Censors' Stamp was at first legislated final authority, so that municipal police could not overrule their judgments. This situation was reversed in 1914, apparently to acknowledge the continued applicability of the federal criminal code against indecency. The mayor's early interest in simply copying the New York system was countered, not necessarily in deliberate opposition, by the Ontario legislature asserting its own authority over the matter. Initial provincewide propositions, however, were not at first supported with a proper bureaucracy to carry out the practical work of censorship. In the metropolitan city of Toronto, still the only municipality with more than a handful of picture shows to patrol, the city police continued to police films in their neighborhood contexts.

In 1909 the film regulations of the Egress from Public Buildings Act were extended to mandate municipal police forces to censor all exhibitions of films depicting crime and immoral acts as they patrolled theaters for proper fire safety standards. As with the initial fire safety regulations, extending a censorship mandate across the entirety of Ontario effectively applied the precedent of Toronto to all places in the province, whether rural or small city, whether everyday picturegoing at theatoriums even existed there yet, let alone problematically. The 1909 regulations to monitor and limit film content still recognized that judgments of indecency

Table 4.1. Cinematograph Legislation for Toronto

By 1890 until 1920. In Toronto, all amusements charging admission are licensed annually for $50.

In Canada, all indecent acts or their depictions are prohibited by the Criminal Code.

In Ontario, all Sunday performances are prohibited along with most Sunday business in general.

1907 Toronto Police Policy
Indecent moving pictures are confiscated on inspection.

1908 Ontario Egress from Public Buildings Act
Handling "combustible film more than 10 inches in length"
must be inspected and licensed by municipal police or fire authorities.

1908 Toronto Police Policy
Amusement licenses become entirely the jurisdiction of police commissioners.

1909 Ontario Egress from Public Buildings Act
Handling "combustible film" requires a provincial license.
Operating a machine without a license is an offense.
Enforcement is a police duty (that is, not a political matter).

1909 Toronto Police Policy
Amusement licenses are not granted if the neighborhood objects.

1910 Ontario Egress from Public Buildings Act
The word "combustible" is removed.

1910 Toronto Police Policy
Formal charges are laid against showmen for exhibiting indecent moving pictures.
Prizefight pictures are banned.

1911 Ontario Theatres and Cinematographs Act
Renews provincial licensing and inspection.
Creates Ontario Board of Censors for film.
Requires adult accompaniment of children under 15.

1911 Toronto Police Policy
Stages and vaudeville acts are banned in picture shows without a full theatre license.

1912 Ontario Theatres and Cinematographs Act
Specifies previously vague sections of 1911 Act.

1913 Ontario Theatres and Cinematographs Act
Creates an official provincial inspector of theatres.

(continued on next page)

Table 4.1. *(continued)*

1913 Toronto Police Policy
Construction of a theatre cannot begin until a license has been approved.

1914 Ontario Theatres and Cinematographs Act
Requires annual statistical returns for picture theatres.
Specifies adult accompanying children must be of the same household.

1915 Ontario Theatres and Cinematographs Act
Reverts to simple "adult accompaniment" of children under 15.

1916 Ontario Amusement Tax Act
Tax ticket for all admissions to entertainments. In policy, tax is graded to cost
of admission.

1917 Ontario Theatres and Cinematographs Act
Clarifies the provincial cinematographs act takes priority over municipal licensing.

1918 Ontario Theatres and Cinematographs Act
Extends jurisdiction of Board of Censors to amusement advertising
(and in 1919 to slides).

1918 Ontario Theatres and Cinematographs Act and Amusement Tax Act
Notarized returns must be done by designated officials, who may not charge a fee.

1919 Ontario Theatres and Cinematographs Act
Allows Saturday and Holiday children's matinees if an official matron is present.
Requires playing the National Anthem after every performance.
Allows municipalities to ban building new theatres within
200 feet of places of worship.

fell to municipal police forces. In Toronto, this seems to have been taken up with integrity. Shortly after Staff Inspector Kennedy took over supervision of the morality department, he began a campaign to clean up moving picture shows, paying special attention to pictures of crime and vice that made heroes out of criminals. During the first months of the new vigilance police only issued warnings, allowing the city's showmen to adapt to the new standards expected of them. The *Star* quoted Kennedy, "I am notifying the manager of every moving picture theater in Toronto to be careful in choosing his films, and to be sure that no scenes of crime and bloodshed are shown" (*Star* February 5, 1910, 12).

If the effort to trust showmen's self-regulation was sincere, it failed to eliminate crime pictures quickly enough because the *Star* soon noted in March that a "new system of censorship" might be introduced at City Hall (*Star* March 12, 1910). The suggestion was to outfit a room in City

Hall with a picture machine and require all films brought into Toronto by the film exchanges to be projected and inspected by an inspector from the morality department before being sent out to picture theaters. The Toronto picture show market was becoming large enough and the concerns for its supervision pressing enough to make this move necessary for efficiency; this move adapted the systems taken up earlier in Chicago and New York City. The question was how to implement such a system, and as always, whether the city police force had the legislative authority to do so. The Ontario Treasury Department, responsible for regulating filmgoing provincially, responded to these moves by the Toronto police force; but the ministry most likely was concerned about picture shows coming to small towns and rural locations without local police forces. In 1910 the Ontario legislature again rewrote the regulations for filmgoing, this time explicitly stating that monitoring the character of film content was the responsibility of the Ontario Provincial Police force. In principle this ensured some policing of picture content in every part of the province with fairness, equity, and transparency. In practice, however, the Superintendent of the Ontario Provincial Police had no way to enforce the new duties, so he compromised. Early in May 1910 he called a meeting at the parliament buildings in Toronto with representatives from the four film exchanges then operating in the city on the assumption that they controlled distribution of all films in Ontario. The exchange men were simply told to behave themselves and refrain from distributing objectionable material (*Star* May 7, 1910). The provincial police, handed this new duty, thus decided an honor system at the distribution end of the film industry would suffice.

This honor system of self-regulation among the Toronto film exchanges undercut the strict municipal policing in the city and undermined Kennedy's municipal policy of holding individual showmen accountable. With the new wording of the law in 1910, if the existing on-the-ground censorship practices of the Toronto city police force could continue was not even clear. When copies of the amended regulations were officially received, Chief Grasett wrote to the assistant provincial treasurer in charge, asking if the usurping of authority from city police was intended (*LCC* July 14, 1910, 194). Because of the lack of clarity in the chain of authority and imprecision in the scale of governance, the existing policing of picture shows in the city was threatened, despite the apparent intent of applying the quality of supervision in Toronto to the entire province. The Toronto police force continued with their prior practice, ignoring the suggested new chain of authority under the Ontario Provincial Police and continuing to defer instead to the Treasury Department. When the superintendent of the Provincial Police sent copies of the 1910 amended regulations to Chief Grasett, after official copies already came from the provincial treasurer, only a brief and cordial reply followed in contrast to the lengthy inquiry to the Treasury previously quoted (*LCC* July 16, 1910, 214). The matter was left in some dispute because censorship took place both through the urban policing of the morality patrol and also the provincial attempt at self-censorship among the film exchanges. The only consistent result at this time was that all agreed to ban moving pictures of prizefights in Ontario, in particular the Johnson–Jeffries heavyweight championship (*News* August 27, 1910; *LCC* August 12, 1910, 473; *ROC* May 25, 1911, line 1772).

After issuing warnings for several months, late in August 1910 Kennedy crossed the line and laid the first ever criminal charges for exhibiting prohibited films. It might have been partly a political response to the conflicting jurisdiction of the Ontario Provincial Police because he reiterated the need to inspect films at the exchanges before they were sent around the city to theaters. Caught in the middle were independent showmen. The first censorship conviction was against Robert Burke, independent showman-owner of the Fairyland, one of the smallest shows in town, where "the seizure and destruction of 1,000 feet of films brought to a timely end a most bloodthirsty concoction of 'deeds of violence' " (*News* August 27, 1910, 7). According to the *Globe* (August 27, 1910), the film was "Life among the Brigands," described as a "hotch-potch of revolver-shooting and hold-ups" (See also *Telegram* August 26, 1910; *ROC* August 26, 1910, line 1878). Days later, the *News* reported the second offender, Morris Spiegel, manager for Canada Moving Pictures Ltd. at the Cosmopolitan downtown, was charged with showing the "wrong kind of moving pictures" and fined $50. The showman's only defense was that he should have been given a warning first, to which the police explained that warnings of the new regulations had been given for months (*News* September 1, 1910; *ROC* September 1, 1910, line 11). According to the *World*, the film was "The Political Dispute," about "political campaigns conducted in France, showing the Jesse James manner of the politicians and the pugilistic qualities of the police" (*World* September 1, 1910, 11). The dramatic editor of the *News* agreed with the police. With regard to censorship and the moral character of the moving pictures, there was no excuse. "No private opinion ever made much immediate headway against the swing of a bobbie's baton; under most circumstances acquiescence is the better part of valor" (*News* September 3, 1910, 7).

The phrase "most circumstances" is important because the same newspaper editor was eager to write articles mocking Inspector Kennedy when films of *Hamlet*, and later *Romeo and Juliet*, were banned. In February 1910, just weeks after Kennedy publicized his new concerted attempt to clean up Toronto's picture shows, the *News* ran the headline, "The Melancholy Dane Is Muzzled, Local Censor Cuts Out Hamlet." Explaining that the police had stamped Shakespeare's play a spectacle of violence and dangerous to young folks. The columnist did not simply let the quote speak for itself but took the care to explain the lesson carefully. "No more Hamlet for this city. No more at any rate in the inexplicable dumb shows to which the immortal Shakespeare referred with prophetic instinct so many years ago." Kennedy's ignorance was quoted in his own words, "I witnessed a moving picture show of Hamlet written I think by Shakespeare at a Yonge Street picture theater this week. . . . That's all very well to say it's a famous drama, but it doesn't keep it from being a spectacle of violence" (*News* February 26, 1910, 7). Aside from demonstrating uncertainty about who wrote *Hamlet* and dismissing its cultural importance as merely a famous drama, the police censor's inability to distinguish cops-and-robbers crime stories from important literary works was ridiculed. The newspaper writer blanketed acceptance of police authority in sarcasm, "The man of law has spoken. Hamlet is a thing of the past."

Such cases, as Uricchio and Pearson (1993) have shown for the literary and historical Vitagraph Quality films, could open rifts among the various voices of governance and moral reform. Censorship in the hands of police followed a strictly rational logic. The ethic behind police duties was consistency above all, thought to remove bias from policing, and in turn corruption and politics. Kennedy was acting according to the rules he was given, applying the regulations as if no interpretation were involved. In those circumstances, all murders and love affairs, even those in Shakespeare's plays, had to be censored. To newspaper editors, and all but the most stringently unbending moral reformers, censorship instead needed to be linked to education, parenting, aesthetic judgment, knowledge of the arts, and culture. Once the police banned *Hamlet*, the consensus of support for film censorship soon shifted; the issue stopped being strictly a matter of the efficient and centralized administration of police duties. Kennedy later retracted his decision, at least for stage plays (*Star* May 7, 1910). An editorial a few months later testifies to the persistence of the problem, harking back to Kennedy's lack of discretion, "a too strict censorship would rule out *Hamlet, Macbeth, Othello,* and *Romeo and Juliet*" (*Star* September 7, 1910, 6). But police censorship in Toronto persisted as if the authorities felt that too-strict censorship was advocated as a good thing.

Just a few weeks later, Kennedy banned a film version of *Romeo and Juliet*. Unlike the $50 fines against showmen a month earlier, the ban on *Romeo and Juliet* affected the business of the Griffin Amusement Company. Griffin was still the dominant showman in town and by then all of Ontario. An exasperated Peter Griffin outlined the situation as dire and an embarrassment to Toronto across the continent. "Men with thousands invested in the moving picture business are simply driven to the wall in this city. Fines have been imposed right and left . . . We are given absolutely no chance in comparison with the picture showmen in any other part of America" (*News* October 8, 1910, 17). Neighborhood showmen were being convicted and fined for showing pictures that the film exchanges, under discretion of the Provincial Police, had already passed. The city police seemed to be increasing constraints on what could be shown and were also moving to amend the city building code bylaws to prevent vaudeville and theatrical acts on stage in places licensed only for moving pictures; these bylaws were meant to prevent "exploiting children" as laboring performers (*Star* August 27, 1910). To continue with smalltime vaudeville acts in January 1911, picture shows had to take out an additional $100 theater license and pass the more stringent fire code inspection required of theaters (*News* December 31, 1910). Some sort of censorship prior to distribution had to happen if only for efficiency and fairness for all concerned. The question was who would administer it, the municipal police force, Provincial Police force, or some other government bureaucratic branch of either the city or the province.

The Toronto chief constable proceeded as if eventually he would have to administer a municipal solution. For example, in September 1910, Chief Grasett informed barristers Morris and Jameson, perhaps representing the then-dominant Dominion Film Exchange, that the police commissioners had refused their offer "proposing that films be censored at the Film Exchange." (*LCC* September 21, 1910, 806). The New York National Board of Censorship corresponded with Toronto's new Mayor G. R. Geary about cooperating in the censorship of films. In November 1910, Chief Grasett, after considering this correspondence in relation to existing protocol, wrote an extensive reply to the mayor outlining the situation and options for municipal censorship. The police were responsible for censorship, but Chief Grasett admitted that "of necessity it is limited and incomplete" and acceded that if all films could be examined "by a competent Censor" at a central location before being exhibited and a certificate issued attesting to the examination, "the undesirable exhibitions could be largely if not entirely eliminated" (*LCC* November 17, 1910, 491–92).

The offer of the National Board of Censorship to send their weekly bulletins would have clearly helped an official censor in Toronto if such an office were created. Some suggested local film exchanges should produce a certificate that each film submitted to the Toronto censor had already been passed by the body in New York. Nobody in Toronto, however, argued that the work of the U.S. censorship board could in any way replace the surveillance and work of local policing. Misunderstandings added to political discomfort with allowing a U.S. body to act as guideline for the supervision of the moral values of Canadian society. Some confusion existed in Toronto about the work and effects of the National Board of Censorship. Local showmen appear to have claimed the New York censors effectively prevented banned films from being imported to Canada. The claim found its way to the pages of the *New York Dramatic Mirror*, then to the National Board of Censorship itself, who sent a letter back to Toronto clarifying that the Board had no such power to prohibit films entering Canada (*News* December 10, 1910).

The balance finally tipped in favor of a bureaucratic, provincial solution. By November 1910, reports were circulating that the Ontario government was drawing up a Motion Pictures Act to install a new bureaucratic administration in a board of three censors. Peter Griffin, quoted in the *News* as if speaking for all picture showmen, said the unpredictability of city police censorship was "demoralizing the business" and that an Ontario Board of Censors was needed to solve the present difficulty (*News* November 5, 1910). In 1911, a film censorship board was created as a branch of the Ontario Treasury (Ontario 1911). Soon after, censorship boards were created in Quebec and Manitoba to prevent Canadian film distributors from dumping films prohibited in the Ontario market into adjacent territory (*News* November 25, 1911).

An article in April 1911 noted how Toronto showmen were actually relying on the new regulation to diffuse criticism leveled against moving pictures (*News* April 22, 1911). The function of government regulation was more than surveillance. Limitations set by bureaucratic governance lent legitimacy to commercial amusements, evident here as exactly the point for Toronto showmen. Censorship regulation would limit nonprofit competition from churches and social groups, freeing commercial shows to focus on improving showmanship and of course profits. Educational shows were seen as unfair competition. No doubt the mothers and ministers who were organizing these community shows felt that the appeal of everyday cheap amusements was unfair competition against their purposes as well. Indeed, the irony of having government censors stamp their approval on senseless entertainment was sarcastically compared in the libertine muckraking pages of *Jack Canuck* (October 28, 1911) to the mark of the beast from Revelations in the Bible! The paper pointed out that the National Board of Censorship in New York City had many prominent and respectable names associated with its work, in contrast to the "three wise men" of the Ontario Board of "Senseless Censors" who had the greatness of their task thrust upon them. On the first board, two of three censors were showmen, including one whose show was rented in daytime as the censors' screening room.

The scandal-sheet criticism in *Jack Canuck*, while directly opposed to religious reformers, equally recognized government censorship was facilitating rather than reforming commercial moviegoing.

The *Star Weekly* (April 20, 1912) took a more level-headed but progressive editorial stance in support of the popularity of filmgoing and against harsh censorship, which it saw as an overreaction. On June 3, 1911, the weekend newspaper wrote a sweeping endorsement of the potential of moving pictures' mass audience, lamenting how cheap amusements and mass culture were drawing audiences away from loftier cultural forms. "The average may not be as good, but wait." After waiting almost a year for the state of filmgoing to improve, editorials throughout 1912 in the *Star Weekly* took up the cause directly. One of its editorials claimed censorship was not enough, that "public-spirited people should bring influence to bear on the enterprise in a constructive way, so that the full benefit of the invention shall be reaped by the community" (p. 20). Emphasizing community control rather than censorship and policing and noting with disdain continued bans on films of Shakespeare in "one of the Western States," the editors advised clergymen to "keep in touch with the public amusements" to try understanding their appeal instead of condemning them with willful ignorance (*Star Weekly* April 27, 1912). Again lamenting the "inadequate use of a magnificent invention," the *Star Weekly* (September 7, 1912), distinguished its stance from that of the *Montreal Herald*, which had dismissed moving pictures entirely "as little better than a nuisance." The Toronto paper had its own, more progressive idea. "The main point is that more censoring and prohibition is not enough. You must apply thought and sound sentiment and culture in a constructive way. You must have competent people thinking out new subjects" (p. 20). Although the newspaper suggested improved writing and film production, a few months later the women of Weston's TIS took a more practical, hands-on approach with their proposal to operate a town picture show themselves. Neither route could really undermine the continued importance of the Ontario Board of Censors.

Once the Board of Censors began its work, some initial confusion resulted over the exact meaning of the law. The first move to fix the ambiguity in the regulation was, not surprisingly, taken on the ground by police patrolmen in Toronto. In October 1911, "Police Seized Pictures of Crime" at a suburban film show (*Star* October 5, 1911). In this case, a film lecturer was used specifically to circumvent the new censorship board. Frames were extracted from a film depicting some well-known U.S. crime and an accompanying lecturer described in detail the sensational circumstances of the no-longer-moving pictures. The lecturer was arrested for an indecent exhibition anyway. This event set the precedent that censorship of

Figure 4.2. Like most early picture shows, Griffin's Auditorium featured both pictures and vaudeville, the latter banned in 1910 unless the show met the safety standards of a proper theater. 380 Queen Street West. *ca.* 1909. (Photograph by William James, City of Toronto Archives, Fonds 1244, Item 320C.)

moving pictures prevented cut scenes from being shown even as photographic stills, thereby enforcing the spirit rather than the letter of the law. The case shows local police implicitly favored standardized film production, in fact insisted on it within the territory of their jurisdiction after films left the censor board. Many film historians have strongly argued that local variations provided by lecturers and music accompanying film shows gave early film a neighborhood, regional, or national context (Lacasse 2000). With official film censorship in Ontario, local authorities worked to eliminate much of this regional and neighborhood variation. On top of censorship, recall how city licensing bylaws were amended to ban vaudeville and amateur stage acts from picture shows unless the building could pass the safety codes required of large theaters and pay for the additional theatrical license on top of the picture show license. The impetus for standardizing music and film programming came from local authorities as much as capitalist production companies. Both relied on efficient management and supervision. In effect, local policing and censorship shared common interests with the production and distribution branches of the film industry.

Centralized bureaucratic regulation and strong policing of violations were implemented earlier in Ontario than in any other Canadian province or American state. The mechanisms supporting moral conservatism in Ontario ensured film regulations were installed quickly and thoroughly with relatively little protest, in an apparently obvious consensus. This arrangement allowed U.S.. films to be imported freely while also allowing regional censorship to prevail. The Toronto police showed they could not distinguish Shakespeare from Wild West shows; at least a professional bureaucracy could do that. It could also achieve regional homogeneity because its decisions covered the entire territory. The Ontario Board of Censors and other aspects of the regulation of filmgoing through the Provincial Treasury's Theatres Branch were instituted without court injunctions or any organized effort to thwart its authority on the part of the film industry. There was hardly any protest.

Routine Theater Inspection and Everyday Violations

No bureaucracy could replace the necessary patrolling of blocked and unlit theater exits, crowded aisles and entrances, or unlicensed operations of projection machines. Newspapers reported all the incidents around censorship in detail. The urgency of the issue masked how infrequent violations against standards of decency actually were. A different story lies within the routine paperwork of the *Register of Criminals* and *letterbooks* of the chief constable. In terms of everyday policing, censorship was a minimal problem despite receiving so much attention. The centralized bureaucracy that emerged to deal with the censorship of films reflected a generalized call for the surveillance of film content rather than a reaction against an actual preponderance of indecent films. Out of about 100 charges against theater managers and employees spelled out in the *Register of Criminals*, only the three already discussed in detail cite the exhibition of prohibited pictures. This means the detailed reports of censorship violations were only as frequent as the violations themselves. This contrasted starkly with the day-to-day routine of less problematic infractions. Of greatest consequence to neighborhood showmen was the 1911 requirement that children had to be accompanied by an adult. This measure hit the bottom line of independent showmen, especially those operating older theaters in poorer working-class neighborhoods. Not only would the number of children's nickels be less, but accepting those nickels risked significant fines in the police court.

Showmen managing theaters along Queen and College streets in neighborhoods closest to downtown received a disproportionate number of charges. As the city expanded in these years extending its official city limits and filling in residential areas both inside and just outside the city limits, these inner-city neighborhoods became increasingly identified with Jewish, Italian, and other immigrant-run businesses and populations. Ethnicity and class perhaps prompted extra police patrolling in these areas; importantly, however, they were still relatively middle-class domestic neighborhoods, not the poorest parts of town. The Jewish-identified Ward had only one picture show at any one time, and the largely Irish-Catholic "Cabbagetown" just east of downtown had only a couple of picture theaters. There is no sign these shows in the poorest parts of town were singled out. The more heavily policed zones for filmgoing, then, were the areas just further out from downtown and the poverty of the ghettos. The cause of stricter patrolling there was most likely a simple result of the dense agglomeration of theaters along Queen and College streets, which would have facilitated heavy policing. Some violations are recorded for theaters in all parts of town; but only the largest, newest theaters in suburban neighborhoods consistently avoided trips to the police court to pay a fine. The archived records show a conspicuous absence of citations against uptown theaters along Yonge Street north of downtown; and no charges are levied against the largest picture shows, the Madison and the Beaver picture palaces, and just one notice was ever given to Daniel Lochiel at the Park Theatre. In contrast, some smaller theaters were cited up to ten times in just a few years.

Before regulations specific to picture shows, only occasional charges were cited against the large downtown theaters. The manager of the Star Burlesque was fined $5 for obstructing theater aisles in November 1907, but that was still extraordinary enough to be reported in the paper (*Star* November 25, 1907). In contrast, frequent fines ranging from $5 to $20 for obstructed aisles began appearing regularly in the *Register of Criminals* in 1909, the last year charges against legitimate theaters were on par with theatoriums. In the second half of 1910, just as the handful of censorship charges for exhibiting pictures of crime are laid, the frequency of citations for minor violations shot up dramatically while charges against the downtown stages almost disappeared. In 1909 the *Register of Criminals* showed three citations against theaters and four against picture shows. In 1910 seven citations were logged, all against picture shows. In 1911 a single charge for obstructing a passageway at the Royal Alexandra Theatre was logged and thirty-four charges laid against managers and employees of picture shows. Not surprisingly, 1911 was the first year statistics for Breaches of the Theatres Act and Breaches of the Moving Pictures Act appeared in the annual report of the chief constable, and were no longer in the miscellaneous column.

By 1911, as well, fines reached as high as $50, the amount specified as the minimum for censorship violations and for permitting children to enter, but soon applied to the occasional charge of blocked aisles. The magistrates at police court were issuing sentences that corresponded in severity to heightened inspections from police. Moving picture theaters in 1911 and 1912 were a significant part of police work, although the matter practically disappeared from newspaper columns after the Board of Censors was created. This contrasted with other cities, such as Ottawa, where late in 1915 theater managers were caught off guard by a sudden strict enforcement of previously lenient prohibitions against overcrowding (*MPW* November 6, 1915, 1169). Aside from generally stricter policing in Toronto, smaller cities such as Ottawa and Hamilton had never experienced the same dramatic proliferation of picture theaters and the resulting problem of efficiently inspecting them all. In Toronto the number of picture shows rose from just a dozen at the beginning of 1909 to about fifty by the end of 1911, exactly the period when the police force, film industry, and audience needed to adjust to new regulations. The growth of the Toronto picture show market stagnated in 1912, before picking up momentum again in 1913 and finally doubling in number to almost 100 locations by 1914. This second boom period was not accompanied by a proportionate increase in surveillance from the police force. Quite the opposite. At that time, moviegoing received much positive attention from journalists, as theaters began regular advertising in newspapers, reliably attracting mainstream mass audiences.

Perhaps surprisingly, showmen made only limited protests at first about the ban on admitting children. Some leeway was given even in this case because the 1911 Ontario law required children be accompanied by an "adult." The chief constable responded succinctly to a parent's complaint in 1913: "The Police Court has held that this means any adult person, therefore we cannot interfere" (*LCC* November 5, 1913, 683). An Ontario legislature attempt to restrict this aspect of filmgoing came in 1914 when the wording was amended to prohibit any child younger than fifteen from attending "unless accompanied by its parent or guardian or by an adult member of the household to which it belongs" (Ontario 1914). It must have proved unenforceable because it was reversed in 1915 to the more lenient wording (Ontario 1915). Perhaps having an unenforceable law leading to systematic violations was politically unpalatable in Ontario. In English Protestant "Toronto the Good" minor corruption received big headlines, such as an investigation into the city architect's office in 1914, which was ironically a demonstration of how rare graft was

(*Star* November 25, 1913; Toronto 1914). When a journalist attempted a series of feature articles on graft in the city, it had to define tipping as a form of corruption to discuss the issue in a local context (*Star Weekly* November 2, 1912; November 16, 1912; January 4, 1913). Montreal exhibitors and distributors were several times reported to be systematically circumventing regulations. The Quebec legislature had to rewrite its Cinematograph Act constantly to plug loopholes (*MPW* June 6, 1914, 1426; February 13, 1915, 1023). A similar situation in Ontario prompted the censor board to change its procedures quickly, but it specifically noted a problem in remote northern towns, not the city, and further justified as trimming expenses (*Star Weekly* June 28, 1913). Strong regulation in Ontario seems to have allowed the film industry to proceed full speed in the pursuit of better showmanship and bigger profits. Once the limitations, however strict, were set, the sense was that they had to be reliably administered in transparency and fairness.

By 1913 all film and show poster censorship had been usurped from the duties of the Toronto police force and placed in provincial bureaucracies. The chief constable wrote he was "glad to be rid of it" although he had always practiced censorship with integrity. The Theatres Branch of the Ontario Treasury soon had final say on licenses for projectionists, theaters, and film exchanges; on censoring films; and on inspecting projecting booths. Lee Grieveson (2004) strongly argued that parallel calls for censorship in the United States responded to anxieties about the special character of widely distributed films dealing with racial and sexual relations. He has persuasively shown that films of Jack Johnson winning prizefights against white opponents provoked racist attempts to censor and ban those moving pictures, as well as to have film distribution defined as interstate commerce and thus restricted by federal law (pp. 135–45). Grieveson also goes into detail about the growing ineffectiveness of the National Board of Censorship, whose stamp of approval was adopted voluntarily. Because the New York–based censorship association had its roots in the Progressive educational movement of the People's Institute, it approved on educational grounds a documentary nonfiction film, *Inside the White Slave Traffic*. This undermined its moral authority when the film became notorious and was widely denounced, prompting the activation of a dormant state censor board in Pennsylvania and the creation of censor boards in Ohio and Kansas (Grieveson 2004, 193–208). The Ontario Board of Censors emerged in parallel to these regional U.S. cases and was at least as effective in installing local standards. As in Canada, regulations and legal disputes over interstate and local film censorship grew in importance in the United States between 1910 and 1915. However, the federal interstate commerce jurisdiction was a decisive resource without a Canadian equivalent. Neither did Canada have a constitutional right of free speech beyond the precedents of common law. Where U.S.. local censor boards had the great expense and trouble of court injunctions and appeals, Canadian boards had authority without recourse. Not until 1915 did the U.S. Supreme Court rule that film was legally limited to "only" harmless, commercial entertainment, without the protection of First Amendment rights. By then state and local censor boards had largely reigned in their initial bravado, while centralized film production in Hollywood studios had in turn begun to self-impose restraint simply to ensure maximal markets. Thus, in the United States, the fight over the local autonomy largely fell away as the dominance of Hollywood became clear.

In Toronto, local censorship mattered because it was a direct outgrowth of the responsibilities of urban policing, and accepting an external authority, let alone the voluntary efforts of a self-regulating industry, was unfathomable and politically unpalatable for territories, especially across international borders. But just what difference did censorship have in Ontario in terms of what ended up projected onto picture screens? With U.S. film studios more attuned to censorship efforts closer to home such as the National Board of Censorship in New York, how did the Ontario Board of Censors really change what was being seen? While the reciprocal effect on production is likely minimal, the Ontario Board of Censors, under its first Chief Censor G. E. Armstrong, made rampant cuts to reshape film according to a perceived particularity of the Ontario audience.

Most obviously and widely commented on was the decision to bar images of the American flag if being used with patriotic fervor. Just months after Armstrong's work began, a brief controversy erupted when a film based on the War of 1812 portrayed the American perspective to the detriment of the Canadian victors. British Loyalist Canadian soldiers had, after all, burned down the White House and won that war. In Toronto picture shows, the movie drew hisses and was interrupted by patriotic protests. Reports of the incident even reached the U.S. film trade press. Censoring overt American patriotism in imported films became the first urgent matter of the Ontario Board of Censors. Beginning late in 1911, scenes of Old Glory were cut from imported films before they were shown to audiences in Toronto. An article in *Jack Canuck*, the same one that sarcastically compared the censor's stamp to the mark of the devil, facetiously acceded that waving the American flag was a "heinous offense indeed, far worse than the murders so vividly portrayed this past week!" (October 28, 1911, 8). An editorial in the *Star Weekly* reviewed how U.S. film producers were at first just perturbed with the moral strictness of the Ontario censors for banning films "not considered injurious to the honest people of Kansas and Michigan." Movie studios' indignation escalated, and they took the banning of the Stars and Stripes to the Secretary of State as a trade issue spilling over onto concerns of sovereignty. The Toronto editor remarked that the more valid concern for sovereignty actually lay on the other side of the border with Canada:

> This must be considered one of the most curious appeals ever made to a Government. These men bedeck their films with their own flag because they know their own flag appeals to the sentiments of their own people. Yet they actually fail to understand that our people want to see our flag bedecking similar pictures if they are to get equal pleasure out of them. . . . Let them substitute our flag for their own on their total output for a month, and see whether the people of the United States would be as tolerant for one night as we have been for years past in a matter of this kind. (*Star Weekly* November 4, 1911, 20)

Such sympathies with the Canadian side were not entirely unheard of on the other side of the border. The New York trade journal *Moving Picture World* recognized that patriotism run amok in films cheapened the possibilities of the art of filmmaking and limited profits from the international market for American films (*MPW* October 28, 1911, 272; November 11, 1911, 487; December 9, 1911, 795). On a simple matter of good management, one Chicago film exchange representative later dismissed the continuing contention over American flags on Toronto movie screens (*MPW* October 17, 1914, 317). His inspection of the Canadian territory convinced him that the centralized censorship boards of Ontario and Quebec were liberal in judgment and efficient in practice, in stark contrast with the local censor nuisance then rampant across the United States. Once passed through the board, film exchanges had full and unobstructed access to the vast territories of Canadian provinces. Even the movie business realized that efficient censorship could bring greater profits.

5

Everybody's Going

Introducing the Mass Audience to Itself

All hats off to that editorial man. The poor, despised moving pictures have at last received recognition. . . . It is the culmination of a long fought battle for the recognition of motion pictures as a legitimate offering.

—*Moving Picture World* June 25, 1910

⚶

IN LARGER CITIES SUCH AS TORONTO the first theatoriums opened almost anonymously downtown, in particular ignored by journalists. Perhaps because early film showmen were not advertising clients, five-cent shows first turned up in newspaper pages only when something newsworthy happened. One of the first hints of the nickelodeon craze in Chicago, for example, was a small report of a fire at an "electric theater" in the ethnic ghetto on the near West Side (*Chicago Tribune* May 15, 1906). At that early point in the moving picture fad, the poor Jewish neighborhood was of as much interest as the novelty amusement or even its flammability. The only show in Toronto's Jewish-identified Ward is actually the best-documented early picture house, including an incident in September 1908 that drew the attention of all the city's daily papers. During a Friday night show at the People's Theater, loud cat-calling on the main floor led people in the gallery to lean over to see what was going on below. The balcony rail gave way and a dozen, mostly children, fell over with it.

The *Globe* printed the most succinct synopsis, but still managed to flesh out the story with somewhat exotic details of "Hebrew" theater and life in the Ward.

> The news of the accident flashed through "The Ward" with all kinds of exaggerations. . . . A squad of [police]men stationed around the theatre to keep back the excited foreigners. Fathers and mothers ran to and fro vainly trying to find children whom they knew had gone to the show, and it was fully an hour before order was restored among two or three thousand people who gathered around. (*Globe* September 5, 1908, 24)

The brief account in the factual, plain-worded *Globe* was newsworthy less for the safety issues or injuries than for the chance to witness and report on audience norms (or lack of them, compared to the downtown stage theaters). The writer described the panic to exit instead of helping the injured, and the dramatic melee of the immigrant neighborhood panicking itself, and hundreds rushing in the opposite direction toward the theater. Similarly, the headline in the *World* stated, "Yiddish Crowd Have Narrow Escape." The *World* also emphasized the neighborhood's panicked response, writing colorfully that "the news spread like wildfire thru the gossiping knots 'in the ward' . . . sobbing and shrieking parents soon pressed upon the police calling in Yiddish" (*World* September 5, 1908, 1). The *Telegram* and the *News* added an account of the instigating disruption, heckling the illustrated-song singer to get a friend hired in her place. Of more interest, both papers carried photographs of victims and of the theater.

The lengthiest treatment was in the *Star*, which curiously mentioned only "the Ward" to signal the Jewish context, and waited until nearly the end of the article to note that "the songs and plays are nearly all in Yiddish, and the audience is composed almost entirely of Hebrews" (*Star* September 5, 1908, 1). The writer seemed to assume the Jewish character of the theater, the Ward, and the injured victims. Finding room for such insider's knowledge opened up a more nuanced explanation of the cause of the accident: a few "young Polanders" had objected to a song sung in English, implying diverse Jewish cultures, classes, and even levels of orthodoxy might have been involved. Not everyone reacted with panic; the paper noted how "the ushers, assisted by the police, were working like heroes to get the excited crowd safely out" (p. 1). The *Star* also explained the role and appeal of the Ward's cheap theater. "These shows are put on each night," reported a resident of the neighborhood:

> and as ten cents admits the women and children to the main floor, hundreds take advantage of it. It is not necessary for the women to dress up, and so they go and take the children with them. They meet their neighbors and gossip from 7:30 until 11, although they are supposed to leave after seeing the show for which they pay admission. It is really worth ten cents for the women to sit there and talk, so you can imagine how popular the place is. (*Star* September 5, 1908, 1).

Finally, the article details the manager's renovation of the building into a theater, including the installation of the gallery and its railing, noting ominously that because the electric wiring for the stage ran along under the balcony, "had the wires broken, the terrible element of fire would have been added, and the result would have been frightful." Then again, a separate article quoted the city architect's defense of his original inspections: "A railing in any theater will have to be exceptionally strong to stand such a strain as that last night. The crowd forced themselves against it" (p. 1). The culprit was the crowd, not the construction. A prompt test of all theater railings in the city would be done, however, to ensure the accident could not be repeated in any of the mainstream theaters downtown.

As much or more than the plain facts of the event, the reporting of the People's Theatre accident was fascinated with the social context of the theater, its audience, and the sociable space that it provided in its neighborhood. Earlier reporting about theatoriums state their facts plainly: the wife abuse trial of John Griffin, the small fire at Griffin's Theatorium, and the Firemen's Fund donation, or the failed attempt at Sunday picture shows in Kingston. These incidents drew no apparent interest in the audience or the social context of five-cent shows, whereas the quantity and quality of reporting on the People's Theatre betrays a sociological fascination with the marginal amusement site. Although no fire erupted and the accident did not involve the moving picture machine at all, the story—framed in terms of theater safety in general—shows the dangers of a panicking theater crowd. The lesson (or public interest, at least) of this accident was in learning about what went on there; this would surely have been a mystery to most readers of the mainstream press. As the only audience meriting attention, the ethnic audience of Toronto stood in for picture show audiences in general. While not empirically true, the point here is that reporting illustrates clearly that the movies were not yet mainstream, and its audience not yet a mass audience.

Early theatoriums were part of a general dispersal of carnival attractions and confections into everyday life, staking a claim in neighborhood domestic areas. An earlier chapter describes how picture shows met police and reformers' calls for oversight at the same time minor crises erupted over the social place of ice cream and popcorn vendors, billiard halls and bowling alleys, even fortune telling and special Sunday religious lectures in theaters. For the most part, the other activities became naturalized as unthreatening, ordinary, perhaps banal options in the everyday life of the city. But the movies became a mainstream, mass cultural practice, fully instituted through corporate conglomeration and state bureaucracies. A significant part of this process was the incorporation of publicity and promotion of moviegoing, especially in mass circulation newspapers.

Parallel to the regulation the police provided and the well-intentioned stewardship of moral reformers and legislators, journalists occasionally drew attention to early moving picture shows and their audiences. In the years before film advertising and publicity became a regular part of newspapers around 1913, journalistic reviews of picture shows and audiences described the novel urban practice with intense fascination, as if the writer were trying to understand the appeal of moving pictures and relay the excitement to a curious readership still unfamiliar with the nickel shows. Throughout North American cities, urban tourism was still an exceptional activity, often framed as an adventurous trek through the neighboring foreignness of poor, ethnic quarters (Cocks 2001; Olsson 2004). Newspapers, too, in large cities experiencing mass immigration, used illustrated feature stories to provide a safe foray into city ghettos (for example, *Chicago Tribune* August 18, 1895). Yiddish and "foreign" theaters also drew attention (*Chicago Tribune* December 24, 1898 and May 31, 1908). Early journalism about moving picture shows in Toronto adopted this almost ethnographic curiosity about marginal audiences in forging an understanding of film as part of modern life. This overlap in the turn-of-the-last-century work of newspapers, social work, moral reform, policing, government, and sociology goes well beyond filmgoing of course. Some experts have strongly argued that these social forces often approximated a consensus over which spaces, practices, and people required study, sharing techniques of observation and interpretation (Bouman 1991; Walkowitz 1992). Newspaper exposés of the perils of early nickelodeons coincided with efforts at reform and police surveillance of lower-class ethnic audiences and of exploitative fly-by-night entrepreneurial showmen, especially those from the same lower-class or ethnic backgrounds. Perhaps the earliest muckraking campaign and one with the greatest effect was a series of articles in the *Chicago Tribune* in April and May 1907 that was linked to the institution of police censorship of films there (Grieveson 1999). Antagonistic editorial policies continued to concern the film industry as a whole. As late as 1913, *Moving Picture World* expressed surprise and relief when the mainstream press profiled the film industry in a positive light (*MPW* March 15, 1913, 1093; April 5, 1913, 32).

Outright antagonism between journalism and picture shows did not surface in Toronto. When the prospect of film and stage censorship was first addressed in Toronto's City Council in April 1907, an editorial in the *Star* firmly stood against it, wondering if amusements really necessitated such "despotism" and calling the proposal part of a "dangerous and growing tendency to meddlesome legislation, interfering with individual liberty" (*Star* April 25, 1907, 8). Although this editorial primarily considered theater censorship, a week later the *Mail & Empire* sent a reporter undercover to investigate five-cent shows specifically. Of course, unlike the hundreds of nickelodeons in Chicago or New York, Toronto had only four theatoriums, all run by John Griffin. The newspaper saw no cause for concern, let alone censorship (*Mail & Empire* May 4, 1907). In contrast with antagonizing reformers, politicians, or the police, when Toronto newspaper reporters occasionally turned attention to picture shows, they usually verified some positive social value of the existing state of affairs. Unlike Staff Inspector Stephen, in charge of the morality department, who claimed late in 1908 there was "no lesson to learn" from the reportedly dire state of picture shows in New York City (*News* December 29, 1908) the *Star* (September 7, 1910) noted that it was "absolutely true" that local picture shows were under stricter censorship than the theaters. This attitude was in stark contrast to Montreal. The *Montreal Herald* (August 27, 1910) had just published the results of its own undercover survey of the moving picture business in Quebec, proclaiming it was "in a state of anarchy, paying no heed to Sunday observance, the $500 tax, the public safety, or decency" (p. 4). The *Star*'s only complaint for Toronto was that the entertainments were "not very instructive or elevating stuff," suggesting better use of "the poor man's" theater by showing more actualities of Canadian landscape, history, and industry.

Reporting on local filmgoing nonetheless contributed advice about how to improve the situation, making the lack of antagonism a reflection of the distinct way picture shows in Toronto were regulated. There was more cooperation among showmen, police, politicians, reformers, and the city's population at large, a theme well covered in previous chapters. The role journalism assumed in Toronto would correspondingly be different from other cities. In general, the journalistic survey of the scene of moviegoing mediated calls for clarity and improvement, demanding stronger, more transparent cooperation among those operating and regulating filmgoing. Any difference in the tone of press coverage in Toronto thus reflects differences in the organization of filmgoing in the city itself.

This chapter examines how the space of moviegoing in the city was mediated and mapped in newspaper pages. The circulation of reporting and promotion in newspapers is perhaps key to understanding how the movies became a communal, mass practice, as opposed to a merely prevalent or routine pastime. The gradual shift from local investigative journalism to promotional advertising reflected a change in who was assumed to be the subject of filmgoing; the shift was from a marginal audience (specifically distinct from newspaper readers) to a mass audience nominally including everyone. But why suppose that the relationship between film and journalism is distinct from showmanship or regulation? Why suppose that moviegoing as a social practice is inextricable from its mediation in newspapers, putting the emphasis on newspaper reading as part of showgoing? The supposition is that the space of filmgoing, of audiences, was embedded in mediated conceptualizations of neighborhood, city, region, nation, and mass culture more generally. If moviegoing was to become a mass activity, distinct audiences needed ways to understand their commonality. There had to be a discourse reshaping the approach to disparate theaters as part of a common pastime. Clearly this shared experience does not happen for specific films, barring exceptional blockbusters. This chapter uncovers a more abstract idea of moviegoing with the gradual introduction of a rhetoric of commonality among temporally and spatially separate audiences. The movies became an almost universal practice, with nearly everyone seeing the same films and participating in the same culture despite actually being separated by time, place, cost, and class. Centralized management and oversight facilitated this process, to be sure, as the previous chapters traced an emergent, broad social relevance for civic showmanship and bureaucratic regulation. But centralized management alone did not communicate that all films and all movie theaters provided a common product. Moviegoing needed to be explained, written about, promoted, and above all, advertised as a common product. No matter how numerous, individual theater buildings on city streets did not achieve this. Newspapers were key to such mediated interpretations, concisely tracing the emergence of a mass market and its organization of actually dispersed urban practices into an apparently common culture. They introduced the mass audience to itself.

Newspaper Pages as a Map of Urban Life

To recover the importance of the metropolitan press in reflecting and shaping the city at the time moving pictures and the mass market emerged, reviewing, albeit in a rudimentary fashion, key essays from the sociology of the University of Chicago is helpful: Robert E. Park's (1923) "The Natural History of the Newspaper," Ernest W. Burgess's (1925) "The Growth of the City," and Louis Wirth's (1938) "Urbanism as a Way of Life." Chicago sociology, which these essays in a sense paraphrase, remains a vital and thorough record of U.S. urban modernity, which had just taken shape in the early twentieth century (Bulmer 1984; Lindner 1996; Weber 2005). These essays contain theories of the historically situated American city, context for the period when moviegoing had just become an inescapable part of everyday urban life. In doing so, an interpretive theory emerges for the method of using newspapers to trace the emergence of the mass market.

Park's essay on "The Natural History of the Newspaper" was included in the Chicago School of sociology's principal text, *The City* (Park et al. 1925). Park, a journalist before becoming a sociologist, wrote an important outline of the social relations the newspaper encouraged: an integrator and educator of immigrants in the American city; an agent of sophistry, or sophistication at least, in the modern world; an orientation to the newsworthiness of the local; an opposition to political partisanship; either a way to recognize oneself or a flight from reality. A newspaper makes a city habitable, makes it feel local and coherent, makes vast metropolitan regions seem like sensible entities with knowable orders of place and histories. The emphasis on social integration as an explanation of the importance of the newspaper will resonate with urban sociologists. This is, after all, the textbook synopsis of the orientation of the Chicago School of Sociology and nearly a century of criticism against it. Indeed, the historical affinities and shared concerns of Chicago Sociology, progressive reform, professionalized policing, and popular journalism is well documented (Burgess 1923). Historicizing the moralistic context in which Chicago sociologists studied urban heterogeneity as a social problem is important. Nonetheless, their studies of social integration were embedded in lived experience and provided the topics that gave American sociology a distinctive focus on class and ethnicity, and especially race and gender (Bulmer 1997). What is only implicit in Park's essay is why it belongs in a textbook on how to study the city as a social object, a book where every other essay is more clearly relevant to urbanism, referencing in their titles neighborhoods, communities, mobility, or city life itself. That the essay is included implies that the natural history of the newspaper is as vital to *The City*, both the book and the place, as Ernest W. Burgess's more widely cited essay on "The Growth of the City," which offered the oft-cited classification of concentric zones as a way of seeing the city.

Burgess's model has been revised, tested, and criticized continually since its publication (Quinn 1940; Zukin 1991). Initially called into question as an empirical hypothesis, theoretical models such as Burgess's have since become criticized as rhetorical and active agents in the reshaping of space and social relations (Harris and Lewis 1998). With the zonal hypothesis more overt, abstract, and diagrammed, Park's equally theoretical elaboration of the role of the collective action of reading journalism and advertising has been left untested, unconsidered as a theory of urban space. One need not make too much of an effort to see the newspaper's sections as another way of zoning the city, of mapping its movements and possibilities and seeing the whole thing at once (Goist 1971). Park was careful to be somewhat skeptical of the efficacy of the newspaper, for example, noting its failed promise to reproduce the sociability of village gossip on a metropolitan scale. A newspaper might be composed to offer the possibility of seeing the whole city at once, but offered to whom and at what cost? Of course options are left off this menu by its editors and advertisers, and others exaggerated by puffery. If the press is an alternative way to map everyday urban life, it is as partial and inscribed with ideology as any statistical table or map.

Park does not provide a key to his half-toned map of the city, but Wirth's relatively straightforward definition of urbanism gives a standard to stake out a claim that reading the newspaper was a part of urbanism. Still discussing urbanism in the abstract, Louis Wirth's "Urbanism as a Way of Life," was overtly influenced by Georg Simmel's essay "The Metropolis an Mental Life" (Simmel 1950; Levine et al. 1976). Wirth starts by distinguishing a quantitative study of urbanism from his own; size and density alone do not describe the urban way of life. Only with the combination of places that are geographically larger, more populated, and culturally heterogeneous is the urban character accentuated. The heterogeneity is key, not only in terms of ethnicity and class but more important with the pace, variations, and rhythms of daily life found in the city. Going back to Simmel, the relentless change and variety in the city, overstimulating the senses, allows explanations for the reserve and blasé anonymity of urbanism. These are way of "immunizing" the self against the endless personal claims and expectations of others. Rationality itself, in the stylized form of sophistication, is the way that city dwellers make intelligible a potentially anonymous and transitory form of urban life, an imaginative and uniquely sociological definition of urban life that was briefly espoused by Weber as well as Simmel (Kemple 2005). Wirth mentions newspapers along with other mass media as a "leveling influence" in the city, one of many institutions that serve the needs of the average person by serving the largest mass of people. But here is a chance to apply his definition of urbanism (a rational way of immunizing the self against the claims of others) by focusing on the way the newspaper is created and distributed to mass readerships, rather than simply read and interpreted by particular readers. Consider how the edited stories, surrounded by advertising, organize and offer a planned life, styled from the fullest range of available, constantly seductive calls for attention in the city. In an exemplary way, through the newspaper the city becomes navigable for the middle class and at the same time is understood to make new places, new things, new people constantly accessible, but in a managed way. The managers, in a sense, are those whose interests pursue mass markets through readers, spectators, and consumers.

Yet, the appeal to those who comprise the mass is far from false consciousness. This is, finally, a point that Park (1923) makes clear when he writes, "reading, which was a luxury in the country, has become a necessity in the city. In the urban environment literacy is almost as much of a necessity as speech itself." He turns to the immigrant in the United States as the proof of newspaper reading's urban centrality, providing "a window looking out into the larger world outside the narrow circle of the immigrant community in which he has been compelled to live" (p. 274). As an example, then, the immigrant experience made clear that this is the function of newspapers for anyone. The urbanism indicated by the compulsion to read a paper, exemplified by people supposedly trapped in their locale, becomes a necessity especially for those urbanites who feel a need to know how they are living in narrow circles. Recalling Wirth and Simmel, the newspaper provides a means to know what is just outside the everyday for people who need to rationalize their place, to define themselves, to put order to the place where they live. In the North American city, especially as presented in newspapers, the order is supposed voluntary, self-selected, chosen from among an offered range.

This use of the newspaper as a menu of components fitting together to make up an urbane life and an urban self is far from the open debate inspired by the political press comprising the democratic public sphere (Habermas 1989). A cosmopolitan turn away from the political press to the popular press has been traced to attempts to avoid a tax on publishing opinion, a point Park did not miss writing in the 1920s (Park 1923 and 1927). He mentions, too, that the emergence of the mass press, the penny paper, accompanied by its new features of editorial independence and impartiality, became transfixed as part of the virtues of metropolitanism, not through the impartiality of liberal judgment but through the impartiality of the urban blasé. Recognizing that the public sphere of inclusive rational debate over ideas and ideals is not, or not only, what is laid out for consumption in the popular press is not difficult. Instead, the new ideal becomes a metropolitan lack of avowed ideals, an attention to the trivial, the superficial, the interesting, the human interest, and emotional turmoil of reporting of sports, entertainment, and wordplay, of all the innovations introduced to city life, commercial, bureaucratic, and technological. Walter Benjamin famously proposed such an emphasis on "room for play" as a form of critique, as his own method (Benjamin 1968; Hansen 2004). The newspaper as a menu of urban possibility, not so much a map charting every possibility as a synopsis of key diversions, is also akin to Michel de Certeau's operational concept of urban practice in everyday life. The "city" produces a space of its own, substitutes a range of options outside of traditions, and promotes a more universal, anonymous subject "walking in the city," clearly a companion to the more historicized figure of the flâneur (Certeau 1984; Frisby 2001). These qualities are even more cogently applied to the way a metropolitan newspaper interprets the city and offers it to a general readership. The newspaper is equally, if not more so, an advertiser of local products and services presented as opportunities rather than mere distractions.

The development of the modern metropolitan newspaper can be tracked in tandem with the advertising industry, from the earliest mercantile reports of shipping and trade news, to early ads for received dry goods, and to the lavish, full-page ads for department stores, theaters, patent medicines, and prepackaged foods (Johnston 2001; Laird 1998). Innovations in newspaper printing, in graphic and photo reproduction, and in news content and formats arise from the symbiotic relationship among larger readerships, increased advertising content, and expanding news content. As papers became more popular and more ads were purchased in them, a corresponding addition of written content was needed to keep a balance. The larger the paper became, the more formally organized its contents became to make sense of the volume of both news and ads. The line between promotional journalism and advertising has always been fluid, and the emergent entertainment, automotive, sports, travel, and women's sections of the paper were organized around ad sponsorship in those categories. The sections of the newspaper, the orderly organization of its content and advertising, emerged out of the necessity to make the ever-increasing size of the paper manageable and useful, especially in the United States with special Sunday editions that date to the 1880s and soon emphasized color and photographs (Baker and Brentano 2005). These Sunday editions from "great cities in America" were available in Toronto at newsstands such as John P. McKenna's, advertising in the *Telegram* in January 1890.

To summarize this characterization of the newspaper as a key instrument of urbanism, the main point is to link the composition of the paper to excitement with the idea of urban living in the abstract. The urbanism described is not meant to be a synthetic overview that combines coexisting habits and concerns but a more or less deliberate overall orientation to the possibility of the city for its inhabitants. The entire paper, all of its sections and features, encourages and facilitates a way of living in the city that specifically aims to understand the whole unwieldy and unmanageable sprawl, not as a burdensome task but as a skill and a challenge. Of course, this imagined experience translates the mass market into practice. Simmel and Wirth evoke urbanism and the mental life of the metropolis as a series of coping mechanisms, as if the city stands in the way of an enjoyable, pleasant daily life. Here, this model is strengthened by observing how mental life in the metropolis can be taken up as a practice of knowing the city as an insider. Perhaps the clearest explanation of how reading the newspaper encourages a particular way of organizing city living is how the entertainment section orders the practice of going out (Erenberg 1981; Nasaw 1993). Knowing what is on where and when is essential to the skillful and successful night out. People must be able to find out when and where to go accurately in a timely, easily legible and accessible way. Newspapers display the range of options, but their listings and advertising serve a dual role, both to seduce the urbanite to participate and to offer a degree of predictability in timing, location, and what to expect. The call for punctuality even in amusement highlights an important feature of urban living, one facilitated by wristwatches and ever-present clocks, bells, and whistles. The advertised display of all the city's amusements in one place implores the newspaper reader to take part in the city, to participate in publics, in audiences, crowds, and queues: waiting and anticipation are part of the excitement. The lists of showtimes and promotions remind readers daily to place themselves in the mix.

From Marginal Audience to Entertainment News

Newspaper journalism on early filmgoing in Toronto did not begin covering the movies in the way theorized above, presenting it as an exciting option in daily life. From 1907 to 1911, when filmgoing was mentioned at all, it was approached at a critical distance, explained for its sociological importance. While not quite in the same muckraking fashion as in Chicago or Montreal, journalists in Toronto at first also treated the early audience as outside the respectable everyday readership of literate, hard-working, middle- and upper-class daily readers. Journalism shifted from being investigative to being more promotional only as film advertising became a regular part of weekend editions after 1910. Sympathetic journalism and prominent advertising do not have to be oversimplified to an instrumental relation based in the financial transaction of showmen purchasing ad space.

Another factor is the time moviegoing took to become instantly understood and widely recognizable.

Just weeks after the flurry of reporting surrounding the broken balcony rail at the People's Theatre, the *News* introduced a more formal, weekly page of local entertainment news. Heavily illustrated with an elaborate banner, puff piece promotion was for the first time combined with local news about entertainment and its business deals. Also on the page was a weekly editorial column on amusement, "The Left Box," penned under the pseudonym Thespis, beginning October 10, 1908. Regular reports on the theater scene in Toronto and the expansion of the Griffin Amusement Company were already appearing in *Billboard* and *Variety*, distributed throughout North America. Thespis might have even been *Billboard* correspondent Joseph Gimson because several articles from the *News* appear almost verbatim in the U.S. magazine. The move from reprinting puff piece promotion to local investigative entertainment journalism made the audience itself an object of interest, such as Thespis's analysis of theater matineegoers. This still-exceptional local theater journalism about audiences in Toronto is as thoughtful, observant, and analytic as later well-known critical writers, such as Siegfried Kracauer (1995), on the same theme. Thespis wrote:

> No one came to learn: it was the fruitless craving for amusement, something that would kill time pleasanter than minding a baby or darning stockings, or shopping, or idling. Had the distraction so much desired been possible from reading a book, the theatre would have been empty. . . . Careless, good-natured, indiscriminate, indolent, and bored. . . . The folks with the least to do are always the busiest. (*News* December 5, 1908, 10)

On the periphery of the new entertainment journalism were occasional reports about the still-novel moving picture industry. A few months after the start of the *News'* column on music and drama, a story next to "The Left Box" set down some figures for the rise of the popular new picture shows and the effect they were having on business at the big playhouses. "Moving Pictures Injuring Theatres: To-day Canada Has 500 Picture Houses—Five Years Ago only 35 Existed—Business Is Booming" (*News* April 3, 1909). A follow-up article quantified the rising popularity through its profits, "One House $300 Weekly" (*News* April 24, 1909). Other articles responded to each new legal regulation of picture shows. The *Star*, for example, profiled police actions, citing how the officer responsible had harassed a show in the center of the city for displaying suggestive posters and the same class of films. "The place didn't last long after the official housecleaning was completed. It no longer exists now" (*Star* April 10, 1909, 8). This place forced to close was most likely the People's Theatre, especially because it surely had trouble recovering from the balcony rail accident. Based on all available sources, the Ward's only picture show is the only picture show to close around this time, and was thus probably this same cheap theater censorship policies shut down.

In fact, the Ward's audience was the first to grab the attention of journalists as well as police crackdowns. Aside from all the newspaper reports of the accident in 1908, the *News* actually covered the Jewish theater's opening night in 1907, and it ran occasional although not frequent articles from that point on. This is somewhat curious because only one theater existed in the Ward at a time, and the many other theatoriums on main streets opened and operated almost entirely without comment. A combination of circumstance, exoticism, singularity, and marginal location makes the Ward's audience the best-documented space of early moviegoing in Toronto. Unlike cities throughout the United States, the earliest theatoriums in Toronto were neither predominantly run by Jewish entrepreneurs nor aimed in any discernable way at Jewish or immigrant neighborhoods. Instead, as discussed earlier, the first Toronto picture shows were almost all operated by the older, Toronto-born Irish-Catholic John Griffin along the main shopping streets downtown. Audiences at these earliest theatoriums were rarely the subject of investigative journalism in local newspapers. The lack of attention comes at least in part from Griffin's reluctance to advertise. In contrast, when a small picture show opened in the Ward in 1907, it immediately caught the interest of a journalist.

The People's Theatre, the first permanent Jewish theater in Toronto, was converted from a small vacated synagogue on University Avenue at Elm Street. Charles Pasternak, a small-time real estate mogul who successfully bought properties in and around the Jewish-associated Ward, purchased the site and opened the theater. On Thursday evening, April 25, 1907, just as the issue of theater and film censorship was making headlines in Toronto, a reporter for the *News* attended the opening of the People's Theatre as an opportunity to look inside a moving picture show. The report was meant not as a generalization of the city's theatoriums; instead, circulating talk of regulating moving pictures might have made looking at the novel Jewish theater a topical story. The *News* reporter found much of interest at the People's Theatre, and the overall tone of the article was one of pleasant surprise. The subheadline stated the case plainly, "the audience combines freedom with pleasure to a remarkable degree." The curiosity and strangeness of the place was still overt, however, as the article began by proposing "some day, perhaps, some oriental historian may undertake to chronicle the story of the interesting Jewish building" (*News* April 26, 1907, 12). While the banners on the building promised a show of the 1904 films of the infamous Toronto fire that destroyed much of downtown, the reporter was disappointed to find these moving pictures absent from the program.

The cost was twenty-five cents downstairs and just fifteen cents upstairs, no seats reserved, and the box office operator automatically sold the more costly downstairs ticket to the reporter, "a Yellow pasteboard printed in Yiddish, which proved an effective passport." Paying to sit "down" turned out to be a relief because the gallery upstairs "was filled— even thronged" with women and children. "Down was the location of the aristocracy who came late, of course, and were clothed for social ceremonial. The young swain with his lady love here held sway." Good music, supplied by a piano and violin, continued all evening as "five or six little business lads" went around selling candies, fruit, and ice-cold drinks, "stopping neither for pictures or singer." The front of the gallery was the domain of women with children, while men, "in accord with Jewish custom, wore their hats, even those who 'had company.'" The article ends with the note that "there was little applause. The whole production was accepted most stoically and there was practically no demonstration," despite the moving pictures being "for the most part amorous and humorous." The detailed description of aspects thought particularly Jewish is striking, especially because selling snacks, sitting silently, and entire families attending together distinguished movies from theater in general. At this early stage, Jewishness, not moving pictures and not the class of the audience, helped comprehend a public place that welcomed children, hawked food, and where the audience showed only silent appreciation.

According to histories of Jewish theater in Toronto, the small size of a nonetheless linguistically and culturally diverse Jewish population doomed earlier attempts to establish Yiddish theaters (Speisman 1979, 1983). The People's Theatre took hold more strongly because Pasternak relied on moving pictures and American touring theater troupes, which were familiar to the larger numbers of more secular Yiddish-speaking Jews in Toronto without entirely alienating those who spoke other languages or were more religious. Perhaps harassed by police, never really recovering from the broken balcony rail accident, the People's Theatre on University Avenue remained open only another year before becoming the African Methodist Church. Early in 1909, the People's Theatre owners, Charles Pasternak now in partnership with Simon Rabinovitz, bought and began renovating another religious building in the Ward, the Agnes Street Methodist Church at the corner of Terauley Street, now Bay and Dundas Streets (*Building Permits* February 27, 1909). It opened with some fanfare and the great support of the Jewish community as the Lyric Theatre, most likely presenting some combination of touring or resident stock Yiddish theater or vaudeville (*News* May 8, 1909). Thespis noted its endorsement by a local Rabbi, uniquely sanctioned by religious leaders as an important force in the community (*News* May 22, 1909). But it seems Pasternak could not make it pay. After just a few months, it was leased to the Griffin Amusement Company and became its flagship theater. The Lyric, as Griffin's Agnes Street Theatre, could seat 1,400 patrons with its ornate proscenium and theater boxes flanking the stage, just what Griffin needed for his expansion into a small-time vaudeville chain. Although the arrangement was short-lived, for about a year the only theater in the Jewish-associated Ward was also the largest showhouse of the Griffin Amusement Company. It was also the first Griffin theater to advertise regularly, almost daily for five months in four of the six Toronto papers. There was still a problem. Although only a block away from downtown's Yonge Street, the theater was still in the Ward; and the public was unsure about just whom it was meant for. Was Griffin's Agnes Street Theatre primarily for the Jewish population of the Ward where it was located? Or because it advertised prominently and was twice as large as any other Griffin theater at that time, were the pictures and vaudeville at Griffin's Agnes Street Theatre meant for mainstream theatergoers? Was it Toronto's first movie palace?

In retrospect, judging the Agnes Street Theatre the city's first major movie house is tempting. Certainly Griffin treated it that way. However, in the dramatic page of the *News*, the location in the Ward trumped the entertainment offered. Shortly after Griffin's opened it, a profile appeared under the headline, "The Ward's Entertainment." As with articles about the earlier People's Theatre, even as a Griffin theater the focus was the strange audience and its neighborhood. The review explained how Toronto's "fifteen thousand Hebrews find amusement" by providing "a glance into the Agnes Street Theatre." The constant daily advertising in the papers had not yet convinced Thespis that the theater was meant for his own typical mainstream reader of the weekend dramatic news (*News* October 9, 1909). Although treating the Jewish-identified theater with the investigative techniques of exposé, the tone is nonetheless sympathetic rather than muckraking. The Ward's theater might have been out of the ordinary routine of the mainstream theatergoer, but it was not some scandalous site of social problems. The difference between the Agnes Street Theatre and the more refined stages of the city was presented instead as a matter of taste and class.

The review begins with an almost anthropological theory of the universal appeal of entertainment in its wildly diverse national forms before turning to the particularities of the theater in the Ward. The writer reminds the reader of the need to be tolerant of diversity. "It has been a notable feature of public and private amusement since the beginning that one man's pinch is another man's poison. Palates differ." Having argued for the taste of each age and nationality, the article then notes within Toronto "a division in the heart of the city containing fifteen thousand Hebrews, known in street parlance as the Ward," thus restating plainly the common-sense association of the Jewish subculture of the city with the area associated with them. This was exactly the confusion that guaranteed a degree of success for Griffin's Agnes Street Theatre as much as it ensured this picture playhouse remained marginalized. The article even admits that the audience was mixed and that the theater aimed "as much for the Gentile patronage as for that of the Yiddish quarter" (*News* October 9, 1909, 7). Ultimately, however mixed the audience might have been, the undeniable fact that it was indeed mixed made the theater "peculiarly the playground of the Hebrew people in this city." Before turning attention to that ethnic audience, the previous week's cheap vaudeville acts are held up to dramatic scrutiny. Why their cheapness or crassness fails as entertainment is never fully explained. Of a blackface comedian, the journalist concludes by mimicking the schtick, "Didn't his audience admit him to be funny? Yes, it didn't." The article then reviews the scenario of a comedic drama that made a middle-class wife her husband's slave driver while she "jogged off to teas, matinees, and school board sessions," but the journalist repeats the sexual innuendo of the conclusion as the husband asserts himself as master. "She took him at his word, and the curtain cut off the possible rest of the story." Other acts are rattled off without detail: impersonators, soprano-voiced popular songs, and the moving pictures. The investigation of the Jewish audience is confused with the crass humour of cheap vaudeville, taboo at the better class of vaudeville and melodrama theaters, reliably censored at the burlesque theaters, but here in the Ward staged without shame. The explicit purpose is to juxtapose the lack of aesthetic quality with the raw enthusiasm of the Jewish playhouse.

Finally, the *News* writer exclaims, "But the audience!" Reminding the reader of the price and policy of the picture show, "pay only 5 and 10 cents and stay as long or as short as you like," the article notes that entire Jewish families attend together, apparently unusual for audiences at the costly mainstream theaters. For the remainder of the article, the journalist lists numerous observations that fuse stereotypical Jewish appearance and behavior. In the gallery: curly heads and strong beards, mighty lungs and ready hearts, sharply intelligent to distinguish amusement gold from alloy. On the lower floor: prosperous, stout waists, glistening diamonds, fashionable Gentiles, and one humble, wistful man who "laughed and clapped his hands apologetically lest someone should see him." The sociological study of these details concludes with an invitation for curious, cosmopolitan Torontonians to witness the scene for themselves. "As a piece of unique study, not so much in its entertainment as its people, the meeting place of the amusement seekers of The Ward is worth a couple of Bohemian hours" (*News* October 9, 1909, 7). Here, finally, the purpose of investigating Jewish showgoing is stated explicitly: a voyeuristic local urban tourism for the adventurous public, no doubt the very same people interested in entertainment news and the astute opinions of Thespis. Drawing on the model of exoticism fairground midways provided, the articles described the site and the audience at Toronto's only theater in the Ward and made a spectacle out of the experience of attending the picture show rather than the pictures themselves. Some people attending the theater could distance themselves from the pleasure of the amusements and make the ethnic audience the entertainment.

This exoticism extended even to Griffin's vaudeville at the Agnes Street Theatre in 1909, at best mixing marginal with mainstream but not mass entertainment in itself. The moving pictures in Toronto late in 1909 were clearly still cheap entertainment, and the novel high-profile of Griffin Amusement Company's large new theater only reinforced its marginality through its location in the Ward. Ascertaining to what degree this audience was working class or even what proportion of it was actually Jewish is impossible. The more important point is to note how the largest picture playhouse in Toronto in 1909 was the only one in the Ward and the only one whose audience was observed with interest. Griffin's lease with Pasternak and Rabinovitch lasted only one season. Reverting to the name Lyric, the Ward's theater continued with Yiddish vaudeville until 1922 when it briefly housed a Chinese playhouse after a more substantial Jewish theater, the Standard, was built on Spadina Avenue. In 1910, Griffin's leased the Majestic Theatre as their main vaudeville house, now squarely downtown in a long-standing mainstream playhouse. Griffin's frustrating inability to shake the stigma of the Agnes Street Theatre might have even finally convinced him to swing strongly toward vaudeville and away from moving pictures as the main attraction. In retrospect, it was a fatal error because it left open the door for a first-run movie palace in Toronto, a lavish playhouse focused on the promotion of motion pictures.

Surveying the General Picture Show Audience

Although the earliest journalistic investigations looking at the moving picture audience began in the Ward, other more abstract surveys soon stepped back to look at moving pictures as a business phenomenon spreading rapidly throughout the city. These tended to be more concerned with easily listed regulations and easily quantified counts of the number of shows, seats, and thousands of people attending. Against the fascination with the enigmatic appeal of cheap amusements for supposedly ethnic and working-class audiences, there was thus a corresponding mystery in nailing down a measure of the popularity and profitability of the film business. The *Star* (May 22, 1909) surveyed the "fad" of moving pictures across the city with facts and figures. Eighteen shows were open with two more planned. The total capacity was about 3,000 seats and a daily attendance of up to 15,000 people. While the $50 cost of a license was noted, a question mark gave the only estimate of profits.

Unlike the more sociological question of how Toronto's 15,000 Jews found amusement, the *Star*'s only consideration of the audience was the estimated statistic of average daily attendance. In a sense, the alternative to undercover investigation was statistical abstraction. If the descriptive details of a Jewish audience in the Ward acted to objectify the practice of filmgoing and distance the newspaper reader from the event, then a general overview provided a different kind of distanced perspective. The distanced, measured calculation of the pros and cons of the picture show fad involved the newspaper reader in the debate over filmgoing rather than presenting a spectacle out of curiosity. At this point in 1909, the statistical and regulatory overview seems a more appropriate framework to consider the vast majority of the picture shows serving middle-class audiences of families outside the Ward.

Descriptions of mainstream moviegoing were soon written but continued to take a relatively abstract form, tending not to specify the ethnicity of the audience or which theatorium and neighborhood was involved. For the next few years, subsequent reviews combined, sometimes awkwardly, statistical overview and descriptions of shows to grasp the growing significance of moving picture shows. Shortly after the creation of the *Star Weekly* in May 1910, it ran a feature on Toronto's five-cent theaters, noting that the city now had thirty-five of them and giving an overview of a typical program. For this subject to be of interest, the entertainment was perhaps still outside common knowledge, although the *Star Weekly* was for the wider region and needed to assume the inexperience of people in rural areas, small towns, and what were already called the "suburbs." Still, whereas a year earlier the review of the Agnes Street Theatre juxtaposed its cheap entertainment against the hurrah of the audience, this time in 1910 the quality and appealing character of the entertainment was upfront. Combining a statistical summary with undercover investigative reporting, it was perhaps the first Toronto newspaper coverage to distinguish among genres of film stories and the various audiences and districts of the city that corresponded with them. "Downtown and near the centre of the city, the shows cater to a different audience. Here love stories abound" (*Star Weekly* May 14, 1910, 18).

The reporter managed to meet the singer of an amusing song to copy the lyrics, "too captivating to leave behind entirely. . . . The place was full of little boys and girls, and when the words of the chorus were thrown on the screen the audience joined in deliriously with the singer: . . . *Too many guys with too many eyes are making eyes at you.*" Although the risqué innuendo of the lyrics was questioned, the problem was cited as an outcome of the positive, inclusive social space that the cheap picture shows created, ably serving young and old, male and female, families and romantic couples courting. The caution was against young women's desire for romantic comedy, which might need to be reined in to accommodate the sensitive morals of the children. Having noticed that the claim, "We aim to please the ladies," was a common slide shown on the screen, the writer wrote that he hoped "it will not 'please the women' much longer for the sake of the children." The details of a romantic melodrama were written out to typify this type of moving picture plot, and early silent film acting was even noted for its novel technique. "Doomed to silence in the moving picture show, the young women in these stories express their feelings by beating madly on their bosoms. . . . Love with them is a violent exercise." The palpable glee of the children, however, seemed well worth it despite these concerns. "The youngsters who sat near me had a strong feeling of good will to each other, and even to their elders, who had come to share the evening's revelry" (*Star Weekly* May 14, 1910, 18).

After recounting the measures taken against the theatoriums in New York and Chicago, and the censorship system under negotiation in Toronto, the *Star Weekly*'s investigation could summarize "nothing [was] very seriously wrong with the Toronto theatoriums just at present." Reversing aspersions against darkened auditoriums, encouraging social evil among single young girls, the powerful stories of the picture shows were cast as softening the hard hearts of young boys. "In some of the downtown shows there is an element which looks rough. . . . Three hard-looking young specimens gazed . . . the pity and the beauty of it kept them quiet and with grave faces. It was hard to tell what they made of it, but at least they did not laugh, which may be considered a tribute to the moving picture." Overall, the article seems to conclude that amusement and storytelling, in whatever form, were an important civilizing force for all elements of the city. If moving pictures were a bit crudely acted and melodramatic in their exposition, their inexpensive price allowed everyone to take part; that collective participation seemed worth the crude theatrics.

In February 1911, with the debate over censorship and limitations on children's attendance at its peak, the *Star Weekly* again went undercover to profile the city's picture shows, concluding with the headline that the "idea that they are demoralizing (was) not borne out by investigation." Doling out the requisite statistical recap (the city now had forty-four of them, which mostly paid good dividends), the journalist still assumed the reader was unfamiliar with the picture show, asking rhetorically, "Have you ever been in one of these places? Perhaps not." For the benefit of the inexperienced, willfully ignorant reader, the article noted the price (most often a dime, not the nicknamed nickel), described the interior (a long and narrow transformed store, neatly decorated, very comfortable), even mentioned the darkness and told how recent projecting machines had perfected the clarity of the image and removed its flicker. The typical program consisted, according the article, of three or four pictured stories. "Some of these are perhaps 'silly,' but not more so than those enacted at the more pretentious playhouses" (*Star Weekly* February 25, 1911, 9).

The entertainment was rather infectious: "The writer has to confess that in at least one place he stayed longer than was absolutely necessary for the purpose of his investigation." Stating flatly that he witnessed nothing objectionable (to the contrary, he caught a picture version of an opera with a small orchestra accompaniment), the reporter directly confronted the allegations that moving pictures were a social problem. At this point in 1911, the overriding question was still an intense curiosity about the audience and what they were doing together in the dark:

> What sort of people compose the audience? Do some of them go there not to be entertained but for other reasons? Do loose women make use of the place? Do young men go to the nickel shows looking for evil adventure rather than to look at the pictures? The present investigator can only record his own experiences and observations. He doesn't look in the least like a private detective or a morality scout, yet in none of the places he visited did he come within range of an evil eye. (*Star Weekly* February 25, 1911, 9)

In no uncertain terms, the moving picture shows were described as ordinary, everyday amusement attended by ordinary, everyday people. Moving pictures were easily dismissed as a fad in 1909, but just two years later were sensibly presented as an important mass practice. "A few years ago when the picture show was a novelty, many people of excellent standing in the community used to make a night of it at these places for a lark or 'just to see what they were like.' Now the merely curious visitors are scarce and audiences are composed largely of regular patrons, to whose purse and taste the picture stories appeal." Again the differences between outlying and downtown shows and audiences were cited. Neighborhood shows were for families and children, whereas "downtown the crowds are most listless, more sophisticated; they don't applaud." Differences between afternoon, evening, and Saturday picture shows were vaguely noted in terms of the crowdedness, age, and proportion of women attending. Ultimately, the mark of respectability was rooted in the business organization. "Professional and business men have in several instances formed small companies to operate them. Naturally they seek to make their places decent and inviting." The worst that could be said was that the picture shows encouraged idleness. Against this stood the economic productivity recognized by financial investors. Although reformers continued to object to the entrepreneurial character of commercial amusements, journalism took the capitalist backing of the theatoriums as proof the pastime was becoming a big business fully integrated into the financial organization of the city.

All aspects of the picture show business were going mainstream, the technology, stories, audiences, and locations of Toronto picture shows, as well as the financial investments that helped operate them. A few months later, another *Star Weekly* (September 2, 1911) review of the nickel shows in Toronto encouraged newspaper readers to interpret the pictures as responding to a universal human interest, quantifying that explanation with the estimate that 50,000 people were drawn to attend the city's picture shows daily. Here, late in 1911, the audience has completely disappeared from the journalistic survey; the lengthy article deals entirely with explanations of the lessons learned from the typical genres of the picture stories. In just two years since the sociological curiosity over the enthusiasm of Jewish families at the Agnes Street Theatre, the repeated investigations of the *Star Weekly* now combined the perspectives of the audience, newspaper reader, and journalist into a type of universal subject of moviegoing assumed to be interested primarily in the featured stories. At least in Toronto, discernibly ethnic audiences were always the exception, but only as moviegoing became mainstream did this marginal audience stop standing in for the general appeal of moving pictures. The new work of the Ontario Board of Censors seems to have coincided with a growing consensus that filmgoing was not a fad but a new mainstream amusement. Also, just in these months in 1911, weekly advertising began for the first time, promoting film titles and stories in advance.

A key distinction existed between the journalistic and advertised presentation of filmgoing. Whether reporting in allegiance with the film industry, its opponents, or attempting to maintain a critical objectivity, journalism of filmgoing relied especially on statistics to argue the importance of the subject. This was also, however, true of promotion inside the film industry and advertising printed by the distributors. Before regular display advertising presented specific movie theaters and films by title as individuated sites for public consumption, newspaper journalism primarily acted to mediate understanding of the still-novel practice of filmgoing for readers that were assumed not to be filmgoers. The primary tools were detailed descriptions of the state of regulation and statistical measures of the industry, still rapidly expanding. Thus, even in a city such as Toronto, whose journalists were relatively sympathetic to filmgoing, the techniques of observation and reporting still could be interpreted as acting to mediate how mainstream readers were incorporated into the mass cultural practice of filmgoing. With advertising, a more direct

Figure 5.1. The Odeon in suburban Parkdale was one of more than fifty theaters to open in 1913 and 1914, bringing the city's total to nearly one hundred. 1558 Queen Street West. *ca.* 1914. (Photograph by J. V. Salmon, City of Toronto Archives, Fonds 1231, Item 758.)

relation emerged based more on the assumption that this relation was established.

Editorials in 1911 and 1912 grasped for the potential of cinema, persistently argued for the general elevation of moving pictures and lamented the "inadequate use of a magnificent invention" (*Star Weekly* September 7, 1912). Feature articles about audiences, and later film genres, were another approach to the same problem of understanding moving pictures in society. Already hinted at in the synopsis of early articles, an important device to track film's influence was the tabulation of growing profits and a count of the current number of theaters. Almost all feature stories give a count of picture shows in Toronto at the time: from eighteen shows in the *Star* article on May 22, 1909, and subsequently reported in *Star Weekly* articles as numbering thirty-five in May 1910, forty-four in February 1911, sixty in June 1912, sixty-five in June 1913, eighty-five in October 1913, to a maximum of eighty-nine in May 1914. After the total plateaus in 1914, such local statistics were rarely mentioned. On the other hand, that May 1914 article is entirely an exercise in estimating theater statistics for the city. The eighty-nine moving picture theaters were supposed as having an average of 400 seats each, providing two-thirds of the 53,000 theater seats in Toronto's ninety-seven theaters (*Star Weekly* May 2, 1914). The method of such estimations appears to be an amusement in itself, repeated about once a year.

The newspaper could turn the police force's licensing statistics into a puzzle for readers' fun. The game of guessing the annual box office revenues at theaters had an even longer history, always tinged with a hint of collective guilt at the lavish habits of Toronto's public (for example, *Star* September 14, 1907). Tens of thousands of dollars spent on entertainment had social and moral—not just economic—consequences. Toronto was supposedly the only city in North America to show a profit in the 1909–1910 season, but no box office figures exist to substantiate the claim, just the "happy" portraits of the city's seven theater managers (*News* April 9, 1910; April 23, 1910). Because these articles were always estimates rather than reports from the theater managers, they hardly stand the test of objective reports. The point was to hold up amassed figures to put the nickels, quarters, and dollars of individual tickets into their modern social context, implicitly explaining how each person's pleasure could collectively and statistically become an incredible mass medium. Late in 1912, one journalist's stab at estimating the city's annual box office revenue translated the quantity into a fantastic image, hypothetically using the city's ticket sales to cover the width of the streetcar tracks on Yonge Street with dollar bills ten miles all the way to suburban Thornhill (*Star Weekly* December 21, 1912).

Statistical measures were as important as regulatory measures for those business interests whose concern was the unimpeded growth of the picture show industry. One of the first articles drew on information the Dominion film exchange supplied, estimating 500 picture houses in Canada, 150 in Ontario, 65 in Montreal alone (*News* April 3, 1909). More to the point, careful management had to counter moral reformers who were keeping an equally attentive watch. Furthermore, getting this information reported in newspapers encouraged investment from local capitalists or shifted the business of small entrepreneurs from one distributor to another. All of the counts made of the local market serve as promotion of the industry in general, whether they come from actual police statistics or not. In May 1911, the Toronto picture machine operators' local of the International Association of Stage and Theatrical Employees presented a resolution to replace mere bureaucratic licensing with an examination by technical experts. The operators' representative presented to the *Globe* (May 8, 1911) evidence that seven fires had occurred in the previous two years in nonunion projection booths, whereas no unionized projectionists suffered fires in their theaters. Even the projectionists' union had the evidence of numbers to argue their trained, tested, skilled employees contributed to the success of the industry. This style of entertainment news, however, presented a general overview of an industry rather than direct encouragement to buy a ticket to a particular picture show. Such prompts to imagine going out were introduced for moving pictures only later. Once introduced, regular advertising for theaters playing specific films reflected a growing geographic and architectural hierarchy among picture shows. Even as filmgoing was becoming mainstream, was becoming a mass medium, a fine scale was forming that would set intricately differentiated prices, places, and times when films would be shown. In fact, the appearance that filmgoing was becoming a mass medium for the entire population depended exactly on subsuming these fine distinctions in the way people went to the movies under the umbrella of a generalized practice of going to the movies. A key step toward this situation was the opening of the Strand, a downtown movie palace that advertised its coming attractions in weekly newspapers.

The First First-Run Downtown Movie Palace

When Alfred and William Hawes opened the Garden Theatre in July 1910, they ran a small ad in just one newspaper, offering a free cold soft drink to summer patrons at the roof garden above the main auditorium. Sporadic ads followed, still only in the *Star*. Nonetheless, it seems the Garden quickly became the most prominent moving picture house in the city, at least judging from a description of the theater and its management in *Billboard*. Its success was certainly noticed by a chain in nearby Buffalo, which purchased it early in 1911 and installed Leon Brick as the new manager (*World* June 11, 1911). He increased the scale of ads, now in several papers, trumpeting the superior quality and high-class character of the orchestra, vaudeville, and moving pictures offered as "A Rendezvous for Particular People." American-style puffery and overstated advertising had arrived in Toronto via Buffalo, although under Brick's management the Garden Theatre seems to have lived up to the self-promoting accolades (*MPW* November 28, 1914, 1257). The key to the Garden's success was the opposite of Griffin's expansion beforehand, as Brick put the focus on motion pictures, making their proper showcasing a point of pride. An ad printed in the *Moving Picture World* even quoted an editorial in the *Star*, "there is about this theater, the management, the audience, and the arrangement alike, an air of refinement as unmistakable as it is rare, and which cannot fail to impress even the most casual visitor" (*MPW* June 28, 1913, 1395).

This style of presentation and promotion claimed motion pictures were a respectable, mainstream pastime. And yet these early ads for the Garden rarely mention in advance which film titles would play. Furthermore, its ads did not appear predictably every week or month, let alone daily. However successful the Garden Theatre was under Leon Brick's skilled showmanship, at just in excess of 600 seats it was still a modest neighborhood theater. Another team of Buffalo showmen, Mitchell Mark and Henry Brock, brought the movie palace to downtown Toronto when they secured a long-term lease for the old Shea's vaudeville theater on Yonge Street later in 1911. The Mark–Brock chain originated in Buffalo but became an early and predominant force in establishing moving pictures as a force that could displace theater and vaudeville as the entertainment for the masses, even on Broadway in New York. Here in Toronto in August 1911, their first "Strand" opened, three years before the Broadway Strand on Times Square. For several years the Strand was Toronto's premiere picture palace. A rare article about moving pictures in the white-collar *Globe* (April 18, 1914) later reviewed a series of children's educational films at the Strand. The writer seems dumbfounded by the ability of the picture show to hold its audience. "We sat beside a small boy. . . . 'Gee! This is some place,' he went on, looking around approvingly. 'I was never here before and I thought it was just an ordinary show' " (p. 11). It is easy to imagine middle-class mothers, white-collar workers, and other *Globe* readers expressing the same surprise with the Strand picture palace as the boy at the educational film show. This was no ordinary show.

Mark and Brock had a proper theater license for the Strand to permit stage acts and vaudeville, by then outlawed in smaller picture shows without an additional license and increased safety standards. But, the newly renovated and renamed theater was unmistakably pitched to the public as a picture theater, albeit in another league from the other fifty picture shows in town. The Strand advertised the titles of its films every week without fail in the *Star Weekly* and the Sunday *World*. The Kinetograph had been part of the Keith's vaudeville bill at Shea's for almost a decade, but its films were never named or reviewed with the stage acts. The moving pictures at Shea's were the proverbial "chasers" on the bill, week after week noted only as "all new pictures." Feature films were not an important part of Shea's Toronto theaters until 1915, and even then one of its two theaters kept a feature-film-free vaudeville show until 1926. Similarly, in 1909 Griffin's Agnes Street Theatre did not name its film titles despite daily advertising, and from 1910 Griffin's Majestic billed its films only as "The Majesticograph." Because it was the old Shea's theater, film had long been part of quality entertainment at the Strand, but for the first time the balance shifted to spotlight the pictures as the stage entertainment became supporting acts. Other picture shows offered the same entertainment as Mark–Brock; some theaters, such as the Garden, might have surpassed it in quality. The difference was regular weekly advertising, the same size and as well-illustrated as theater ads. More than the building itself, the Strand's advertising shifted the spatial organization of moviegoing toward a hierarchy favoring large picture palaces downtown. In 1906 and 1907, the early Griffin's theatoriums had existed almost anonymously downtown, certainly no competition against the large playhouses. And it seemed from 1908 to 1911 that filmgoing would be a popular practice associated with residential neighborhoods, practically domestic, the entertainment equivalent of corner stores. Until the Strand opened in 1911, downtown was just one picturegoing neighborhood among many.

The Strand needed to advertise to fill the house for practical reasons. As large as a vaudeville theater, in 1911 twice the size of any other picture show, it was the southernmost theater on Yonge Street, slightly outside the normal path for department store shoppers and audiences at smaller shows. More important was the need to distinguish itself from the small theatoriums and to mark a departure from the status quo of moviegoing. One possible explanation is that the new use of newspaper advertising was caused by the emergence of feature films as the focus of an entire evening's entertainment. But, in its first two years, the Strand program contained the same General Film Company single-reel films as anywhere else, despite the fact that each week only one short film was "featured" in the ad. Mentioning multiple-reel lengths began only in September 1912, and until well into 1913 almost all the films at the Strand were ordinary titles that would soon appear at neighborhood theatoriums with no hurrah. Certainly the name recognition of stars, directors, and studios were all gaining prominence; but the new policy at the Strand of promoting whatever was playing weekly with nearly equal stature was instituted right from its opening. Altogether, the advertising for the Strand introduced to Toronto a new class of filmgoing, one where the audience would know what was playing ahead of time and travel to the theater with the titles and stories of the films already in mind. This was an entirely new way of entering the picture show. The Strand's ads in weekend papers framed this particular downtown picture show as a peer of the so-called "legitimate" stage theaters. Audiences could antici-pate their viewing and look forward to experiencing what newspapers described. Before the Strand, advertising a particular film title was re-served for extraordinary events only. In 1897 ads leading up to the Veriscope pictures of the Corbett–Fitzsimmons prizefight sparked an at-tempt to ban them. For theatoriums, in October 1907 both Applegath's Crystal Palace and Griffin's Hippodrome played *The Passion Play* with large display ads in several daily papers. The Strand instead promoted its movies indiscriminately, hyping whatever was playing that week with the same size and style ad.

This actually took a few months to settle into such a "branded" pattern of promotion. The first ad on August 19, 1911, states only a general description of the theater address, prices, and opening date with-out mentioning film titles beyond the curiously flowery phrase "exclusive sunlight-shadow plays and novelties." Toward a standardized format, in October 1911 the "Strand Weekly" branded the short "actualities" of the week, not yet quite a newsreel in the sense of current events but called an "animated newspaper" nonetheless. The label "Strand Weekly" turned the weekly nonfiction films into a moving picture version of the *Star Weekly* and Sunday *World* where the Strand ads were printed. Next came the strategy of selecting a single film from the weekly General Film roster and advertising it as the feature, usually with a photo of a scene. At first, these featured films were neither longer, multiple-reel titles nor even always fiction films. They were features simply because the advertising featured them. The Strand style was finally set with a special illustrated border in February 1912. The first border showed a world of human motion: cowboys and soldiers on horseback, camels, rickshaws, steamers and sailboats, trains, automobiles, aeroplanes, hot air balloons—every-thing but a crowded streetcar. This elaborate motif on motion might have struck an unfortunately masculine or juvenile tone with its panoply of adventure. After just a month, a more clearly themed and sparsely illustrated border presented four sides to a show at the Strand: drama (on top, with a locomotive, a steamship, and a fencing duel); comedy (at left, with a the iconic laughing mask, a puppet, a clown, and an aeroplane); music (at right, with various instruments and an automobile); and art (at bottom, showing a serene courtly pool surrounded by mountainous countryside). The Strand advertising artists struck a balance by using generic categories such as drama and comedy while retaining the most thrilling and compelling of modern icons: planes, trains, and automobiles. The regular, weekly hype of whatever was playing was an innovation of showmanship that acted to define the geographic, cultural, and social relation of filmgoing to modern, urban life.

Newspaper Ads Cure "Poster-itis"

Newspaper ads largely displaced more localized promotion. Indeed, one of the reasons urban nickelodeons and theatoriums were absent from newspapers was the widespread use of handbills, programs, gramophones, posters, electric signs, and ornamental façades. Each of these promotional tools remains in some form today. But they all happen on the sidewalk outside a theater. City bylaws cracked down on littering and noise, school trustees targeted coupons and handbills passed out to children, and reformers and censors attacked posters as well as film content. In general, the transition from nickel show to picture palace required tempering and refining this sidewalk ballyhoo. Only the visual spectacle of electric signs and ornamental theater façades grew more sensational as cinemas became larger and moviegoing became mainstream.

The first of these to get curtailed was "barking" on the sidewalks outside theaters, a practice copied from the carnival and exhibition midway although often limited to a simple gramophone playing music. Within a few months of the first nickelodeon opening in Chicago, one picture show's phonograph ballyhoo was suppressed by a judge because it disturbed his own court's proceedings (*Chicago Tribune* March 29, 1906). In Toronto from at least 1908, police followed up noise complaints about theatorium barking, asking managers to cease the practice (*LCC* March 19, 1908, 965). Next came crackdowns on distributing handbills, flyers, and special coupons on crowded city streets and especially at schoolyards. Handbills offered on the street were a sign that film showmanship was still operating without much preparation. Also, because the vast majority of the handbills probably ended up in the trash almost immediately, the police could zero in on them as a cause of litter, especially when showmen were targeting unsupervised children as a potential audience. Board of

Education Inspector Hughes had reported the menace of flyers handed out to schoolchildren, prompting Chief Grasett to instruct officers to treat distributing handbills as littering and loitering nuisances (*LCC* March 11, 1911, 746). Writing to *Moving Picture World* in 1913, George Perry at the U-Kum Theatre in Toronto reported he had turned to delivering his handbills "from house to house once to twice a week in quantities of 1,500 to 2,500. . . . While the cost is considerable," for this blanket door-to-door delivery, "the returns are greater and much better impression is created" (*MPW* August 16, 1913, 736).

Sidewalk posters were not just subject to official censorship; show-men aiming for an upwardly mobile audience restrained the quantity of posters to demonstrate a classy show. In *Moving Picture World* the purpose of posters was reconsidered, and "poster-itis" was seen as a disease, a sign of tawdry, cheap amusements that would never attract refined crowds and reap the profits that came from demonstrating attention to civilized, cultured entertainment (*MPW* June 11, 1910, 987). Thus, storefront the-aters cluttered with posters were disparaged not just for the sensational, perhaps immoral, display of thrills, dangers, and crime scenes that moves toward censorship had tempered (*News* September 22, 1908). As late as 1912, the front-page cartoon of *Jack Canuck* (July 20, 1912) showed the provincial film censors adjudicating a poster, not a film. A theater whose entrance was filled with posters simply betrayed the immaturity of the early years of the nickelodeon when people still had to be taught what to expect and encouraged and prodded into entering. Clear, streamlined passageways from the sidewalk to the auditorium in part showed that people had come to know what to do and what to expect when entering a theater. When Perry wrote of his work at the U-Kum, he also proudly sent in a photo of his theater entrance and noted he had "discarded the poster . . . the seats thus vacated have been taken by the steadily growing automobile trade and by a class who never visited the picture show on account of its cheap appearance" (*MPW* August 16, 1913, 736). Muting the visual "noise" of posters cluttering the sidewalk in front of a picture show was also implicitly part of keeping entrances and exits from theaters unobstructed, a matter of urgent fire safety. Patrolling these regulations was a primary activity of everyday policing of picture theaters by police on patrol, including controlling crowds lined up to purchase tickets or waiting to go inside. On the other hand, this violation for crowding sidewalks could be used to advertise the popularity of a theater (*World* July 25, 1915). The shift away from the sidewalk coincides with the increasing regularity of newspaper advertising.

Aesthetic restraint also applied to the façade of the building itself. Classical architectural motifs had been part of theatorium facades in

Figure 5.2. Poster-itis in the heart of the city at the Red Mill (formerly Griffin's Theatorium.) 183 Yonge Street. *ca.* 1913. (Photograph by J. V. Salmon, City of Toronto Archives, Fonds 1231, Item 638.)

Toronto since 1906, trumpeting angels and cherubs, laurel wreaths, a crest with a "G" for Griffin. These early ornaments tacked on the fronts of existing stores were gaudy compared to the simple brickwork and plain terra cotta expanses of the purpose-built neighborhood movie theaters that followed. Although lavishly decorated nickelodeon fronts were probably the norm elsewhere, at least in Protestant, morally conservative Toronto, established meant refined, and refined meant plain. Even larger theaters that endured as neighborhood institutions for decades, such as the Garden on College Street, the Odeon in Parkdale, and the York in Yorkville, had street fronts as plain as neighboring shops. Sensational posters on sandwich boards laid out on sidewalks and hung as banners from the recessed archways of theatoriums were soon confined to display cases, and diminished in proportion to the expanding heights of electric signs and widths of façades.

If the point of promotion was heightening anticipation for movies, building up desire and expectation for the pleasure of going, then the advance publicity of the newspaper was practically required, despite the cost to local exhibitors. To anticipate and to expect is a disciplined, mannered form of desire; and attending films with anticipation and expectation implies more than just an accumulation of excitement. Planning, scheduling, waiting, and delay became part of filmgoing with the introduction of newspaper advertising as well. Without assuming that historical audiences were necessarily changing their everyday decisions, advance promotion mediated through the daily news was altogether a sign that filmgoing was a refined, established pastime. Compared to displaying lurid posters, distributing stacks of handbills, and barking out loud at passersby, newspaper advertising showed that moviegoing was no longer appealing to immature appetites for instant gratification. Posters were tolerated if censored; but the interaction with strangers required to hand out flyers or vocally "bark" invitations to "step right in" were treated as outright nuisances. If the trend in general was thus toward visual means of promotion instead of direct interaction with crowds and strangers, then newspaper advertising was the pinnacle of modern, mediated promotion.

Representing Showmanship Collectively in Advertising

The *Star Weekly* from its start in 1910 included regular feature stories on the local development of filmgoing as business and social endeavors. It also included news about innovations in film applications and profiles of how sports teams, universities, scientists, and educators used films. It did not, however, include any more than occasional ads for picture theaters, except for the downtown Mark–Brock Strand. In February and March 1913, the paper included a series of full-page ads for the General Film Company, the official distributors of "licensed" Edison Trust films. These impressive and entirely exceptional ads culminated on March 8, 1913, with a full page of film news, almost definitely supplied by the General Film Company, with only one article having local details inserted. To counter this, in April the Allens' Canadian Universal Film Company, the independent distributor, took out a half-page ad in the *Star Weekly* listing twenty-four mostly small neighborhood theaters exhibiting its films. In all of the General Film Company ads from the previous months, only major downtown theaters were mentioned by name, whereas the Universal ad listed the names and addresses of its numerous neighborhood theaters in all parts of the city. In Toronto, then, collecting the field of small shows under a single banner was introduced by film distributors, affiliated with U.S. studios. An alternative, however, had already begun in other cities, a sort of self-organization on the part of showmen in conjunction with the newspaper. It came to Toronto in the Sunday *World* in June 1913.

On its own, the weekly ad for the Strand would not gather the showmanship of dozens of competing picture shows into a mass practice, a way of gathering "everyone" together regardless of which theater was attended or which film was seen. Collective advertising, gathering independent showmen under the same banner "Motion Pictures," soon began to demonstrate this amassing character of filmgoing. This innovation of a Sunday paper "Motion Pictures" page in fact excluded the Strand, whose ads continued alongside ads for established stage theaters. Introduced by the Sunday *World*, the collective banner was meant for small picture shows, most advertising here for the first time. In many Sunday editions of newspapers throughout the United States at the time, including in the nearby *Buffalo Times*, special pages featuring motion pictures were introducing a way for small, neighborhood theaters to advertise regularly. Beginning June 8, 1913, the *Sunday World* began a "Photo Plays and Players" page to complement what were at the time the city's most extensive and best-illustrated Stage and Vaudeville pages. Soon changing the banner to "Motion Pictures," the page included ads for up to twenty theatoriums at a time. The editorial content profiled those neighborhood picture theaters but also included news on film stars and directors, upcoming films and industry gossip, and occasional feature stories on the exhibition business in Toronto. There were ads from film exchanges and distributors, an ad for the projectionists' union, ads for new equipment, news on fire safety and construction, and regular columns on the politics and protocols of theater licensing and censorship. For the first year, the numerous ads for movie theaters did not showcase their films or mention featured titles or movie stars. Instead, the theater itself was showcased, its construction, decoration, ventilation, its refined and select patronage, and more simply its neighborhood location.

The special film page in the Sunday *World* demonstrated how the movies were still largely a domestic or at least neighborhood practice. In contrast with the Strand movie palace ad located amongst the stage and vaudeville pages, the weekly movies page advertised and profiled smaller, independent theaters with little differentiation among them beyond their location. Running weekly for three years, about seventy out of Toronto's ninety movie theaters of the period advertised in the Sunday *World* at least once. Participating theaters varied greatly each week. Half of those included appear only once or twice, usually for their grand openings. Only nine theaters advertised more than one-third of the time; and although these are predictably the largest and most costly movie theaters in the city, they span many neighborhoods and are not centered downtown. Except for the fact that the most costly and largest neighborhood theaters were regularly included (the Beaver, Madison, and Park), there does not seem to be any pattern behind which showmen used the page or not. The dozen theaters advertised and profiled on the first page in

June were from ten neighborhoods, only one of which was downtown. At the maximum twenty theaters, theatoriums from eleven neighborhoods were included, again only one from downtown. The geographic dispersion of the theaters in the Sunday *World* page is so striking that it might even have been deliberate; but no information on who managed, edited, or solicited the ads was printed. Among those present and absent are both older and brand-new theaters, both small storefront theaters with fewer than 200 seats and large theaters with more than 800 seats, both those that ended up affiliated with chains in the coming decade and those that remained independent, both those that were short-lived and those that stayed open into the 1950s and beyond.

In May 1916, the *World* reinvented this film news feature as a daily motion picture column with news and a theater list. This lasted only until August before reverting to a general section for stage, vaudeville, cinema, and other leisure activities indiscriminately. Another newspaper, the *News*, had begun late in 1915 to publish regular columns under the banner, "News from Screenland." In March 1918, the *News* began running a weekly, later daily, list of film shows in the city until the paper went bankrupt in 1919. When the *Star Weekly* finally introduced a banner "For the Followers of the Films" for its film news in September 1914, it was not a new way of organizing showmanship and promotion, but merely a label for the film news that it had long printed, still without significant advertising from small shows. In retrospect, these innovative motion picture advertising features seem to be attempts by the two least successful of Toronto's newspapers to offer something unique that was absent from the four more prominent, more profitable papers. By the mid-1920s both the *World* and the *News* had folded, while the other four daily papers continue in some form today. But whatever the relation to the finances of the newspaper, these advertising features are open, collective representations of filmgoing as an important leisure activity that was part of the everyday life of the entire city.

The Sunday motion pictures feature was a continental phenomenon in these years and may have been a loosely organized outgrowth of the Motion Picture Exhibitors' League of America, organized nationally and in most states from 1911 for several years (*MPW* July 22, 1911, 111). An exceptionally early example of collectively featuring picture theaters was printed in the *St. Louis Republic* for a single week in February 1910. When newspaper journalism was still seen by the film trade press as a hostile enemy, this effort of collective showmanship merited prominent congratulations in *Moving Picture World* and was reproduced in full for showmen across the continent to see (*MPW* February 26, 1910, 289, 295). These same weeks, articles by S. L. "Roxy" Rothaphel on the "dignity" and "art" of the "profession" of showmanship ran in the trade journal as well (*MPW* February 12, 1910, 202; February 26, 1911, 289). Although he would be the most famous film showman for decades to come, Roxy's name-brand hoopla would never apply to cooperation among competitors in a local market (Hall 1966).

Despite the promise of the St. Louis example, a more enduring weekly pictures page would take another two years to debut in a metropolitan Sunday newspaper in the *Cleveland Sunday Leader* beginning in November 1911; it remained a noteworthy exception until 1913 (Abel 2006, 220). The feature mirrored the film trade papers such as *Moving Picture World*, condensed to a single newspaper page, except that the Sunday picture page presented news about the film industry as of interest to the general newspaper-reading public. Scattered articles in Toronto newspapers, as early as 1909, took up the topicality of moviegoing as part of the map of modern culture that newspapers provided. The *Cleveland Leader* innovation was to present this in combination with advertising and promotion and make it a predictable, weekly feature. A variation soon came when the *Philadelphia Evening Times* began a small daily column and insert of ads in July 1912. Even with Cleveland setting a significant precedent, adopting "Motion Picture" feature pages in metropolitan Sunday newspapers took more than a year to spread, even to nearby Buffalo— while Detroit and Cincinnati newspapers seem not to have taken up the model at all. Chicago newspapers developed an entirely different model slightly later.

Cooperation between showmen and newspapers took time to replace muckraking articles, which continued to profile the harmful moral effects and lack of fire safety precautions in picture shows. In the very same issue that the Cleveland innovation was noted in the *Moving Picture World*, a situation in Minneapolis was outlined in detail. The *Minneapolis Tribune* published a feature article claiming unilaterally that all forty-seven picture shows in the city were "unsafe or unsanitary," and the exhibitors' league had formed a committee to investigate the issue, lobby against the newspaper, and meet with city aldermen to preempt an escalation of the paper's exposé into a crisis (*MPW* November 25, 1911, 631). Despite this antagonism, the *Tribune* ironically later brought a Sunday pictures page to Minneapolis in March 1913, just a week before the *Buffalo Sunday Times* introduced a page of "Motion Picture News." Coincidence or fad, similar pages had just begun in newspapers such as the *Milwaukee Sentinel*, the *Indianapolis Sun*, and in both the *Pittsburgh Leader* and the *Pittsburgh Post*. In Canada, the *Vancouver World* began the feature in January 1913. In all these cities, the special moving picture pages often included film news from the showmen's perspective. Censorship, overly strict policing, and other hardships became the subject of articles among the weekly movie advertising.

By the time Toronto showmen organized a protective association and the motion pictures feature page of the Sunday *World* appeared in June 1913, the more drastic measures of censorship and limitations and children's attendance had already been instituted fully in Ontario. Although a handful of stories are found in the Toronto page about legislative issues, they are phrased in terms of fairness, not strident lobbying. One turns attention to licensing disparities among Ontario cities (*World* June 8, 1913), while an article about children's attendance mentions how some Toronto managers are "entirely in agreement with the government," although the majority ask why children should not go alone if the government censors are doing such a good job (*World* September 21, 1913). Instead of positioning local showmanship against governance, the Toronto picture page, as is shown again and again for Toronto's showmen in general, highlighted the integration of filmgoing into local traditions. An article tells of King George's installation of a moving picture theater in Buckingham Palace (*World* June 29, 1913); another, the story of how an Englishman made the first motion picture (*World* August 10, 1913). There was news of one theater's competition quizzing picturegoers' knowledge of the photo players while the newspaper itself rewarded the best essays about photo plays and called for children to send in thoughtful accounts of their filmgoing habits (*World* September 21, 1913). Still, the many theaters advertising collectively in the Sunday *World* at first strongly distinguished one from the other by appealing to the special advantages and neighborhood character of each place. While the collective advertising of the motion pictures page gathered separate spaces under the umbrella of similar promotion, a stronger move toward making film a mass medium came early in 1914. An innovative type of film genre was introduced that would have dozens of separate picture shows throughout Ontario and all over North America collectively present the same film at the same time.

Reading Everyone into the Audience: Serial-Queen Heroines

Sunday motion picture pages demonstrated moviegoing had taken on a respectable place in society, but the variety of ads and articles emphasized differences among separate audiences rather than concretely claiming everyone was doing the same activity. Soon the serial film and its fictionalized story accompaniment in weekend newspapers overtly encouraged an entire continent to "see" the same movie together, even as it solidified a spatial and temporal hierarchy among increasingly distinct

theaters. In September 1912, the Strand Theatre and its weekly advertising in the *Star Weekly* began its second year. The section of the paper in
which the ads appeared had a new title: the "Women's Section." Although
no one component was an innovation, the new banner solidified the
context. Society and fashion columns were grouped with serial fiction
stories, along with suffragette news and articles considering debates over
proper feminine conduct as well as the dramatic pages where the Strand
ad appeared. Coincidently, the Strand featured a special series of films,
the *What Happened to Mary?* series starring Mary Fuller. The first ad
notes that the *What Happened to Mary?* stories appear in print in McClure's
Ladies World magazine (ad in *Star Weekly* October 12, 1912). This was the
prototype for the "serial queen" drama, a fad that acted to bring a regular,
literate, enthusiastic audience firmly to the picture theater in the years
before longer feature films were the norm. The key audience members
were middle-class mothers and working women who were already the
implied readers of serial fiction and would appreciate the mass literary
form of the serial story. The picture versions incorporated exactly those
thrilling genres that had long been the fulcrum in the debate about the
need for film censorship: modern thrills and dangers, crime and suspense,
sordid romantic melodrama.

Putting these elements in the context of a serial drama whose hero-
ine was acted by a famous movie star was, in a sense, merely a film version
of the stage melodrama that was so popular in the decade before this
(Singer 2001). The genius move was to integrate the films with the serial
fiction of women's magazines and weekend newspaper editions. Pretty
much the same constituency that had been organizing against the commercial, exploitative sensational film industry was now made directly part
of the audience through intertextual fiction versions of films. Its elements
of success were regular episodes, prominent advertising in national magazines and weekend newspaper editions, combined with written story versions so that each new film could be read ahead of time and the film
version eagerly sought out in theaters. The promotional strategies were
explicitly directed toward the widespread circulation in multiple forms of
a single "text." The key innovation was regular advertising and story
versions in respectable women's or family mass circulation publications.

Written summaries of the Strand's weekly film features had earlier
been printed in the *Star Weekly* or the Sunday *World* alongside the advertising. Precedent had been set for linking a written version of a film to
its promotion ahead of time. A newspaper reader attending the Strand
after reading its ad would most likely have already read a description of
the film as well. By February 1913, just after the weekly Strand ads began
to note the number of reels or "parts" of the upcoming feature, these

written synopses were also divided into matching parts like chapters. The serial queen story-film brought this phenomenon of promoting local first-run movie palaces to all picture shows—and on a continental scale. The serial story-film made filmgoing a truly mass medium by expanding the promotional logic of theaters such as the Strand downtown in Toronto into a transnational film experience. The promotion of film serials and special movie palaces differed in one key respect, although the difference was mutually beneficial. Elite theater sites depended on distinguishing themselves from other movie theaters. The timing that separated first-run from second- and subsequent-runs of each film title cast each theater site into a particular place in a strict hierarchy, with first-run downtown like the Strand at the top. This differentiated among theater types and spaces, despite the same films being sooner or later shown in theaters everywhere. Each part of a serial film was distributed in the same careful hierarchy of runs. First-run palaces played the first episode first to maximal hype and support of newspaper publicity. But because serial films continued for months, smaller, peripheral, and cheaper subsequent-run theaters could begin showing the series while later episodes were playing first-run downtown. Serial films thus cast the illusion that everyone was watching part of the same film, whether it was the story version in a newspaper or one of the numerous episodes. Yet, a strict hierarchy actually existed of where audiences or readers could begin the first episode of the story. The mismatch of explicit and implicit distinctions and uniformities allowed filmgoing, in the abstract, to be enjoyed as a mass medium.

The early few serial story-films (not yet exactly fitting the serial queen type) had been affiliated with McClure's continentally distributed magazines. At the beginning of 1914, *The Adventures of Kathlyn* brought the story tie-ins to the local level in weekend newspapers throughout the United States, beginning and syndicated through the *Chicago Sunday Tribune*. The most famous of the serials, *The Perils of Pauline*, was prominently syndicated nationally through the chain of Hearst newspapers (Ramsaye 1986, 652–69). Despite the appearance of a more localized outlet for the stories in metropolitan newspapers, the distribution was no less centralized or national in scope than the *Ladies' World* had been for *What Happened to Mary?* in 1912. In Toronto, the *Star Weekly* picked up many of these early syndicated stories, beginning in January 1914 with *The Adventures of Kathlyn* after a couple of weeks' advance promotion. As with the earlier serials, the Strand ads promoted its first-run status showing *Kathlyn*. Unlike the earlier serials, however, the Strand's own ad was not the only place to find out where the films were showing. The *Star Weekly* printed lists of where to see the *Kathlyn* episodes. New locations were added to the bottom of the list each week as peripheral theaters began with the first episode over the twenty-six weeks of the serial story. Twenty-five theaters in Toronto were cited in the newspaper as playing *Kathlyn*. The theaters were big and small and located in all parts of the city; the paper even included a note that the films were playing in the smaller cities of Hamilton and Galt.

In its mature form, the serial story-film lasted at least fifteen episodes, so that it took four months or more to follow the drama to the end. If all of the film episodes, all of the fiction installments, and the nationally syndicated promotion in key magazines and newspapers were considered altogether to comprise a single film text, then by 1914 and 1915, a significant part of the filmgoing audience of North America would have been aware that the film they were watching was in some form being seen by almost everyone else, everywhere else. A good local indication that this innovation was of an entirely different character and status than earlier moviegoing in Toronto came with the second serial film-story; *Lucille Love, the Girl of Mystery* began in the *Globe* in April 1914. This was Toronto's firmly white-collar, serious newspaper, which had given attention to films beforehand only in legislative reports about new regulation. It was the *Globe*'s only dabbling in film promotion, an exception to the rule. The third to appear, again in the *Star Weekly*, was *The Million Dollar Mystery*. More than one-third of Toronto's theaters played it, as the newspaper listed thirty-three participating theaters in the city. This time mention was also made of fully thirty-eight theaters throughout the rest of Ontario, including at least ten in the Griffin's chain, but all followed far behind the first-run Strand downtown. By August 1914, the Sunday *World* joined the fad with *The Trey of Hearts*. For a few weeks in February 1915, the *Star Weekly* was running three serial stories concurrently. In April 1915, even the *News* found a way to compete by running the serial *Who Pays?* in small, daily installments. However, the gimmick for *Who Pays?* was having autonomous stories last only a week, in contrast to the "long tedious serial," to quote its ad (*News* April 10, 1915). By the end of 1916, the serial craze had pretty much run its course, although Chicago papers continue with serials a bit longer. In Toronto, a final serial in the *Star Weekly* ran in the fall of 1915. The last in the Sunday *World* began late in 1916.

Without the printed story versions, film serials continued for decades with great success, developing into a cliffhanger genre with a visual grammar and clichés all of its own. The appeal of reading along in the newspaper was short-lived; in retrospect, it served primarily to boost female and lower-class readership for newspapers such as the *Chicago Tribune*, which had been missing that demographic. The sensationalist Hearst newspapers such as the *Chicago Examiner*, on the other hand, are

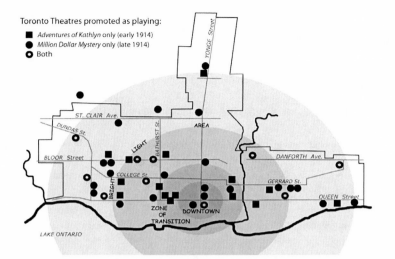

Figure 5.3. In the six-month lag between the first and second movie serials in the *Star Weekly*, a suburban shift has occurred, and the Strand's first-run status downtown is reinforced by nearby second-run competition. (City Limits in 1914 with zones evoking Burgess's "The Growth of the City.")

said not to have picked up much new circulation from serial fiction tie-ins (Ramsaye 1986, 660–62; Wilinsky 2000). Although the phenomenon was short-lived, its importance in constructing the appearance of a universal audience for a mass medium cannot be underestimated. In just two years, the sixteen serial film-stories that appeared in Toronto newspapers were advertised as showing in eighty-six picture theaters in the city, all but a few of those open at the time. Perhaps more important, 124 picture theaters in the rest of Ontario were noted in Toronto newspapers, too, as many as one-third of those theaters then open. Certainly, the idea was to expand the circulation of the weekend newspapers; but simply noting that the time had come when film could be trusted for that purpose supports the understanding that the serial film craze was instrumental in creating a mass audience—bringing together the whole province of Ontario through one film and one newspaper.

Serials explicitly showed exactly how your own movie theater, wherever it was, whatever its size, was part of the same big business, was connected to the most palatial downtown cinema. The newspaper circulation of the stories and advertising relied on the appeal of a mass audience over a vast territory watching the "same" films, most likely aware other newspapers ran the stories and other theaters the films all over the continent.

The flipside, of course, was the incredibly strict hierarchy of who could see the first episode when and at what cost. Theaters downtown in Toronto charged the highest prices and played the films first for the entire province of Ontario. Theaters downtown in other big cities had the same position in their regions. Peripheral theaters in neighborhoods and outlying cities were pegged farther down. It was the first time that films were openly promoted as circulating in a run-zone pattern. Zones ranked importance, within cities roughly geographically from downtown outward, and in the wider territory roughly by population from big city to small village. Within each zone, each theater had a priority in the ability to access films, ranked from first-run onward, which roughly corresponded to its size of theater and filigree of construction. Although any theater's audience could see the "same" film as elsewhere, a series of distinctions actually existed in terms of cost, comfort, location, and time. The largest theaters even had sections of seats that cost more than others, and matinees were cheaper than evenings. For example, from 1911 to 1913 at the Toronto Strand downtown, tickets cost five, ten, twenty, and thirty-five cents in the evenings, and five, ten, and twenty-five cents at matinees.

As serialization provided a semblance of simultaneity for film programs at a majority of Toronto's picture shows, the architectural and geographic disparity among movie theaters was widening. Recall how 1913 and 1914 witnessed a building boom, nearly doubling the number of movie theaters in the city. Some were movie palaces in every sense of the word. The Madison, Park, and Beaver each had distinguished façades and interiors designed by prominent local architects. They each seated 1,000 people or more, advertised their openings with large display ads in newspapers, and were soon running daily newspaper ads. Many others were only slightly less palatial. But even as late as 1914, some new theaters continued to be modest conversions of existing stores, in particular a few theaters downtown that opened only briefly. By the start of the serial queen fad, many of the earliest theatoriums were still open and joined the fad, too, although well down the hierarchy from the downtown Strand. What could possibly have been the appeal of watching a serial in a small, shabby neighborhood nickel show, months after it played in a downtown or uptown palace? There is no reason to assume audiences at small shows in the margins of the run-zone hierarchy automatically treated their status negatively. Rather, different locations, surroundings, and admission prices probably allowed for a sense of the variety of occasions movies provided. The expensive, elaborately decorated palaces downtown probably made a special event of a first-run film. Of course, the sense of occasion was highly constructed to justify the high ticket price. Audiences there were well serviced by ushers, attendants, orchestras, and professional managers, even though the Strand, for example, offered some balcony seats for just a nickel as late as 1914. At the other extreme were cheaper seats in theaters closer to home, less ornate and open to informal, even rowdy, socializing. Families, children, and friends at neighborhood nickel shows could feel at ease and perhaps have more play and fun. Many gradations between these could be found. While one drawback was waiting months to see a particular film, social benefits of moviegoing close to home with friends or family came along with the cheap ticket price.

Going to the movies could be done as an occasion to match many social situations. But whether part of a refined, "high-class" audience downtown or at a laid-back "nabe" close to home, the many occasions that could be made of filmgoing were all recognizable as part of the same mass cultural system. Serial films and their intertextual promotions made this explicit. It also translated the complex system of film distribution, pricing, and zoning into an instantly legible and understandable format that positioned a newspaper reader or filmgoer immediately as part of the system, assessing an expense and prescribing a practice based on her level of interest. The episodic series of films played against the series of differences among theaters and their audience. That these films were serialized in written form added yet another distinction in how people approached and consumed the story. There was even an important order in which newspapers were tied to the films. In Toronto, the *Star Weekly* was not just first but most important, followed by the Sunday *World*. The *Globe* had a different type of importance, picking up an early serial but abandoning the gimmick first as well. In Toronto, the other exception was the apparently desperate attempt of the *News* to fit a serial story into its readers' routines in a daily format, although daily serializations were common in U.S. papers without Sunday editions.

If the film serials partly explain how the mass cultural character of filmgoing was circulated to audiences to gather their differences under a single rubric of seriality, then an important underlying structural change was that it was the first time distributors took responsibility for local promotion and advertising. In 1914, a tight cooperation among film exchanges and newspapers in Chicago, Detroit, Cleveland, and Buffalo (but not Toronto) led to daily picture stories, another form of intertextual allegiance between films and newspapers. Daily movie stories were published in newspapers with the help of film exchanges, often presented as an early form of film criticism. The *Chicago Record-Herald* began "making movie history" with a daily story version of a Universal picture beginning February 7, 1914, within a few days supported by a listing of what was playing at over 300 Chicago picture shows. Soon after, Universal Pictures arranged to publish the daily stories in the *Detroit Free Press* and the

Figure 5.4. Variations of this promotion for Universal Pictures daily stories appeared in cities such as Detroit, Buffalo, and prominently here in the *Chicago Record-Herald*. Another ad in the series quite literally combined the newspapers' front page with a movie theater entrance. (Adapted from ads printed on February 4 and 23, 1914.)

Buffalo Times. Not to be outdone, the *Chicago Tribune* took the idea and reframed it as movie criticism with "Today's Best Moving Picture Story" beginning early in February 1914. The idea was an instant success and was soon accompanied by a list of special feature films playing at "High-Class Moving Picture Theaters." By July ghostwriter Audrey Alspaugh had taken on the pseudonym Kitty Kelly; and before long, she had gossip column competition when Louella Parsons began her movie reporting in the *Chicago Herald* in December 1914 (Barbas 2005). Picking up on this new more formal alliance of print and moving pictures, *Mary Pickford's Daily Column*, ghostwritten by the incredibly popular star's screenwriter Frances Marion, was syndicated to newspapers across the continent. It began in Toronto in the *News* on December 18, 1915, more than a month after it started elsewhere.

Gossip and portraits of movie stars (most less famous than Pickford) became the centerpiece of feature film pages in weekend newspapers. When in March 1914 the *Chicago Sunday Tribune* began a regular motion picture page, *Right Off the Reel*, its stories—primarily about the film industry and its stars—were laid out around a large picture of a different film star each week. *Right Off the Reel* was soon syndicated, for example to the *Buffalo Courier* within weeks of its Chicago debut. Throughout 1914, newspapers across the continent introduced new film pages to their daily and weekend editions. Unlike the pages from 1913 and earlier, these later versions included few ads from neighborhood showmen, let alone conspicuously promoting moviegoing as a locally organized practice.

By 1914, when newspapers included film pages, they no longer focused on local showmen boosting theater spaces as desirable sites of pleasure and congregation. By then advertising dwelt almost exclusively on first-run films starring well-known celebrities changing weekly at downtown theaters. The promotional journalism that supported the advertising no longer focused on local showmanship, censorship, or regulation, but on the industry and its high-profile stars and studios, now almost all located in California—soon nicknamed Hollywood. Beginning in February 1916, the Sunday *World* held a competition where readers mailed in ballots voting for their favorite movie stars. The winner was Mary Pickford, who was so popular that she might have won a similar contest in any city. In Toronto, however, Pickford was repeatedly noted as a hometown girl, continually rooted in her University Avenue birthplace despite her international fame and celebrity. After Pickford won the contest as Toronto's favorite movie star, her mother reported in an interview that she was proud of her daughter's hometown support (*World* May 11, 1916). An earlier biography in the Sunday *World* began with the headline, "A Toronto Girl Who Earns $104,000 a Year" (*World* February 28, 1915).

Figure 5.5. Inside a maple leaf, Toronto's own Mary Pickford was recast as Canada's Sweetheart as well as the best paid, most famous movie star of the day. (*World* February 21, 1915.)

Promoting smaller picture shows run by independent showmen continued in various forms. Most typically, a list of what film was playing where offered information about the many movie theaters in the city as if all were equivalent. Never again would newspaper promotion advertise individuated showmanship and distinctive neighborhood theaters in the way the *World*'s Photoplays page did in 1913 and 1914. In the summer of 1916, the *World* turned to a simple list of film titles each day at theaters across the city. Although fifty-six theaters were listed at some point, more than half the movie theaters in the city at the time, the daily directory was abandoned in August 1916 just as a new downtown movie palace, the Regent, opened. Entirely rebuilt on the foundation of the Majestic vaudeville theater downtown, the Regent overtook the Strand as the city's premiere first-run picture palace. Its publicity promised a steady supply of

Famous Players-Paramount feature films. Although the Regent was an entirely local operation, its investors and managers went on to build Famous Players Canadian theaters, affiliated with Paramount-Famous Players in the United States. The Regent was later fondly recalled as the first step in the vertically integrated chain.

The film industry had matured into a mass media system supported with promotion and journalism about its celebrities and their latest feature films. By 1915 the typical feature film was more than an hour in length and could anchor an entire evening's vaudeville show. Even when compared to the early film serials, let alone the earlier attempts at collective advertising on the part of local showmen, newspaper promotion of filmgoing barely mentioned individual theaters, except for the largest first-run palaces downtown. In 1911 and 1912, only the Strand had purchased regular advertising for its first-run films. After a few brief years when almost all picture shows ran ads on special picture pages or were mentioned in ads for a specific film serial, the situation had come nearly full circle by 1916 when only the largest first-run theaters still bought ads. First-run downtown could stand in for the entire system.

Conclusion
Wartime Filmgoing as Citizenship

Why not show some typical Canadian Western scenes instead of pictures illustrating a wild and wooly West which does not exist in Canada? Why not illustrate the life in our lumber camps and mines? . . . Cutting out objectionable features is well enough, but the greatest results will be obtained by constructive action.

"The Moving Pictures," Editorial, *Star* September 7, 1910

We had so much trouble when we first took up our duties because of the flaunting of the Stars and Stripes in moving picture stories that we have cut them out entirely, and now the Stars and Stripes is not allowed to wave in any of the pictures that have passed our inspectors.

"Ban Stars and Stripes," *Telegram* October 17, 1911

❧

D URING THE WAR THE PROCESS of making cinema legitimate and regulating its fun and amusement crystallized around a central focus in the war effort. Within weeks of the ultimatum signaling the start of World War I in August 1914, entrepreneurial showmen in Toronto made moviegoing an explicit part of the city's homefront war effort. They did not turn to propaganda but simply publicized that box office receipts at many moving picture shows across the city would be donated to the War Relief Fund used to support the families of soldiers. For two weeks, apparently without changing the form or format of their entertainment, showmen in Toronto attached the war effort to the regular pleasures and purposes of their amusement. Dozens of showmen, theater employees, and local branches of U.S. film distributors waived their ordinary fees and wages so that every nickel passing through the box office was passed along to the War Relief Fund. Similar patriotic uses of everyday film shows continued in Toronto, soon sanctioned and supplemented by provincial government edicts and a wartime amusement tax. Cinema was a constant part of Toronto's war effort from August 1914 until the Armistice in November 1918. But only occasionally did this civic showmanship rely on war films or propaganda. Without patriotic production or state-sponsored films, the network of showmanship, regulation, and promotion that had just taken shape as the war began allowed moviegoing easily to become an act of citizenship as long as the fighting lasted.

For the years before the war, the production of standardized filmgoing was rooted in urban commerce and transnational trading, in urban policing and rationalized bureaucracies, in urban journalism and routine advertising campaigns. In Toronto, these standards for film showmanship, regulation, and promotion crystallized into an overtly nationalistic practice of moviegoing integral to the city's war effort and in turn central to Canada's participation overseas. As in U.S. cities, film regulations and collective showmanship began as a way to wrestle with the local particularity of mass amusement, but then during the war the prior focus on regional distinctions became more squarely a way to articulate Toronto's unique position as a British colonial metropolis (Crerar 2005). Mass culture in all forms played a significant role in this transformation (Litt 2005). For the first time in any systematic way, moviegoing in Toronto was repositioned apart from the U.S. domestic market by showmen, governments, and presumably audiences as well.

There was no break, however, with the regular and regulated practices introduced before the war. In a sense, the complexity of showmanship, regulation, and promotion was eventually condensed into a list of theater names, sites, prices, and ever-changing titles of films. Each theater, ticket, and film continued to be given local context by the particular theater's entrepreneurial or corporate management. Each theater, ticket, and film continued to be carefully licensed and inspected, censored and taxed by local offices of bureaucratic governance. And many theaters, tickets, and films continued to be carefully promoted and profiled in newspaper columns. This interconnected process among commerce, oversight, and advertising was well underway by the start of the war in August 1914. Local practices of filmgoing in Toronto were included among the many ways the people came together to enact being a city in a nation at war overseas. Little to no effort was made to produce Canadian films or import British and Allied pictures. Rather than deliver propaganda, showmen, government, and audiences attached the banner of the war effort to ordinary, everyday moviegoing. Showmanship, regulation, and promotion had developed with attention to the particular people of Toronto, and political circumstances—the city's British character—meant its regional particularity was now nationalistic. Does this mean that a nationalist cinema was produced out of Toronto without producing films in Canada? To even ask this question is to recognize that the production of cinema is not equivalent to the production of films, that the conditions of moviegoing are effectively distinct from and independent of the production of movies, that what is on screen is part of a complex institution.

The Life of a Film in Canada

Nationalism stemming from the war effort, even when it involved attitudes and advertising about films, was hardly identical with actual movie production. A patriotic or boosterist fervor for filmgoing and the viewer's experience in the theater did not depend on Toronto-based, or even Canadian, film production for its success. This was the case even before the war. The journalist in the *News* writing about the People's theatorium in the Ward in 1907 mentioned that colorful posters outside the theater promised films of the Great Toronto Fire. Yet, the actual show did not include those local films (*News* April 26, 1907). Thus, the earliest apparent description of a Toronto moving picture show already indicates the problem of Canadian content on the screen: that the prospect of it could gather a crowd but its absence did not dampen the excitement of the show. This book has not detailed the production of films in Toronto, even for these early years when there was little to none. Previous film historians, especially Peter Morris, have taken up this task in earnest and confirmed little to no local or regional film production in Ontario in these years. Morris (1992) writes, "it is perhaps more surprising that there was *any* production than that there was so little" (p. 55). As the movies flourished around 1913 and 1914, so did regional film production all over North America, especially early newsreels and actualities. A few Canadian studios released a handful of feature fiction films. Most received a fair deal of press coverage and advertising, all of it emphasizing the local appeal of Canadian films. However, in the context of moviegoing as an everyday practice, where perhaps a dozen new films appeared each week at any one theater, the attention garnered by this handful of Canadian productions would have come and gone from any location in just a few days. Out of Montreal came a single feature film from the British-American Film Company, *The Battle of Long Sault* (Pelletier 2007). Although the *Star Weekly* (February 8, 1913) published a feature story about the film and its production, it played at the Toronto Strand for just one week (*Star Weekly* February 22, 1913). Another feature drawn from Canadian history was the Canadian Bioscope Company's *Evangeline*. Although it was prominently promoted for distribution in the United States in *Moving Picture World* (June 20, 1914, 1749), it was not advertised as playing at any of Toronto's first-run theaters. The fleeting character of any single film was not unique to Canadian titles, of course. Even the famed "first feature" *Queen Elizabeth* starring Sarah Bernhardt lasted only one week at the Strand in November 1912. *The Birth of a Nation* was exceptional not so much for its epic success, playing for three weeks when it debuted in Toronto at Massey Hall in September 1915, but for its ability to sustain many repeat engagements, returning for three more weeks at Christmas 1915, again in August 1916, and many times more in the future. Almost every other film, whatever its quality, star power, or reputation, left an imprint as immaterial as its flickering projection—entirely in the memories of audience members. In this way, cinema was like other mass cultural aspects of city life, a passing barrage of impressions that only collectively added up to an institution through regulation and predictability.

The emergence of regular, predictable showmanship, governance, and promotion of movies each adopted a veneer of nationalism during the war years from 1914 to 1918. The potential for a nationalist cinema was both built on the entrepreneurial urban roots of nickel shows and a consequence of the earlier recognition that the widespread proliferation of nickel shows was a problem that required state intervention. And yet, in Toronto during World War I, the state's role in making moviegoing a form of patriotic citizenship lagged behind collective, civic showmanship at ordinary picture theaters. This is consistent with the recent move to define national cinemas in terms of their cinema cultures rather than their film production output in itself (Abel 2006; Higson 1989). National cinemas weigh heavily in the very structure of film studies as a discipline; yet study of the relation between nationalism and cinema as contemporaneous global practices are relatively rare, especially if framed in such abstract, conceptual terms. Although the rise of cinema has been thoroughly linked to women's suffrage (Stamp 2000), to southern U.S. black people's modern subjectivity (Stewart 2005), to mass immigration in the United States (Cohen 1990), and the embourgeoisement of the working class (Rosenzweig 1983), it remains to gather these cases under the collective banner of the citizenship of cinema. The apparent near-universal inclusivity of moviegoing as a mass cultural practice constituted "going to the movies" as a form of citizen-ship, at least during World War I.

Nationalism—flag waving patriotism—was not imposed on filmgoing in Toronto, but taken up, largely voluntarily, within the existing collective forms of the Toronto showmen's protective association, the Ontario Board of Censors and Treasury, metropolitan newspapers, and implicitly by audiences themselves. Altogether these efforts turned Toronto into the indisputable headquarters of the Canadian film industry, reflecting how the city's stalwart British patriotism anchored the national war effort and filled its war coffers more than anywhere else, in particular Montreal. Even before the war began, the practices developed for Toronto set pre-cedents for Canadian provinces, at least implicitly forming a national paradigm for filmgoing. The further development of the same tendencies during the war was qualitatively different only insofar as the war effort was often deliberately attached to moviegoing. Toronto became a center of cinema production for the whole of Canada, *not by producing films but by producing a nationalist mass practice of filmgoing.*

The problem of patriotic films had been part of the talk circulating around film before the war, part of the practice of censorship, part of measuring the moral effects of cheap amusements. A dichotomy of na-tionalist approaches had already been articulated, either to produce de-pictions of parochial life and Canadian history or to censor the worst flag-waving of imported U.S. films. Advocates of neither side demon-strated a nuanced or complex understanding of the appeal of moviegoing as a mass practice: charming films of lumber camps were proposed and images of the Stars and Stripes were simply cut, as if either action could produce a nationalist cinema for Canada. Altogether, the reason standard-ized practices of filmgoing developed the way they did in Ontario was often overtly against the ill effects of incipient nationalism in U.S. films. Garth Jowett (1975) speculates this sentiment did not emerge until after the war, when "the nation was in no mood to tolerate American movie claims which showed the Americans winning the War almost single-handedly" (p. 60). In fact, resentment of American flag-waving was ex-pressed well before the war; this problem was one of the first issues the Ontario Board of Censors engaged in 1911. During the war, movie the-aters were directed in a more positive way toward producing nationalist practices of gathering to watch films, no matter what type of movies. Patriotic exhibition, however, could not alone be a basis for a national cinema. A nationalist cinema, a national system of filmmaking, can only emerge within the development of urban and regional systems of film exhibition. Richard Abel (1996; 1999) has shown for both France and the United States before the war (implicitly for the dominant cities of film production, Paris, New York, and Chicago within those nations) that an increasingly nationalist and protectionist cinema emerged only after the *ciné* and the nickelodeon became geographically widespread. Recognizing national film production as distinct from the local social processes embedding film into communities opens up the possibility that nationalist moviegoing can happen without the films themselves being produced nationally. This appears to be exactly what happened in Toronto during the war.

The relative absence of openly nationalist propaganda films might have allowed filmgoing to become an everyday part of the war effort exactly because the films viewed continued to be merely harmless entertainment for the most part. The trope of escapism being a valuable community resource was hauled out within weeks of the start of the war. "Public Needs Amusement in This Time of War Clouds" ran a headline in the *Star Weekly* (September 12, 1914), even as voluntary censorship and discrimination against German and Austrian vaudevillians began at Shea's. At the same time as wartime newsreels were packing in crowds at the Strand, film audiences were said to have shifted attendance to crowded downtown theaters, leaving smaller suburban theaters in a brief financial crunch. Lee Grieveson (2004) has demonstrated that for the United States before the war defining film strictly as commercial entertainment was key to defusing the problematic moral, racial, and gendered aspects of mass filmgoing. This seems to have happened even earlier and with a much stronger consensus in Ontario (or at least there was less protest because of the more centralized authority of provincial governments) exactly because of the latent threat of imported films.

The dominance of the U.S. film market was being felt around the world. In his attempt to articulate "the historical specificity of early French cinema," Abel (1996) successfully demonstrates that the earliest years of the film industry were openly transnational. Technology, film stock, film stories, patents, and production techniques spread rapidly from one company or country to another. Specification of the French nationalist character of films largely emerged in subsequent years, roughly the period covered in this study of Toronto, through protectionist trade policies both by governments and by particular corporations, nationally-particular court decisions and legal precedents policing the status of film "speech" and authorship. This happened in the context of the tremendously disproportionate size of the U.S. nickelodeon marketplace. By late 1909, Abel (1996) notes of the dominant French film studio Pathé, "For every five film prints distributed in France, forty were reserved for the rest of Europe and elsewhere, while 150 were shipped to the United States" (p. 111). The size of that U.S. nickelodeon market and its origins in the northeastern United States bordering Ontario and Quebec meant that even before the first theatorium opened in Toronto, the Canadian film market was already structurally part of the North American domestic market.

There was some success, albeit brief, in getting films made in Toronto. One important case is worth considering in some detail to introduce a concluding discussion of the nationalist character of filmgoing in Toronto during World War I. In the winter months early in 1915, advertising appeared in the *Star Weekly* and the Sunday *World* for the Toronto-made films of the Conness-Till Company, initiated in April 1914 by Edward H. Robins with backing from James and Charles Beury, financiers in his hometown Philadelphia. Some of the money came from the two men whose names formed the company's moniker, U.S. theatrical producer Luke Edwin Conness and Toronto businessman Louis A. Till (Morris 1992, 51–54). The company's first move was a publicity campaign and amateur screenwriting contest, appearing in all six Toronto newspapers at the end of August 1914 as well as in Montreal and other cities and reported in the trade press *Moving Picture World* (September 19, 1914, 1667). Robins, the head screenwriter for Conness-Till, even began contributing a column, "Behind the Screen," to the *World* in November 1914. The company spent $50,000 building a studio in suburban Toronto on the banks of the Humber River. After first releasing a few short films of Toronto scenes, by the end of January 1915 ads for Conness-Till began appearing in the weekend editions' film pages, announcing "All Ready Mr. Exhibitor To Talk Service," with a schedule of four upcoming film titles. The logo for the company was a stately beaver on top of a maple leaf and the films were known as the "Made in Canada" or even just "M in C" films. On the other hand, *Moving Picture World* (January 23, 1915, 550) reported that muckraking *Jack Canuck* printed one of its cynical exposés, citing with glee how the American actress employed as the company's star was complaining about the bitter cold and low pay.

A preview screening of Conness-Till's first film, *On the King's Highway*, was held at the Strand but finally played to the public at a new, small downtown theater opposite City Hall on Queen Street, the Photodrome (*MPW* February 13, 1915, 1021; *Star Weekly* February 6, 1915). The film was screened for a few days in February, and the Photodrome picked up subsequent Made in Canada features as they were released. At least five other neighborhood theaters advertised one of Conness-Till's eleven films between February and April 1915. In the meantime, preview screenings were held for showmen in Montreal, where another feature, *Canada in Peace and War*, played at that city's key early movie palace, the Strand (*MPW* March 13, 1915, 1639; April 17, 1915, 431). Back in Toronto, attempts were made to hype the hometown studio as sharing in the glamour and fame of the movie business. Actors, directors, and managers of Conness-Till appeared at the Garden Theatre for a special "formal opening" of United Features, a new company formed to distribute its films (*Star Weekly* March 6, 1915). The following week Robins and other players from the studio appeared in person at the Mary Pickford Theatre, the former Griffin's Auditorium. After three months releasing new multireel features almost weekly, the *Star Weekly* published a lengthy illustrated article about the company with a photo of the studio, the actresses, a set lit by bright arc-lights, and a dramatic scene being filmed. Although the article began with the understatement, "quite a number of people in Toronto are perhaps not aware that the business of film production in this city is now an accomplished fact," the profile then proceeded with praise:

> These people enjoy the signal honor of being the first in the Canadian market to promote this particular industry, hence their slogan "Made in Canada." . . . Speaking to some of the local talent who have embraced the movies as an occupation, the *Star Weekly* man learned that the business though hard was interesting and in many ways opportunities arose for advancement for those persons who were sincere in their efforts. (*Star Weekly* April 17, 1915, 22)

The story took a tour through the sound stage with a ballroom scene under direction, the prop room, developing room, drying room, printing room, and lunchroom. A sense of the technical expertise and high cost came with a calculation that the high-voltage arc-lights cost $300 a day to keep lit. The studio was an all-in-one, fully operational outfit that could deliver finished prints to the local distributor. The ad just below this article, one of Conness-Till's last, listed ten films available, averaging three reels each. There must have been some dissatisfaction or impatience on the part of the Philadelphia financiers because late in April 1915, the company was reorganized and renamed the Beury Feature Film Company (*MPW* May 8, 1915, 937). A month later, in the middle of production of an antismoking social issue film, *Nicotine*, the suburban Toronto film studio went up in flames (*MPW* May 29, 1915, 1482). The fire made headlines in all Toronto newspapers on June 1, 1915. Despite some insurance on the property, the investors called it quits instead of replacing the investment. No copies of the company's films remain.

The fire destroying the Conness-Till film studio might be seen as an abrupt end to Toronto-made movies. On the other hand, a more "natural" death by bankruptcy seems just as likely, given the promotions alongside its "Made in Canada" newspaper ads. The small, independent

Toronto film company could not even monopolize the local wartime patriotism that was its hook. Indeed, Conness-Till's patriotic advantage paled next to the weekly Strand War Series, which included scenes of preparations and news from Europe. Not really "news" as much as "views," the Strand War Series began in Toronto on September 21, 1914, just two weeks after the films first appeared at the Broadway Strand in New York City. The series had at least sixteen weeks and the films played elsewhere in Toronto after their debut at the Strand downtown. For Conness-Till, there could hardly have been a worse time to enter the film business. In exactly these months the serial melodrama fad was at its peak and six stories blanketed the city in theaters and in print. Even the Toronto-made advantage was lost, as it was announced Toronto-born Lottie Pickford, sister of Mary, would star in the serial *Diamond from the Sky* (*Star Weekly* April 10, 1915). Mary Pickford herself, in the few months of the Conness-Till film releases, had become the highest paid and best-known movie star in the world, and newspapers began claiming her Toronto roots as cause for celebration (*World* February 28, 1915; *Star Weekly* October 31, 1914). The same week in April 1915 that the *Star Weekly* profiled the local film studio, the Strand downtown had a special Pickford repertoire festival, playing a different film of hers every day and offering lady patrons a souvenir book, "Mary Pickford's Own Story."

In retrospect even worse, a parallel promotional campaign began early in 1915 to brand and anchor Paramount feature films from Famous

Figure C-1. Conness-Till's Made in Canada message next to Paramount: the new "household word." (*Star Weekly* February 25, 1915.)

Players—Jesse Lasky productions. Mary Pickford and other well-known stars of the moment such as John Barrymore, Marguerite Clark, and Tyrone Power, were listed as exclusively appearing in Paramount films. Even the local Paramount manager, twenty-six-year-old Philip Kauffman of Allen's Famous Players Film Service, was a heavy self-promoter who got his picture printed and "meteoric" career reported in the paper (*Star Weekly* June 12, 1915). He probably did not exactly intend to sabotage the efforts of the Conness-Till company, but his advertising for the Paramount films of the Famous Players company was often adjacent to the Made in Canada campaign on the film page of the *Star Weekly* in February and March 1915. Instead of the stoic beaver on top of the Conness-Till maple leaf, Kauffman used pithy slogans to argue forcefully and claim the importance of Paramount films: "Give the Public What They Want," "I Am Going to Make Paramount a Household Word," "Does Quality Mean Anything to You?" as well as occasional more direct links to the local audience, "The Toronto Theatres Listed below Show Our Productions." These slogans were followed by a list of several dozen local theaters. In the trade press *Moving Picture World*, Paramount Pictures boasted the advantage to local exhibitors of its national advertising in the *Saturday Evening Post*. One of their trade ads even made the chain store strategy explicit, showing Paramount Pictures as the link between "your theater" and "the public" (*MPW* October 10, 1914, 226). The combination of transnational manufacturing, distribution, and chains of theaters was graphically shown as a cooperative effort that connected the local showman to the local public in contrast to the distanced corporatism of vertical integration.

The emerging corporate transnational structure of the film business was even becoming a topic of general interest for feature stories in Toronto's weekend editions. Better integration with U.S. film networks became something to brag about, despite the United States still being a neutral bystander nation at that point in the war. The *World* printed a story early in 1916, "Life of One Film in Canada, What Happens to a Film after It Reaches Toronto" (*World* January 30, 1916) and another proudly proclaimed, "Canada Is No Longer Graveyard of Features" (*World* February 6, 1916). In general, film distributors used their regional branches both to situate local showmen in a personable and manageable regional context as well as to claim the advantages of economies of scale that the continental reach of a chain structure afforded. In many film trade press ads, for example, for the United Film Service and Universal Film Manufacturing, Canadian cities were listed as equals of U.S. cities. In this solidification of the chain structure of the film market, the Conness-Till Company's Made in Canada films are remarkable not for their failure but for their relative success. Not many other companies anywhere in North America were as small but still managed to release a film each week for three months. Just a few years earlier, it might have really taken off. No other film company in Canada before or for years after (except for those producing newsreels) managed to release a similar volume of films. In the end, only a handful of local theaters picked up the Made in Canada films and promoted them, even as all but a few of the ninety movie theaters in Toronto pointedly offered Paramount, World, or Metro features, as well as serials from Mutual, Universal, or Pathé.

How was it that the predominance of U.S. cinema in Toronto did not prevent moviegoing from becoming a regular and vital part of the homefront war effort? This was achieved locally through collective showmanship rather than being imposed on theaters as government policy. Furthermore, the civic showmanship of wartime moviegoing did not rely on propaganda or escapism. Instead, largely without changing the content of their shows or the running of their businesses, Toronto's showmen simply appended their movie theaters (and their mass audiences) to the more traditional forms of fund-raising or rallying. This differed markedly from the concurrent use of cinema during World War I in Great Britain and the United States. Michael Hammond's (2006) study of cinemagoing in Great Britain during World War I proposes that the social space of cinemagoing adapted to include "new audiences" and shifted squarely away from educational value to entertainment at a time when the nation needed a collective escape. His point is that the role of cinema in wartime Britain solidified cinema's place as a legitimate form of leisure. That is a British history, focusing on the national struggle for solidarity in the face of a war all-too-close to home. In contrast, Canadians were on an overseas homefront, distant enough from the frontlines to need ways to participate collectively and feel connected to the war effort.

Practical Patriotism as an Extension of Showmanship

Leslie Midkiff DeBauche's (1997) *Reel Patriotism* describes the uses of film in the United States during World War I as a matter of "practical patriotism," a phrase I will adapt and apply liberally to Toronto. DeBauche recounts a more centralized, nationwide effort to reshape moviegoing to fit the war effort—successful at a national level primarily because it was organized by film studios. For example, movie stars rallied the cause rather than relying on local showmen to do their best on an urban or regional scale. Her study shows how U.S. exhibition practices were strongly related to studio production, movie star fund-raising, and nationally-coordinated

campaigns. That is an American history, focusing on the practical patriotism of the film industry. It fails to reflect the far more localized, modest
efforts that were used in Toronto to make moviegoing patriotic for local
showmen, for people in the audience, and even for Canadian governments.

Both what Hammond documents in Great Britain and what
DeBauche recounts for the United States demonstrate that moviegoing
during the war followed nationally-sensitive standards—but less as a result of government edict than as a form of showmanship. The film industry and local showmen made moviegoing into an act of citizenship, but
in ways attuned to the local, and now national, culture of their setting.
Concepts of citizenship have eclipsed a simple focus on how states deter-
mine the boundaries of the nation, although state-defined membership
remains foundational. At the most basic level, a distinction between the
lived experiences of substantive citizenship and the status of formal citizenship has allowed a nuanced understanding of how people participate
in their communities, at whatever scale and many simultaneously,
specifically beyond state categorizations of citizens and associated rights
and responsibilities (Isin and Wood 1999; Marshall 1992). Such a move
toward redefining citizenship delimits at least two distinctions, from formal state-defined rights, and from social action in general. Citizenship is
neither merely a bureaucratic category nor an entirely cultural lifeworld,
but rather an analytic conceptualization, for citizens themselves as much
as for scholars. It is a form of association between the social and the
communal, or at least distinct from both. Citizenship, then, constitutes a
field of practices in which individuals engage a relation to "everyone,"
neither so abstractly as to be defined entirely by structural or undeliberated
relations, nor restricted to the wholly interpersonal world of everyday
life. Citizenship thus becomes an important middle-ground conceptualization of intentional interactions, of conditions understood as affect-
ing the shape of everyday action. In short, citizenship is practical, in the
double sense of being practices with norms and standards to be embraced,
adapted, or rejected, and in the somewhat functionalist sense of being the
means to an end.

The very inclusivity and novelty of everyday moviegoing can be
understood as the basis of an act of citizenship, as the site of both a
nominally and an apparently universal voluntary association. This was not
a trivial or inconsequential achievement in the context of rapidly expanding, extraordinarily heterogeneous populations of early twentieth century
North American cities. This is not to say that the commercialized wel-
come of a movie theater achieves a state of justice, of equal inclusion in
the public sphere. Nonetheless, the availability of everyday mass practices
is always also an opportunity to address and perform the commonality of

everyday experience within a locality as part of the world. Moviegoing was thus a latent form of citizenship, at least once it became a mainstream mass practice, overtly so within the war effort.

The collective experience of World War I was inherently a mediated and visual culture for North American city dwellers. The "homefront" war effort in cities so far away from soldiers' battlefields, gravesites, and hospitals required a degree of abstraction, or rather mediation, with the valor and horror of the frontlines. There was a need to enact being at war, to make collective sacrifice an everyday practice and a visible part of the culture of cities. In Toronto, moviegoing was a constant part of making the war effort concrete and visible. The homefront's participation was a continual public performance: in reading newspapers—often in crowds as the latest headlines were publicly posted—in parades, mass rallies, and on occasion in riots. In gathering together people could recognize and actually see the collective bonds of civic life. Newspapers and advertisements were explicitly linked to the war. The way people shopped and spent or saved money shifted to respect the nation's war resources. Moviegoing became an everyday way to feel a shared bond, an effect perhaps latent in the standardization of filmgoing but made explicit and deliberate right from the start in August 1914. Local showmen in Toronto used their theaters for the war effort almost immediately, apparently voluntarily right from August 1914 to the armistice in November 1918. Any practicality behind showmen's patriotism was a local and largely sincere attempt to do their part. Economic benefits were to be had, too, especially as taxation and conservative fiscal policies took hold in later years, threatening to shut down luxuries and optional consumption. Overall, however, collective actions by theater managers had the important and productive role of redefining filmgoing as an important force in society.

Although everything was now directed toward victory, the war effort of Toronto and other cities in North America happened without drastically disrupting the form or rhythm of economic (and in turn visual) culture. The department stores referenced the war in their daily advertising, display windows, and showrooms, early on proclaiming that it was "Business as Usual," and later selling gift packs to ship to soldiers overseas. Advertising for many commodities used war images, especially any that might seem extravagant, such as chocolates, beer, or chewing gum. Types of consumption were promoted as a way to save money to buy Victory Bonds, such as using Gillette safety razors as an alternative to going to a daily barber, or buying furniture on credit to save cash for war bonds, and even buying ready-to-wear instead of made-to-measure suits. Prepackaged brand-name consumption was thus legitimated as part of the war effort. Many of these ads were directed at older businessmen and employers who remained in Canada to carry on with business while young soldiers fought. One recruiting campaign made this explicit, imploring employers to encourage their own employees to become soldiers. Government Victory Bond advertising, too, singled out the duties that came with the businessmen's privilege, asking what returning soldiers would think if someone at home did not do enough. The sensibility of advertising was carried over into impromptu recruiting efforts, such as when a streetcar in a military parade offered a "Free Trip to Europe" with a destination of Berlin. Parades and rallies had a constant public presence during the war.

Gender roles, family life, household economy, and religious and political allegiances were all upended and rearranged during the war. But judging from newspapers, maintaining the pre-war form of everyday consumption was vital to the morale of the war effort. In other words, modern urbanism was already a practice of acting collectively, so that when the collective act of being at war was imposed on the culture, the city's people were easily able to openly demonstrate their part in the nation at war. The pleasures of modern consumption and visual display were thus, perhaps, already infused with an element of collective sacrifice, something hinted at, for example, in the link between potlatch and consumption, as noted by Bataille (1989). Within Canada, Torontonians took part much more enthusiastically than did the nation as a whole. The British patriotism of Canada's predominantly British-heritage population at first had to be tempered to accommodate reticence among rural farmers (often central European in ethnicity) and Quebec's francophone culture, both of which were set against participation in the war. Eventually conscription was enforced. Within Toronto itself, a differently bifurcated culture, structurally American yet culturally British, allowed cinema to emerge as an important force of cohesion, created by the city's showmen despite their films coming from across the border. Thus, a pastime that was almost entirely American in content was presented in a context that was resolutely local and patriotically Canadian (or perhaps British). The space off the screen gave moviegoing Canadian content.

Early in the war recruiting soldiers was still a relatively easy matter of soliciting volunteers enthusiastic for adventure. The local war effort focused instead on fund-raising for humanitarian efforts, such as the War Relief Fund for local soldiers' families, the Red Cross, or the Belgian Relief Fund, to help civilians rather than the military. Still, even in these relatively optimistic first months of the war, theaters and cinemas quickly and publicly took part, providing places for mass fund-raising rallies and donating box office receipts to relief funds. For a week at the end of August 1914, not a full month since the start of the war, large newspaper

"This shall not be war upon our women and children"

HUSBANDS and fathers, sons and brothers may go to battle, but all the hordes of warring Europe shall not force them to leave grim privation and terror of want encamped at their hearthstones.

Not while we Britons who remain at home have a dollar left shall the women and children of our soldiers suffer!

Give! Give! Give! to the War Relief Fund

GIVE in the name of our own women and children, fortunately not robbed of their husbands and fathers.

We are face to face with the realities of war, more dreadful than we at home yet understand, but imagination needs no help in picturing what the war means to the women and children whose natural protectors have been taken from them.

With rent to be paid--with Winter coming and no fuel in the house--with the little children crying for warm clothing--with foodstuffs rising in price, war is, indeed, carried to the very hearthstones, unless we defenders at home stand in the way.

Give! Give! Give!
$500,000 in Four Days

Every dollar will be spent under a thorough business-like administration.

HEADQUARTERS: KING EAST and VICTORIA STREETS

Patron : H.R.H. Duke of Connaught.
Hon. Presidents : Sir John Gibson, K.C.M.G.; Sir James Whitney, K.C.M.G.
President : Hon. Sir William Mulock, K.C.M.G.
Hon. Treasurer : E. R. Wood.   Hon. Secretary : E. T. Malone, K.C.
Asst. Sec.-Treasurer : A. S. Muirhead.

GO TO THE "MOVIES"

The following moving picture shows will very generously give the whole day's receipts to the fund on the days and nights designated:

GARDEN THEATRE, 395 College Street, Wednesday, Afternoon and Evening.
ACADEMY THEATRE, 1145 Bloor St. West, Thursday, Afternoon and Evening.
VERMONT THEATRE, 1184 Bathurst St., Thursday, Afternoon and Evening.
CRYSTAL PALACE, 1424 Yonge Street, Thursday, Afternoon and Evening.

CRYSTAL PALACE, 141 Yonge Street, Friday, Afternoon and Evening.
DORIC THEATRE, Gladstone and Bloor Streets, Thursday, Afternoon and Evening.
CRESCENT THEATRE, 1091 Dundas St., Thursday, Afternoon and Evening.
CROWN YONGE STREET THEATRE, Thursday Evening.

P.S.-- *GREAT BENEFIT CONCERT* --Massey Hall, Friday, 8.15 p.m.   Massed Bands of Royal Grenadiers, 48th Highlanders, Queen's Own, Governor-General's Body Guard, 12th York Rangers, and a splendid lot of soloists and patriotic dancers. Tickets, 50c, $1.00 and $2.00, at FUND HEADQUARTERS and MASSEY HALL.

Figure C-2. Going to the "Movies" was a simple way to contribute to the War Relief Fund during the first month of World War I, the first time many picture shows were advertised in any newspaper. (Ad in all Toronto newspapers August 26, 1914.)

ads for the War Relief Fund campaign contained a special box, "Go to the 'Movies.' " Altogether that week more than one-third of the city's movie theaters and all nine film exchanges had donated their nickels and dimes of revenue to the fund (*News* August 24, 1914).

The movies were a way to make the war effort collective, public, and enjoyable. This collective effort of the local movie industry was unique among corporate donations that week because it implicitly argued that routine forms of everyday urban consumption could be at the core of a successful homefront war effort. Fun could be patriotic (and patriotism could be fun). Unlike picture theaters, but like perhaps tens of thousands of individuals, other businesses had made donations directly to the fund without openly signifying that these amounts relied on their customers' continued practice of shopping and consumption. Only at the listed movie shows was the collective act of consumption redefined as an important part of the war effort, and only with these specific audiences was routine commercial practice made to double as a patriotic contribution, a small sacrifice to the nation now at war.

In facilitating an easy way for audiences to act patriotically and participate in the fund-raising campaign, showmen were taking a type of responsibility for their audiences. This argument is strengthened even as it is qualified by considering exactly who was considered to compose the typical audience for movie shows: children, young women, and foreign-born families. Those least able to give, and probably considered least likely to give, were brought into the patriotic efforts of the city at war by showmen's attaching to the mainstream campaign a cultural space developed specifically to include them. Thus, Toronto's showmen collectively used their sites to make the sacrifice of contributions effortless, indeed entertaining, without the speeches, hymns, and prayers of the traditional mass meetings, and without the altruistic charity of coins flowing straight out of the pocket. In a sense, then, showmen recognized and accommodated aspersions of immaturity of moving picture show audiences, long associated with the movies' appeal to the most disenfranchised members of the population.

This move was not pragmatic merely on the part of showmen, part of what DeBauche has described as the "practical patriotism" of the U.S. film industry later in the war. In a much more nuanced way, showmen provided a pragmatic relation to the war effort for their young, female, and foreign-born audiences, exactly those persons excluded from formal citizenship and exactly those who would remain on the homefront. The emerging mass practices that included them in the marketplace and gathering places of commercial leisure had long welcomed their nickels and dimes in exchange for a limited, commercial version of enfranchisement. Toronto's showmen quickly turned their existing practical mass practice into a practical patriotism for the disenfranchised masses. In this case, patriotism was not merely a show of support for soldiers, but a way for those who could not fight to participate in the war effort regardless.

Symbolically, the movie business moved close to the "front." In the Labor Day parade just after this fund-raising effort in 1914, unionized locals for the moving picture operators, stage hands, and bill posters were sixth, seventh, and eighth in line out of seventy unions, nearly leading the procession (*Telegram* September 5, 1914). Movies became, almost immediately, a nightly part of soldiers' last days on the homefront, too. By December 1914 the YMCA showed films each night to thousands of soldiers encamped on the exhibition grounds in Toronto, and "the number of demands for 'night leave' from the soldier boys [was] reduced to almost nil" (*MPW* December 5, 1914, 1404). In the meantime, George Schlessinger, American manager of the Strand, installed an illuminated portrait of King George over the entrance and a sign reading "For King and Country" over the box office (*MPW* December 12, 1914, 1563).

By 1916, voluntary recruiting was waning, and movie theaters again stepped in and offered their unique ability to bring together crowds for rallies all over the city. Theaters were legally closed on Sundays at this time; but to lure recruits, the novel thrill of a Sunday entertainment in Ontario was permitted. As an initiative of Toronto showmen, perhaps because the Toronto Protective Association had just recently formed, film exchanges would supply the films free of charge; and theater managers, picture machine operators, and musicians would all donate their time. Two automobiles would be at call at each theater to whisk away recruits to the armories as soon as they signed up (*News* October 26, 1915). Late in 1915, Toronto correspondent to *Moving Picture World* W. M. Gladish noted, "the idea of Sunday performances is something entirely new—almost shocking for Toronto" (*MPW* November 13, 1915, 1335). Soon afterward, the Ontario government sanctioned the Toronto showmen's effort, at least to ensure the legality of what was happening; and a temporary provincewide measure brought Sunday movies to Ontario if the purposes were for recruiting soldiers (*MPW* April 1, 1916, 115). At least fifty movie theaters participated, about half of the city's total (*Globe* May 15, 1916). Later in 1916, and restricted to soldiers' camps, not just Sunday movies but even otherwise banned films of prizefights were permitted. Further, those picture theaters in the soldiers' camp were some of the largest in Canada at the time. The Strand in Camp Borden held 2,200 soldiers, also used for training during the day (*MPW* August 19, 1916, 1274).

The Practical Patriotism of the Amusement Tax

Using film to assert sovereign borders became central during World War I from August 1914, notwithstanding the fact that censoring U.S. flag-waving had long been a preoccupation. Soon after the start of the war, Ernest J. Chambers was installed as a national war censor to manage press content and imported writing and images, especially those written in foreign languages and espousing socialism. The duties of the national war censor in Ottawa were largely practiced through voluntary and sympathetic editorial policies in the newsrooms of the major Canadian metropolitan newspapers (Keshen 1996). Specifically for film, provincial censor boards created before the war adopted more or less standardized policies with regard to themes related to the war effort. The Ontario Board of Censors took the lead and set precedents for the other provinces. For example, within weeks of the start of the war, the Ontario censors initiated a patriotic policy of banning all images of war from movie screens, regardless the intention or context of the story. Intended to keep morale and recruitment high, this idea was soon adopted as an informal national policy among provincial censorship boards (*MPW* November 28, 1914, 1236).

In March 1916, on top of the showmen's ballyhoo that was working so well, the Ontario government announced a more totalizing patriotic use of moviegoing in the Provincial Treasurer's budget announcement: a war-time amusement tax, one of the first "sales taxes" graded to a purchase price. With the tax, nationalist sentiment became symbolically connected to film regulation and filmgoing was now directly serving the state. The war effort and war economy ultimately allowed a new form of regulation far greater in its oversight than censorship had ever been. In May 1916 the Ontario wartime amusement tax introduced a massive system of total regulation (Ontario 1916). Ledger sheets counting every ticket sold at every theater, including nonprofit fund-raisers, now had to be reported to the Treasury on penalty of losing the theater's license. The tax was also graded based on the cost of admission. Theater patrons paying a dollar or more at downtown Toronto theaters purchased an additional ten cent tax ticket, while those attending, say, a dance hall for fifty cents or more paid an additional five cents. Movie palace patrons who paid twenty cents or more were charged a tax of two cents, while people attending small movie theaters in neighborhoods and small towns paid just a cent for their tax ticket to accompany any admission below twenty cents. Interestingly, although it was thus a tax on all commercial amusements, everyone understood that movie patrons' penny taxes were the main point, not the nickel and dime taxes of theater patrons. According to an archived memo, in the first nine months of the amusement tax ending January 1917, more than 27 million one-cent tax tickets were sold, and some 3 million two-cent tickets. This compared to less than half a million five-cent tax tickets, and only 60,000 tickets of ten-cent value. Even converted to revenue, these first seasons of the amusement tax generated more than $300,000 from movie patrons paying one and two cents each, compared to just more than $25,000 from the more costly amusements (Ontario *Amusement Tax Files*).

Even before the war, and well before the amusement tax, the Ontario legislature already required less detailed annual reports of every licensed theater's operation. The amendments to the Theatres Act in 1914 mandated "every owner, lessee, or manager of a theater and the user or exhibitor of every moving-picture machine, cinematograph or other similar apparatus shall make returns to the Treasurer." The Theatres Branch received statistics on the seating capacity, construction of the theater, aisles and exits, number of performances, number of persons admitted, admission prices charged, total receipts from the box office, and "such other matters as the Lieutenant Governor may deem advisable for better carrying out the provisions of the Act" (Ontario 1914). With the new emphasis on statistical surveillance, the police patrols of the everyday conduct of the actual audience were finally and officially peripheral to the proper functioning of the film regulation bureaucracy. None of this statistical box-office information appears to have been archived. Instead, it was kept strictly confidential; and queries over the years to the Theatres Branch about specific theater information, even from Members of Parliament, were rebuffed firmly because the cooperation of the theater owners depended on the confidentiality of the statistics. Presumably, any theater manager who could compile and return this detailed information, or even hire someone to do so, could be more or less depended on to act responsibly overall.

In 1916 with the wartime measure of an amusement tax on every admission, the bureaucratic surveillance of showmen's paperwork was accelerated. The statistics of the war tax returns had to be legally notarized and submitted monthly. At least initially the Ontario Provincial Police constantly policed box offices. In July 1916 the Provincial Treasurer instructed the official inspector of moving picture theaters, R. C. Newman, to investigate and take action against reported irregularities. Just a few weeks after the amusement tax began, two theaters in Toronto were threatened closed when suspicious paperwork prompted inspections that confirmed tax fraud. The first suspicious case was Albert Perks's Queen's Palace, the smallest remaining storefront theatorium in Toronto with just 285 chairs (*MPW* July 15, 1916: 411). Inspector Newman was told to shut Perks down, informed by the Treasurer that the showman "has been re-selling tickets already used, and has refused to put in a chopper" to destroy tickets as they were handed over (Ontario *Amusement Tax Files*). Perks, charged in provincial court and his license confiscated by the Ontario Treasury, still did not close his doors. A week later he was charged by the city police for operating without a license and permitting a minor to enter his theater (*ROC* July 18, 1916, lines 1747–748). A similar situation was occurring at the Alexandra Theatre, run by Mrs. MacDonald. This time Inspector Otto Elliott was called. He was a former government censor and, earlier still, an independent showman himself. Archived correspondence shows that Elliott had instructions to revoke Mrs. McDonald's license until she obeyed the law, filed returns, and began to act honestly. Here the inspector was more lenient, apparently because the licenseholder was a war widow and was being polite, giving the run-around instead of the open contempt Perks had shown. The total surveillance of bureaucracy could shut down an errant showman faster than any police beat.

The amusement tax was about to tie the profitability of movie business to the coffers of the government at war. The previous decade had seen calls for limitations on the commercial character of film showmanship and proposals by churches and social service groups to establish educational picture shows as a community service. Now, with the ban on war scenes lifted, films of the battlefields of France filled downtown movie palaces with a patriotic public, paying both the cost of admission and the amusement tax. The harmless entertainment of moving pictures was hard at work in service of the nation and its soldiers.

This is not to say that Ontario showmen, or even those in charge of the exchanges distributing imported films from the United States and Europe, won out over their reformist competition. At the most basic level, they paid the fees and fines that allowed the work of police inspections and the bureaus of censorship to operate. The cost was more than financial because allowing the state to set limitations involved showmen relinquishing some autonomy over the shows they presented. However, as they realized that regulation was their ally in doing business without objections and protests, showmen worked in tandem with state supervision of the public. A corresponding subtle shift in the definition of the audience occurred here because entering a picture show became tacitly authorized by the government. Perhaps no individual moviegoer ever thought this consciously, but the opposite sentiment—that moviegoing was anti-social—was certainly expressed during the contentious years beforehand when the norms of filmgoing were being worked out and revised annually in government statutes. In a sense, the Ontario government and bureaucracy gave up its ability to resist film as a mass practice.

Government's own regulatory efficiency replaced strict policing, in effect establishing the importance of film in society as an indisputable fact.

Filmgoing by 1916 occurred with codependence among the public, commercial amusements, and government. Film showmanship needed government sanction to demonstrate that amusement was not wasteful but patriotic. Audiences needed the gathering space and images of wartime to enact their participation in an overseas war. Government needed these spaces of everyday mass gathering to communicate with the people, especially women and children. The wartime amusement tax objectified these relations into a fixed and fiscal transaction. With this, the mutual dependencies of audience, showmen, and government became economic as well. Going to the movies had become a small but significant way for everyone in Ontario to be a proper Canadian.

Newspaper-Sponsored Propaganda

The most complete integration of newspaper promotion and filmgoing happened during World War I as well. As with showmanship (through a collective use of theaters as spaces for fund-raising and rallies), and with regulation (through the wartime amusement tax), innovative film promotions were introduced in support of the war effort. Some of the first filmed news footage from the battlefields was taken by *Chicago Tribune* journalist Edwin F. Weigle, helped along by the deep pockets and resources of the American paper. Although the United States did not enter the war until 1917, early neutrality did not translate into disinterest on the part of the American public. At first banned in Ontario, the Weigle films were apparently so important this decision was quickly overturned (*Star Weekly* December 5, 1914). Although local showmen organized to support the war effort through donations and rallies, their film programs continued basically unchanged. The first campaign of the War Relief Fund late in August 1914 included a call to "Go to the Movies" in its advertising. It was the first time many small shows were ever mentioned in the paper (and for almost all, the first ad outside the Sunday *World*). The campaign established a public display of cooperation between movies and newspapers, now allied in the war effort. This continued with the occasional rally or fund-raiser at downtown theaters and in the spring of 1916 was again connected directly to moving picture theaters, which were used as sites of recruiting rallies all over the city at a time when recruitment was still voluntary (Miller 2002). In the fall of 1916, as strategies for recruiting shifted toward compulsory service and became more heavy-handed, the censors became less concerned about portraying the horrors of fighting and more concerned with allowing the Canadian public an explanation of why they were at war. Films showing battle scenes from Europe arrived in Toronto to help justify the war effort.

These films were presented as news, despite being exhibited in regular picture theaters to paying audiences. Allied-produced films *Britain Prepared* and *Canada in Action* were released by arrangement of the war office and played at Massey Hall in May 1916. Some films were not just promoted in newspaper advertising but actually sponsored by newspapers. An early important set of films, *On the Battlefields of France*, played at the Royal Alexandra Theatre in December 1915, sponsored by the *World*, which supported it with full-page advertisements. Even more important was the film *Battle of the Somme* in October 1916, when the *World* provided exclusive daily large display ads for its promotion; the film played a week at the new Regent movie palace and another week at two other downtown theaters. Ultimately, the war provided a situation in which newspaper promotion of filmgoing became standardized and routine and also served an unquestioned social purpose. Filmgoing, as an alternative mass medium to journalism, was boosted as a means of civic participation, practically a responsibility in the practice of good citizenship. Being "Canadian" included having fun.

In the last months of the war, something finally affected the normal operation of cinemas: Spanish influenza (J. Barry 2004). For four years the war effort had worked to support the economic, industrial, and capitalist systems in Toronto's urban culture. Now everything stopped. Few rationalized methods existed for controlling the epidemic, and people were simply urged to stay home, remain isolated, and refrain from gathering in public places. In other words, all of the social mechanisms that formed the city's war effort were interrupted or stopped. Many public buildings were closed; business operations were scaled back; teams of volunteers were put in service of managing the health risk (*Telegram* October 12, 1918). For the first time, and perhaps the only time, all cinemas in Toronto were closed. The order to shut their doors lasted two weeks. Up to 100 people were dying each day for the three weeks the flu struck Toronto (*Telegram* October 29, 1918). Yet, the city was lucky, at least partly because of an incredibly vigilant organization of volunteer health workers. The *News* (November 2, 1918) reported that Toronto had eradicated the epidemic in record time, about two weeks faster than other cities. While theaters in Toronto were closed for two weeks, those in Montreal were closed two weeks earlier and remained closed after those in Toronto reopened (*News* November 1, 1918).

The closing of theaters because of the flu epidemic coincided exactly with the scheduled 1918 Victory Bond campaign. This year was to include a special set of Victory Bond films starring famous movie stars from the United States, some of them in specially-made Canadian versions (DeBauche 1997; *News* October 18, 1918). The Victory Bond films were delayed by the flu epidemic, but a few showmen found a way to exhibit them despite the theaters being shuttered. Even as the flu gripped the city, with theaters still closed, a few movie projectors were pointed in the opposite direction out the windows of projection booths onto the street, turning public space downtown into a cinema. Mary Pickford was seen in *100% Canadian*, while her husband, Douglas Fairbanks, starred in *The Maple Leaf Forever* (*Canadian Moving Picture Digest* November 9, 1918). The outdoor film shows provided a public forum for speeches about the need to buy bonds and save money, and allowed a place for people during the Spanish flu epidemic to continue taking part in the performance of being at war. In Toronto, the Allens offered to the largest purchaser of bonds that evening a pair of movie passes for six months and gave away a pair of tickets for any $50 bond purchase. Other outdoor film shows took place at the Beaver and the Park in outlying neighborhoods, and cities across Ontario followed suit. These movie shows turned out to be the final rallies before the armistice was announced. The Protective Association bought newspaper ads announcing that all of the city's movie theaters were reopening on November 4, 1918 (*News* October 31, 1918). The war had ravaged the city's population of young men, and Spanish flu added tragically to the death toll. However, the city continued to gather crowds, to focus as a public on films and shows, parades and rallies, with two days of victory celebrations (one false call, one for real) filling the streets to make victory tangible.

Moviegoing as Civic Subjectivity

If the filmgoing produced in Toronto was nationalist, at least during the war, it was part of how the city and its institutions actively adopted a metropolitan role within Canada, despite the city retaining a peripheral role in relation to the world, especially the world of film production. The oversight of film became standardized in Toronto with standards forged in relation to those of the United States, but translated into terms seen as fit for Toronto. The practices that composed those standards were usurped from municipal policing and forced on all of Ontario. Subsequently, Toronto influenced other jurisdictions in Canada. A common understanding of Canadian history proposes that World War I was the moment the country's colonial status was finally replaced with a tenuous sense of independence and political autonomy, even if resulting from rushing to fight in Great Britain's defense (Brown and Cook 1974, 275–

93). During the war, just as the city of Toronto became an instrumental source of the men and money needed for Canada to participate as a nation instead of a colony, so too did Toronto supply the practices and devices of mass congregation and culture needed to create the semblance of being a nation. Film was an important part of this. The film industry meant more than making films and included making filmgoing into a form of deliberate congregation in support of the nation.

Recognizing this aspect of filmgoing is merely documenting how the possibility of an institutional, national cinema does not begin with film production or distribution, whether national in scope or nationalist in intention. Neither does it begin with government regulations addressing the problem of film that are national in scope or nationalist in intention. Neither does it start with the promotion of an understanding of film in relation to the nation or nationalism. Everyday filmgoing as a mass medium began with the particularity of urban sites, urban problems, and urban solutions. This is not a politically or theoretically prescriptive claim. It is based simply on the recognition that film showmanship—not just in Canada but everywhere entrepreneurs built a nickelodeon culture—imported its products and translated them into a desirable everyday practice for the particular people wherever the nickel show was located.

The wartime case of moviegoing as a form of practical patriotism for audiences and government through the conditions of civic showmanship provides novel insights for theoretical debates over cinematic subjectivity. The point is not to hypothesize an average, ideal, or typical experience of moviegoing, but to demonstrate that the civic uses of showmanship standardized the gamut of regulations that had been set before the war to constitute moviegoers as civic subjects. This mass subjectivity inscribed moviegoing as an act of citizenship, irrespective of individuated experiences, pleasures, interpretations, and purposes, indeed exactly to allow a multiplicity of these to maximize participation and make moviegoing tautologically an all-inclusive activity. This idea outlines a stronger, more contextual theory of spectatorship, one rooted in urban experience and civic participation in particular publics, which extends the move, made in more recent film theories, away from theorizing universal subjectivity at the level of interpretation, meaning, and cognizant experience (Hansen 1993; Mayne 1993). The idea that early cinema at the nickelodeon was an "alternative public sphere" extends into the subsequent period when movies were a mass practice. Without arguing that entire urban publics found the same meaning in moviegoing, let alone in a particular film, the case of Toronto demonstrates that the moviegoing public was constituted through promotional showmanship and its regulation as if it were providing an activity and space for anyone in the city to enter safely and sensibly enjoy.

This situation set conditions for a municipal or regional universal subject of moviegoing by making the activity sensible as a common practice and public gathering. Before the war, limitations were stipulated to manage material and social hazards, ostensibly to ensure theatorium spaces were safe, clean, and inclusive of the entire city. During the war, this regulated inclusivity took on a nationalist tone, in practical patriotism for audiences, local showmen, and governments, particularly when the social relations of moviegoing were fixed into a tax ticket system.

Mass practices such as moviegoing were integrated into everyday life through regulations and standards significantly determined at the level of the municipality and region. There is an important implication for sociological critiques of cultural globalization and mass culture. A thorough critique and understanding of the emergence of mass practices must grapple with homogenization as a process through which modern civic localities engaged their own internal, situated commonality and used practices such as moviegoing to relate that localized situation strongly to the world beyond. Mass cultural practices and the orientation to the mass market emerged neither just because of transnational distribution and in-dustrialization nor because urbanization provided the mass populations essential for reaping massive profits. Movies also proliferated because of a perceived need for spaces and activities that gathered the rapidly expanding publics of strangers in modern cities voluntarily and sensibly. Before such mass practices, conspicuous consumption and entertainment had primarily been provided through sites of either social exclusion or special "carnival" occasions. Activities such as picture shows were not just affordable, and not just welcoming of women, children, and foreign-born families. The movies could reasonably be said to gather "everyone" under a common practice in a way that overtly democratic practices such as voting, documentation such as passports, or statuses such as citizenship did not provide (and still do not, even in the most inclusive liberal state institutions.)

Furthering understanding of modern citizenship, the case of moviegoing in Toronto demonstrates the value of considering activities that are not formally political. The main point is that practices typically thought to undermine genuine, authentic, deliberated civic participation (mass media and mass consumption, to say the least) must be confronted not as opposed to citizenship but as a type of civic participation itself. The success and proliferation of mass culture might then be productively linked to its very ubiquity because mass practices, in fact, adequately fulfilled democratic ideals. Movies provided the conditions for a genuinely inclusive form of civic participation, albeit passive and commercial. Irrespective of the con-tent of films, moviegoing as citizenship was cheap, mass franchise. This is not to say that the composition of films is unimportant in considering how moviegoing might become an act of citizenship. The literature on national and nationalist cinemas is thorough, and it is self-evident that films themselves are important, in what they depict, connote, and convey. The emphasis on what films represent, however, often comes at the expense of considering the importance of the form and constitution of the local practice of moviegoing as a situated social action of cultural consumption. Mass products and mass practices, perhaps most overtly moviegoing, were actively imported, adjusted, and adapted to regional difference by the local representatives of transnational trade such as showmen as much as by local governments and the police forces that administered their laws.

As Eric Hobsbawm (1987) notes without quite drawing out the implications, moviegoing appeared and flourished at the cusp of a new global, modern era of the mass market (pp. 105–6, 236–42). The brilliance of the mass market was to incorporate, even cater to, those who had initially been systematically excluded from the age of empire. This changed the way business, government, family life, and religious life were practiced. While the public participation in mass culture was limited to the consumption of spectacle and entertainment, the disenfranchised were openly welcomed. Above all else, moviegoing was perhaps the first mass practice, growing to undeniable prominence in less than a decade between 1905 and 1915.

The economically stratospheric success of what became Hollywood was earned one nickel at time; and yet, conditions for moviegoing emerged that allowed all but the most disingenuous of snobs to engage in the practice as a common practice—one that carefully gathered entire cities, regions, and nations together as if they were doing the same activity. This is not to discount the importance of distinctions in moviegoing through location, cost, race, class, and theater architecture; but these differences were successfully rendered subordinate to institutionalized moviegoing as a common practice of entire publics. All parts of society were openly courted as key to the constitution of the public as including "everyone," at least as a public of moviegoers. There was something for everyone at a price almost everyone could afford. Moviegoing became focused on entertainment not just because that specific form of gathering (as opposed to education, illumination, and inspiration) was most profitable but because it was the form most "harmless" to those disenfranchised members of the audience. This became explicit during the war, as Toronto showmen offered moviegoing as a way to enact being an overseas city at war. Watching movies, we became a city, and then a nation, together.

Works Cited

Abel, Richard. 1996. Booming the film business: The historical specificity of early French cinema. In *Silent film*, ed. Richard Abel, 109–24. New Brunswick, NJ: Rutgers University Press.

———. 1999. *The red rooster scare: Making cinema American, 1900–1910*. Berkeley: University of California Press.

———. 2006. *Americanizing the movies and "movie-mad" audiences, 1910–1914*. Berkeley: University of California Press.

Acland, Charles. 2003. *Screen traffic: Movies, multiplexes, and global culture*. Durham, NC: Duke University Press.

Adair-Toteff, Christopher, ed. 2005. *Sociological beginnings: The first conference of the German Society for Sociology*. Liverpool, England: Liverpool University Press.

Addams, Jane. 1907. Public recreation and social morality. *Charities and the Commons* 18 (August): 492–94.

———. 1909. *The spirit of youth and the city streets*. New York: Macmillan.

Allen, Robert C. 1979. Motion picture exhibition in Manhattan: Beyond the nickelodeon. *Cinema Journal* 18 (2): 2–15.

———. 1996. Manhattan myopia; or Oh! Iowa! *Cinema Journal* 35 (3): 75–103.

Altenloh, Emilie. 2001. A sociology of the cinema: The audience. *Screen* 42 (3): 249–93.

Altman, Rick. 2005. *Silent film sound*. New York: Columbia University Press.

Architecture and Building. 1911. The moving picture theater. 43 (8): 319–22.

Aronson, Michael G. 2002. The wrong kind of nickel madness: Pricing problems for Pittsburgh nickelodeons. *Cinema Journal* 42 (1): 71–96.

Baker, Nicholson, and Margaret Brentano. 2005. *The world on Sunday: Graphic art in Joseph Pulitzer's newspaper, 1898–1911*. New York: Bulfinch.

Balides, Constance. 1993. Scenarios of exposure in the practice of everyday life: Women in the cinema of attractions. *Screen* 34 (1): 19–37.

Balio, Tino, ed. 1976. *The American film industry*. Madison: University of Wisconsin Press.

Barbas, Samantha. 2005. *The first lady of Hollywood: A biography of Louella Parsons*. Berkeley: University of California Press.

225

Barnard, Timothy. 2002. The machine operator: *Deus ex machina* of the storefront cinema. *Framework* 43 (1): 40–75.

Barry, John M. 2004. *The great influenza*. New York: Penguin.

Barry, Richard. 1911. Moving picture bubble. *Pearson's Magazine* (January): 131–36.

Barth, Gunther. 1980. *City people: The rise of modern city culture in nineteenth-century America*. New York: Oxford University Press.

Bataille, Georges. 1967. *The accursed share*, vol. 1. Trans. Robert Hurley. New York: Zone Books, 1989.

Baudry, Jean-Louis. 1974. Ideological effects of the basic cinematic apparatus. *Film Quarterly* 28 (2): 39–47.

Benjamin, Walter. 1968. *Illuminations: Essays and reflections*. Trans. Harry Zohn. New York: Schocken.

Bergson, Henri. 1911. *Creative evolution*. Trans. Arthur Mitchell. Mineola, NY: Dover Publications, 1998.

Bertellini, Giorgio. 1999. Shipwrecked spectators: Italy's immigrants at the movies in New York, 1906–1916. *Velvet Light Trap* 44: 39–53.

Blackall, C. H. 1914. New York moving picture theater law: A frank consideration of the aims and methods of the ordinance. *Brickbuilder* 23 (2): 47.

Blumer, Herbert. 1933. *Movies and conduct*. New York: Macmillan.

Bordwell, David. 1985. *Narration in the fiction film*. Madison: University of Wisconsin Press.

Bossin, Hye. 1951. Canada and the film: The story of the Canadian motion picture industry. In *Yearbook of the Canadian motion picture industry*, ed. Hye Bossin, 21–41. Toronto, Ontario: Canadian Film Weekly.

Boulay, Harvey, and Alan DiGaetano. 1985. Why did political machines disappear? *Journal of Urban History* 12 (1): 25–50.

Bouman, Mark J. 1991. The "good lamp is the best police" metaphor and ideologies of the nineteenth-century urban landscape. *American Studies* 32: 63–78.

Bourdieu, Pierre. 1991. *Language and symbolic power*. Ed. John B. Thompson. Trans. Gino Raymond and Matthew Adamson. Cambridge, MA: Harvard University Press.

Bowser, Eileen. 1990. *The transformation of cinema, 1907–1915*. Berkeley: University of California Press.

Boyer, M. Christine. 1994. *The city of collective memory: Its historical imagery and architectural entertainments*. Cambridge, MA: MIT Press.

Brandt, Nat. 2003. *Chicago death trap: The Iroquois Theatre fire of 1903*. Carbondale: Southern Illinois University Press.

Braudel, Fernand. 1982. *The wheels of commerce*. Vol. 2 of *Civilization and capitalism*. New York: Harper and Row.

Brown, Robert Craig, and Ramsay Cook. 1974. *Canada 1896–1921: A nation transformed*. Toronto, Ontario: McClelland and Stewart.

Buck-Morss, Susan. 1989. *The dialectics of seeing: Walter Benjamin and the Arcades Project*. Cambridge, MA: MIT Press.

Building Permits. 1906–1918. City of Toronto (Ontario) Archives.

Bulmer, Martin. 1984. *The Chicago School of sociology: Institutionalization, diversity, and the rise of sociological research*. Chicago: University of Chicago Press.

————. 1997. W. I. Thomas and Robert E. Park: Conceptualizing, theorizing, and investigating social processes. In *Reclaiming the sociological classics: The state of scholarship*, ed. Charles Camic, 242–61. Malden, MA: Blackwell.

Burgess, Ernest W. 1923. The interdependence of sociology and social work. *Journal of Social Forces* 1: 366–70.

————. 1925. The growth of the city. In *The city*, ed. Robert E. Park, Ernest W. Burgess, and Roderick D. Mackenzie, 47–62. Chicago: University of Chicago Press, 1967.

Butsch, Richard. 1994. Bowery b'hoys and matinee ladies: The re-gendering of nineteenth-century American theater audiences. *American Quarterly* 46 (3): 374–405.

Campbell, Lyndsay. 1996. A slub in the cloth: The St. Clair affair and the discourse of moral reform. Paper presented at the annual meetings of the Canadian Association of Law and Society, St. Catharines, Ontario. http://www.rcds-cjls.uqam.ca/campbell.htm (accessed September 3, 2007).

Careless, J. M. S. 1984. *Toronto to 1918: An illustrated history*. Toronto, Ontario: Lorimer.

Certeau, Michel de. 1984. *The practice of everyday life*. Trans. Steven Rendall. Berkeley: University of California Press.

Chanan, Michael. 1996. *The dream that kicks: The prehistory and early years of cinema in Britain*. London: Routledge.

Chandler, Alfred D., Jr. 1977. *The visible hand: The managerial revolution in American business*. Cambridge, MA: Belknap-Harvard University Press.

Charters, W. W. 1933. *Motion pictures and youth: A summary*. New York, Macmillan.

Chief Constable of the City of Toronto. 1907–1915. *Annual reports*. City of Toronto (Ontario) Archives. Reports box 48.

————. 1907–1916. *Letterbooks*. City of Toronto (Ontario) Archives. Boxes 106156 to 106167.

————. 1907–1917. *Register of criminals*. City of Toronto (Ontario) Archives. Boxes 141493 to 141502, and box 109207.

Cocks, Catherine. 2001. *Doing the town: The rise of urban tourism in the United States, 1850–1915*. Berkeley: University of California Press.

Cohen, Lizbeth. 1990. *Making a new deal: Industrial workers in Chicago, 1919–1939*. New York: Cambridge University Press.

Collier, John. 1908. Cheap amusements. *Charities and the Commons* 20 (April): 73–76.

————. 1910. Light on moving pictures. *The Survey* 25 (October): 80.

Cox, Kirwan. 2000. The rise and fall of the Allens: The war for Canada's movie theatres. *Lonergan Review* 6: 44–81.

Crary, Jonathan. 1992. *Techniques of the observer: On vision and modernity in the nineteenth century*. Cambridge, MA: MIT Press.

Crerar, Adam. 2005. Ontario and the Great War. In *Canada and the First World War*, ed. David MacKenzie, 230–71. Toronto, Ontario: University of Toronto Press.

Cressey, Paul G., and F. U. Thrasher. 1933. *Boys, movies and city streets*. New York: Macmillan.

Currie, Barton W. 1907. The nickel madness. *Harper's Weekly*, August 24, 1246–47.

Czitrom, Daniel. 1984. The redemption of leisure: The National Board of Censorship and the rise of motion pictures in New York City, 1900–1920. *Studies in Visual Communication* 10 (4): 2–6.

Dean, Malcolm. 1981. *Censored! Only in Canada: The history of film censorship, the scandal off the screen.* Toronto, Ontario: Virgo.

DeBauche, Leslie Midkiff. 1997. *Reel patriotism: The movies and World War I.* Madison: University of Wisconsin Press.

DeCordova, Richard. 1990. *Picture personalities: The emergence of the star system in America.* Urbana: University of Illinois Press.

Dorland, Michael. 1998. *So close to the State/s: The emergence of Canadian feature film policy.* Toronto, Ontario: University of Toronto Press.

Elias, Norbert. 2000. *The civilizing process: Sociogenetic and psychogenetic investigations,* rev. ed. Trans. Edmund Jephcott. Malden, MA: Blackwell.

Erenberg, Lewis A. 1981. *Steppin' out: New York nightlife and the transformation of American culture, 1890–1930.* Chicago: University of Chicago Press.

Ewen, Elizabeth. 1980. City lights: Immigrant women and the rise of the movies. *Signs* 5 (3): S45–65.

Ewen, Stewart. 1976. *Captains of consciousness: Advertising and the social roots of consumer culture.* New York: McGraw-Hill.

Film daily yearbook. 1932. New York: Film Daily.

Fisher, Boyd. 1912. The regulation of motion picture theaters. *American City* 7 (6): 520–22.

Fisher, Robert. 1975. Film censorship and progressive reform: The National Board of Censorship of motion pictures, 1909–1922. *Journal of Popular Film* 4 (2): 143–56.

Fosdick, Raymond B. 1911. Report on motion picture theaters of greater New York. http://www.cinemaweb.com/silentfilm/bookshelf/17_fi_3.htm (accessed September 3, 2007).

Friedberg, Anne. 1993. *Window shopping: Cinema and the postmodern.* Berkeley: University of California Press.

Frisby, David. 1986. *Fragments of modernity.* Cambridge, MA: MIT Press.

———. 2001. *Cityscapes of modernity.* Malden, MA: Polity Press.

Fuller, Kathryn H. 1996. *At the picture show: Small-town audiences and the creation of movie fan culture.* Washington, DC: Smithsonian Institution Press.

Gaudreault, André. 1990. Film, narrative, narration: The cinema of the Lumière brothers. In *Early cinema: Space, frame, narrative,* ed. Thomas Elsaesser, 68–75. London: British Film Institute.

———, and Germain Lacasse. 1996. The introduction of the Lumière Cinematograph in Canada. *Canadian Journal of Film Studies* 5 (2): 112–23.

———, Germain Lacasse, and Jean-Pierre Sirois-Trahan. 1996. *Au pays des ennemis du cinéma.* Québec: Nuit blanche.

Goist, P. Dixon. 1971. City and community: The urban theory of Robert Park. *American Quarterly* 23: 46–59.

Gomery, Douglas. 1992. *Shared pleasures: A history of movie presentation in the United States.* Madison: University of Wisconsin Press.

Goodson, Steve. 2002. *Highbrows, hillbillies and hellfire: Public entertainment in Atlanta, 1880–1930*. Athens: University of Georgia Press.

Grieveson, Lee. 1999. Why the audience mattered in Chicago in 1907. In *American movie audiences from the turn of the century to the early sound era*, ed. Melvyn Stokes and Richard Maltby, 79–91. London: British Film Institute.

———. 2004. *Policing cinema: Movies and censorship in early-twentieth-century America*. Berkeley: University of California Press.

Grossman, James R. 1989. *Land of hope: Chicago, Black Southerners, and the great migration*. Chicago: University of Chicago Press.

Gunning, Tom. 1990. The cinema of attractions. In *Early cinema: Space, frame, narrative*, ed. Thomas Elsaesser, 56–62. London: British Film Institute.

———. 1991. *D. W. Griffith and the origins of American narrative film: The early years at Biograph*. Urbana: University of Illinois Press.

———. 1993. Now you see it, now you don't: The temporality of the cinema of attractions. *Velvet Light Trap* 32: 3–12.

Gutteridge, Robert W. 2000. *Magic moments: First 20 years of moving pictures in Toronto, 1894–1914*. Whitby, Ontario: Gutteridge-Pratley.

Haber, Samuel. 1964. *Efficiency and uplift: Scientific management in the Progressive era, 1890–1920*. Chicago: University of Chicago Press.

Habermas, Jürgen. 1989. *The structural transformation of the public sphere: An inquiry into a category of bourgeois society*. Cambridge, MA: MIT Press.

Hall, Ben M. 1966. *The best remaining seats: The golden age of the movie palace*. New York, Bramhall House.

Hammond, Michael. 2006. *The big show: British cinema culture in the Great War, 1914–1918*. Exeter, England: University of Exeter Press.

Hanawalt, Barbara A., and Kathryn L. Reyerson, eds. 1994. *City and spectacle in medieval Europe*. Minneapolis: Medieval Studies at University of Minnesota Press.

Hansen, Miriam. 1991. *Babel and Babylon: Spectatorship in American silent film*. Cambridge, MA: Harvard University Press.

———. 1993. Early cinema, late cinema: Permutations of the public sphere. *Screen* 34 (3): 197–210.

———. 2004. Room-for-play: Walter Benjamin's gamble with cinema. *October* 109: 3–45.

Harris, Richard. 1996. *Unplanned suburbs: Toronto's American tragedy, 1900 to 1950*. Baltimore, MD: Johns Hopkins University Press.

———, and Robert Lewis. 1998. Constructing a fault(y) zone: Misrepresentations of American cities and suburbs, 1900–1950. *Annals of the Association of American Geographers* 88: 622–39.

Haskell, Thomas L. 2000. *The emergence of professional social science: The American Social Science Association and the nineteenth-century crisis of authority*. Baltimore, MD: Johns Hopkins University Press.

Heinze, Andrew R. 1990. *Adapting to abundance: Jewish immigrants, mass consumption, and the search for American identity*. New York: Columbia University Press.

Higson, Andrew. 1989. The concept of national cinema. *Screen* 30 (4): 36–47.

Hobsbawm, Eric. 1987. *The age of empire, 1875–1914*. London: Weidenfeld and Nicolson.

Huyssen, Andreas. 1986. *After the great divide: Modernism, mass culture, postmodernism*. Bloomington: Indiana University Press.

Insurance Engineering. 1909. Moving picture regulations: Reports from mayors of cities. 17: 298–321.

Isin, Engin F. 1992. *Cities without citizens: The modernity of the city as a corporation*. Montreal, Quebec: Black Rose.

———, and Patricia K. Wood. 1999. *Citizenship and identity*. London: Sage.

Jacobs, Jane. 1969. *The economy of cities*. New York: Vintage.

Jacobs, Lewis. 1968. *The rise of the American film: A critical history*. New York: Columbia Teachers College Press.

Jancovich, Mark, and Lucy Faire with Sarah Stubbings. 2003. *The place of the audience: Cultural geographies of film consumption*. London: British Film Institute.

Johnston, Russell. 2001. *Selling themselves: The emergence of Canadian advertising*. Toronto, Ontario: University of Toronto Press.

Jowett, Garth S. 1974. The first motion picture audiences. *Journal of Popular Film* 3 (1): 39–54.

———. 1975. American domination of the motion picture industry: Canada as a test case. *Journal of the University Film Association* 27 (3): 58–61, 72.

———. 1976. *Film, the democratic art: A social history of American film*. Boston: Focal Press.

———, Ian C. Jarvie, and Kathryn H. Fuller. 1996. *Children and the movies: Media influence and the Payne Fund controversy*. New York: Cambridge University Press.

Kalberg, Stephen. 1997. Max Weber's sociology: Research strategies and modes of analysis. In *Reclaiming the sociological classics*, ed. Charles Camic, 208–41. Malden, MA: Blackwell.

Keil, Charlie. 2001. *Early American cinema in transition: Story, style, and filmmaking, 1907–1913*. Madison: University of Wisconsin Press.

———, and Marta Braun. 2001. Sounding Canadian: Early sound practices and nationalism in Toronto-based exhibition. In *The sounds of early cinema*, ed. Richard Abel and Rick Altman, 198–204. Bloomington: Indiana University Press.

Kemple, Thomas M. 2005. Instrumentum vocale: A note on Max Weber's value-free polemics and sociological aesthetics. *Theory, Culture, and Society* 22 (4): 1–22.

Keshen, Jeffrey A. 1996. *Propaganda and censorship during Canada's Great War*. Edmonton, Alberta: University of Alberta Press.

Kingsley, Sherman C. 1907. The penny arcade and the cheap theater. *Charities and the Commons* 18 (June): 295–97.

Kracauer, Siegfried. 1995. *The mass ornament: Weimar essays*. Trans. Thomas Y. Levin. Cambridge, MA: Harvard University Press.

Lacasse, Germain. 1984. Cultural amnesia and the birth of film in Canada. *Cinema Canada* 108 (June): 6–7.

———. 2000. *Le bonimenteur de vues animées: Le cinéma muet entre tradition et modernité*. Paris: Éditions Klinksieck.

Laird, Pamela Walker. 1998. *Advertising progress: American business and the rise of consumer marketing*. Baltimore, MD: Johns Hopkins University Press.

Latour, Bruno. 2005. *Reassembling the social: An introduction to actor-network theory*. New York: Oxford University Press.

Lazarsfeld, Paul F. 1947. Audience research in the movie field. *Annals of the American Academy of Political and Social Science* 254: 160–68.

———, and Robert K. Merton. 1948. Mass communication, popular taste, and organized social action. In *The Communication of ideas*, ed. Lyman Bryson, 95–118. New York: Harper.

LCC. See Chief Constable of the City of Toronto. *Letterbooks*.

LeBon, Gustave. 1895. *The crowd: A study of the popular mind*. Mineola, NY: Dover, 2002.

Lenton-Young, Gerald. 1990. Variety theatre. In *Early Stages: Theatre in Ontario, 1800–1914*, ed. Ann Saddlemeyer, 204–06. Toronto, Ontario: University of Toronto Press.

Leupp, Constance D. 1910. The motion picture as a social worker. *The Survey* 24 (August): 739–41.

Levien, Sonya. 1913. New York's motion picture law. *American City* 9 (4): 319–21.

Levine, D. N., E. B. Carter, and E. M. Gorman. 1976. Simmel's influence on American sociology II. *American Journal of Sociology* 81: 1112–132.

Lindner, Rolf. 1996. *The reportage of urban culture: Robert Park and the Chicago School*. New York: Cambridge University Press.

Lindstrom, J. A. 1999. Almost worse than the restrictive measures: Chicago reformers and the nickelodeons. *Cinema Journal* 39 (1): 90–112.

Litt, Paul. 2005. Canada invaded! The Great War, mass culture, and Canadian cultural nationalism. In *Canada and the First World War*, ed. David MacKenzie, 323–49. Toronto, Ontario: University of Toronto Press.

Luckett, Moya. 1999. Advertising and femininity: The case of "Our Mutual Girl." *Screen* 40 (4): 363–83.

MacKenzie, Scott. 2000. A screen of one's own: Early cinema in Québec and the public sphere, 1906–1928. *Screen* 41 (2): 183–202.

Magder, Ted. 1993. *Canada's Hollywood: The Canadian state and feature films*. Toronto, Ontario: University of Toronto Press.

Maltby, Richard. 1983. *Harmless entertainment: Hollywood and the ideology of consensus*. Metuchen, NJ: Scarecrow Press.

———. 1996. A brief romantic interlude: Dick and Jane go to $3\frac{1}{2}$ seconds of the classical Hollywood cinema. In *Post-theory: Reconstructing film studies*, ed. David Bordwell and Noel Carroll, 434–459. Madison: University of Wisconsin Press.

Marquis, Greg. 1991. *Policing Canada's century*. Toronto, Ontario: University of Toronto Press.

Marshall, T. H. 1992. *Citizenship and social class*. London: Pluto.

May, Larry. 1980. *Screening out the past: The birth of mass culture and the motion picture industry*. New York: Oxford University Press.

Mayer, Jacob P. 1946. *Sociology of film: Studies and documents*. London: Faber and Faber.

———. 1948. *British cinemas and their audiences*. London: Dobson.

Mayne, Judith. 1982. Immigrants and spectators. *Wide Angle* 5 (2): 32–41.

———. 1993. *Cinema and spectatorship*. New York: Routledge.

McCarthy, Kathleen D. 1976. Nickel vice and virtue: Movie censorship in Chicago, 1907–1915. *Journal of Popular Film* 5 (1): 37–55.

McNulty, Timothy. 2005. You saw it here first. *Pittsburgh Post-Gazette*, June 19, http://www.post-gazette.com/pg/05170/522854.stm (accessed September 3, 2007).

McSwain, James B. 2002. Fire hazards and protection of property: Municipal regulation of the storage and supply of fuel oil in Mobile, Alabama, 1894–1910. *Journal of Urban History* 28 (5): 599–628.

Methodist Church of Canada. 1907. *Report of the secretary to the executive committee of the Methodist Board of Temperance, Prohibition, and Moral Reform*. May 22. Victoria University and United Church Archives, Toronto, Ontario. 78.102C, Box 1, File 10A.

———. 1913. *Minutes of the annual meeting of the General Board of the Methodist Department of Temperance, Prohibition, and Moral Reform*. October 21. Victoria University and United Church Archives, Toronto, Ontario. 78.102C, Box 1, File 2.

Miller, Ian Hugh Maclean. 2002. *Our glory and our grief: Torontonians and the Great War*. Toronto, Ontario: University of Toronto Press.

Mills, C. Wright. 1951. *White collar: The American middle classes*. New York: Oxford University Press.

Mitchell, Alice Miller. 1929. *Children and movies*. Chicago: University of Chicago Press.

Monod, David. 1996. *Store wars: Shopkeepers and the culture of mass marketing, 1890–1939*. Toronto, Ontario: University of Toronto Press.

Moore, Paul S. 2003. Nathan L. Nathanson introduces Canadian Odeon: Producing national competition in exhibition. *Canadian Journal of Film Studies* 12 (2): 22–45.

———. 2004. Movie palaces on Canadian downtown main streets: Montreal, Toronto, and Vancouver. *Urban History Review* 32 (2): 3–20.

Morris, Peter. 1992. *Embattled shadows: A history of Canadian cinema, 1895–1939*. Montreal, Quebec: McGill-Queen's University Press.

Mosher, Clayton James. 1998. *Discrimination and denial: Systemic racism in Ontario's legal and justice systems, 1892 – 1961*. Toronto, Ontario: University of Toronto Press.

MPW. Moving Picture World.

Münsterberg, Hugo. 2002. *The Photoplay: A psychological study*. In *Hugo Münsterberg on Film*, ed. Allan Langdale, 45–162. New York: Routledge.

Musser, Charles. 1990. *The emergence of cinema: The American screen to 1907*. Berkeley: University of California Press.

———, and Carol Nelson. 1991. *High-class moving pictures: Lyman H. Howe and the forgotten era of traveling exhibition, 1880–1920*. Princeton, NJ: Princeton University Press.

Nasaw, David. 1985. *Children of the city: At work and at play*. New York: Oxford University Press.

———. 1993. *Going out: The rise and fall of public amusements*. Cambridge, MA: Harvard University Press.

Novak, William J. 1996. *The people's welfare: Law and regulation in nineteenth-century America*. Chapel Hill: University of North Carolina Press.

Olsson, Jan. 2004. Pressing inroads: Metaspectators and the nickelodeon culture. In *Screen Culture: History and Textuality*, ed. John Fullerton, 113–35. Eastleigh, England: John Libbey.

Ontario. 1908. An act to amend the act to regulate the means of egress from public buildings. *Statutes*. 8 Edward VII c. 60.

———. 1909. An act to regulate the means of egress from public buildings. *Statutes*. 9 Edward VII c. 87.

———. 1910. Statute law amendment act. *Statutes*. 10 Edward VII c. 26 s. 3.

———. 1911. An act to regulate halls, theatres, and cinematographs. *Statutes*. 1 George V c. 73.

———. 1912. An act to amend the theatres and cinematographs act. *Statutes*. 2 George V c. 54.

———. 1913. Statute law amendment act. *Statutes*. 3 George V c. 18 s. 40.

———. 1914. Statute law amendment act. *Statutes*. 4 George V c. 21 s. 53.

———. 1915. Statute law amendment act. *Statutes*. 5 George V c. 20 s. 21.

———. 1916. An act to increase the supplementary revenue of Ontario. *Statutes*. 6 George V c. 9.

———. 1917. Statute law amendment act. *Statutes*. 7 George V c. 24. s. 32.

———. 1918. Statute law amendment act. *Statutes*. 8 George V c. 20. s. 43, 44, 54, and 55.

———. 1919. An act to amend the theatres and cinematographs act. *Statutes*. 9 George V C. 66.

———. *Amusement Tax Correspondence Files*. Archives of Ontario, Toronto. RG 6-3. Box 1. File 1.

Park, Robert E. 1923. The natural history of the newspaper. *American Journal of Sociology* 29 (3): 273–89.

———. 1927. Topical summaries of current literature: The American newspaper. *American Journal of Sociology* 32 (5): 806–13.

———. 1972. *The crowd and the public and other essays*. Ed. Henry Elsner, Jr. Chicago: University of Chicago Press.

———, Ernest W. Burgess, and Roderick D. Mackenzie. 1925. *The city*. Chicago: University of Chicago Press, 1967.

Patterson, Joseph Medill. 1907. The nickelodeons: The poor man's elementary course in the drama. *Saturday Evening Post*. November 23, 10–11, 38.

Pearson, Roberta, and William Uricchio. 1999. The formative and impressionable stage: Discursive constructions of the nickelodeon's child audience. In *American movie audiences from the turn of the century to the early sound era*, ed. Melvyn Stokes and Richard Maltby, 64–75. London: British Film Institute.

Peiss, Kathy. 1986. *Cheap amusements: Working women and leisure in turn-of-the-century New York*. Philadelphia: Temple University Press.

Pelletier, Louis. 2007. An experiment in "historically correct" Canadian photoplays: Montreal's British American Film Manufacturing Co. *Film History* 19: 34–48.

Pendakur, Manjunath. 1990. *Canadian dreams and American control: The political economy of the Canadian film industry*. Toronto, Ontario: Garamond.

Petersen, Patricia. 1984. The evolution of the Board of Control. In *Forging a consensus: Historical essays on Toronto*, ed. Victor L. Russell, 181–91. Toronto, Ontario: University of Toronto Press.

Peterson, Ruth C., and L. L. Thurstone. 1933. *Motion pictures and the social attitudes of children*. New York, Macmillan.

Popple, Simon, and Joe Kember. 2004. *Early cinema: From factory gate to dream factory*, London: Wallflower.

Potamianos, George. 2002. Movies at the margins: The distribution of films to theaters in small-town America, 1895–1919. In *American silent film: Discovering marginalized voices*, ed. Gregg Bachman and Thomas J. Slater, 9–26. Carbondale: Southern Illinois University Press.

Presbyterian Church of Canada. 1907–1910. *Minutes of the Presbyterian Committee on Temperance, Moral, and Social Reform*. Victoria University and United Church Archives, Toronto, Ontario. 79.169C.

———. 1910. *Acts and proceedings of the 36th General Assembly of the Presbyterian Church in Canada*. Toronto, Ontario: Murray Company.

Preston, Ivan L. 1975. *The great American blow-up: Puffery in advertising and selling*. Madison: Wisconsin University Press.

Quilley, Stephen, and Steven Loyal. 2004. Towards a "central theory": The scope and relevance of the sociology of Norbert Elias. In *The sociology of Norbert Elias*, ed. Stephen Quilley and Steven Loyal, 1–22. New York: Cambridge University Press.

Quinn, J. A. 1940. The Burgess zonal hypothesis and its critics. *American Sociological Review* 5: 210–18.

Ramsaye, Terry. 1986. *A million and one nights: A history of the motion picture through 1925*. New York: Touchstone.

Reisman, David. 1960. *The lonely crowd*. New Haven, CT: Yale University Press.

Riis, Jacob. 1890. *How the other half lives: Studies among the tenements of New York*. New York: Hill and Wang, 1957.

ROC. See Chief Constable of the City of Toronto. *Register of Criminals*.

Rogers, Nicholas. 1984. Serving Toronto the good: The development of the city police force, 1834–84. In *Forging a consensus: Historical essays on Toronto*, ed. Victor L. Russell, 116–40. Toronto, Ontario: University of Toronto Press.

Rosen, Christine Meisner. 1986. *The limits of power: Great fires and the process of city growth in America*. New York: Cambridge University Press.

Rosenzweig, Roy. 1983. *Eight hours for what we will: Workers and leisure in an industrial city, 1870–1920*. New York: Cambridge University Press.

Ross, Stephen J. 1998. *Working-class Hollywood: Silent film and the shaping of class in America*. Princeton, NJ: Princeton University Press.

Ruble, Blair A. 2001. *Second metropolis: Pragmatic pluralism in Gilded Age Chicago, Silver Age Moscow, and Meiji Osaka*. Washington, DC: Woodrow Wilson Center.

Russell, Victor L., ed. 1984. *Forging a consensus: Historical essays on Toronto*. Toronto, Ontario: University of Toronto Press.

Simmel, Georg. 1950. *The sociology of Georg Simmel*. Trans. and ed. Kurt Wolff. Glencoe, IL: Free Press.

———. 1990. *The philosophy of money*. Trans. Tom Bottomore and David Frisby. London: Routledge.

Singer, Ben. 1995. Manhattan nickelodeons: New data on audiences and exhibitors. *Cinema Journal* 34 (3): 5–35.

———. 2001. *Melodrama and modernity: Early sensational cinema and its contexts*. New York: Columbia University Press.

Sjoberg, Gideon. 1960. *The preindustrial city past and present*. New York: Free Press.

Sklar, Robert. 1975. *Movie-made America: A cultural history of American movies*. New York: Vintage-Random House.

———. 1988. Oh! Althusser! Historiography and the rise of cinema studies. *Radical History Review* 41: 11–36.

Smither, R. B. N., ed. 2002. *This film is dangerous: A celebration of nitrate film*. Brussels: FIAF.

Soja, Edward W. 2000. *Postmetropolis: Critical studies of cities and regions*. Malden, MA: Blackwell.

Sombart, Werner. 1967. *Luxury and capitalism*. Trans. W. R. Dittmar. Ann Arbor: University of Michigan Press.

Speisman, Stephen. 1979. *The Jews of Toronto: A history to 1937*. Toronto, Ontario: McClelland and Stewart.

———. 1983. Yiddish theatre in Toronto. *Polyphony* 5 (2): 95–98.

Staiger, Janet. 1983. Combination and litigation: Structures of U. S. film distribution, 1891–1917. *Cinema Journal* 23 (2): 41–72.

———. 1990. Advertising wares, winning patrons, voicing ideals: Thinking about the history and theory of film advertising. *Cinema Journal* 29 (3): 3–31.

Stamp, Shelley. 2000. *Movie-struck girls: Women and motion picture culture after the nickelodeon*. Princeton, NJ: Princeton University Press.

Steven, Peter. 2003. Pleasing the Canadians: A national flavour for early cinema, 1896–1914. *Canadian Journal of Film Studies* 12 (2): 5–21.

Stewart, Jacqueline Najuma. 2005. *Migrating to the movies: Cinema and Black urban modernity*. Berkeley: University of California Press.

Strange, Carolyn. 1995. *Toronto's girl problem: The perils and pleasures of the city, 1880–1930*. Toronto, Ontario: University of Toronto Press.

Strasser, Susan. 1989. *Satisfaction guaranteed: The making of the American mass market*. New York: Pantheon.

Stromgren, Richard L. 1988. The "Moving Picture World" of W. Stephen Bush. *Film History* 2 (1): 13–22.

Taylor, John H. 1991. Urban autonomy in Canada: Its evolution and decline. In *The Canadian city: Essays in urban and social history*, ed. Gilbert A. Stelter and Alan F. J. Artibise, 478–500. Ottawa, Ontario: Carleton University Press.

Thissen, Judith. 2002. Charlie Steiner's Houston Hippodrome: Moviegoing on New York's Lower East Side, 1909–1913. In *American silent film: Discovering marginalized voices*, ed. Gregg Bachman and Thomas J. Slater, 27–47. Carbondale: Southern Illinois University Press.

Tönnies, Ferdinand. 2001. *Community and civil society*. Trans. Jose Harris and Margaret Hollis. Ed. Jose Harris. New York: Cambridge University Press.

Toronto. 1914. *Investigation into city architect's department*. City of Toronto (Ontario) Archives, RG5 Series D, Boxes 17–19.

Toronto Bylaw 2449. Relating to illegal posters and plays. s. 10. Passed January 13, 1890.

Toronto Bylaw 2453. Relating to amusement licenses. s. 43. Passed January 13, 1890.

Toronto Bylaw 3289. Licensing shooting parlors or "any instrument or mechanical device for amusement." Passed December 24, 1894.

Toronto Bylaw 4552. Licensing "slot machines by which pictures are exhibited or musical or other sounds produced." Passed June 12, 1905.

Toronto Bylaw 5319. Licensing amusement park specific attractions "and any other contrivance." Passed May 25, 1909.

Uricchio, William, and Roberta E. Pearson. 1993. *Reframing culture: The case of the Vitagraph Quality films*. Princeton, NJ: Princeton University Press.

Valverde, Mariana. 1991. *The age of light, soap, and water: Moral reform in English Canada, 1885–1925*. Toronto, Ontario: McCelland and Stewart.

———. 2003. *Law's dream of common knowledge*. Princeton, NJ: Princeton University Press.

Veblen, Thorstein. 1998. *The theory of the leisure class*. Amherst, NY: Prometheus.

Walden, Keith. 1997. *Becoming modern in Toronto: The industrial exhibition and the shaping of a late-Victorian culture*. Toronto, Ontario: University of Toronto Press.

Walkowitz, Judith. 1992. *City of dreadful delight: Narratives of sexual danger in late-Victorian London*. Chicago: University of Chicago Press.

Waller, Gregory A. 1995. *Main Street amusements: Movies and commercial entertainment in a Southern city, 1896–1930*. Washington, DC: Smithsonian Institution Press.

———. 2005. Imagining and promoting the small-town theater. *Cinema Journal* 44 (3): 3–19.

Ward, David. 1989. *Poverty, ethnicity, and the American city: Changing conceptions of the slum and the ghetto*. New York: Cambridge University Press.

Weber, Max. 1949. *The methodology of the social sciences*. Trans. Edward A. Shils and Henry A. Finch. New York: Free Press.

———. 1958. *The city*. Glencoe, IL: Free Press.

———. 2005. The comparative sociology of newspapers and associations. In *Sociological beginnings: The first conference of the German Society for Sociology*, ed. Christopher Adair-Toteff, 74–93. Liverpool, England: Liverpool University Press.

Wendt, Lloyd. 1952. *Give the lady what she wants: The story of Marshall Field and Company*. Chicago: Rand McNally.

Weston. 1912–1913. *Council minutes*. City of Toronto (Ontario) Archives. Box 266405. File 4.

White, Peter. 1931. *Investigation into an alleged combine in the motion picture industry in Canada*. Ottawa, Ontario: King's Printer.

Wiebe, Robert H. 1967. *The search for order, 1877–1920*. New York: Hill and Wang.

Wilinsky, Barbara. 2000. Flirting with Kathlyn: Creating the mass audience. In *Hollywood goes shopping*, ed. David Dresser and Garth S. Jowett, 34–56. Minneapolis: University of Minnesota Press.

Wirth, Louis. 1938. Urbanism as a way of life. *American Journal of Sociology* 44 (1): 1–24.

Zukin, Sharon. 1991. *Landscapes of power: From Detroit to Disneyworld*. Berkeley: University of California Press.

Zukor, Adolph. 1953. *The public is never wrong*. New York: Putnam.

Zunz, Oliver. 1990. *Making America corporate, 1870–1920*. Chicago: University of Chicago Press.

Index

239